Readings in Psychology

Core Concepts and Special Topics

Readings in Psychology

Core Concepts and Special Topics

Edited by

Frank H. Sjursen, Jr.
Shoreline Community College

and

Lee Roy Beach
University of Washington

Holt, Rinehart and Winston, Inc.
New York   Chicago   San Francisco   Atlanta
Dallas   Montreal   Toronto   London   Sydney

Copyright © 1973 by Holt, Rinehart and Winston, Inc.
All rights reserved
Library of Congress Catalog Card Number: 72–11211
ISBN: 0–03–084886–5
Printed in the United States of America
3456   090   987654321

Preface

While it certainly can be used with other texts, this book was designed to supplement the introductory text *Psychology: Core Concepts and Special Topics* by Lee Roy Beach. The readings are divided into sections that parallel the divisions of the text and the order of presentation follows the order of the discussion in the text. The guiding philosophy for this book has been the same as for Beach's text—psychology is intrinsically interesting, and introductory psychology books can be scientifically respectable without being dull encyclopedias.

Many of the readings are taken from sources other than the standard psychological journals and a couple of them were written especially for this collection. Whenever possible, the goal has been to obtain scholarly articles that are intended for an audience of intelligent laymen rather than articles intended for professional psychologists; articles in the latter class are often too technical for beginning students. It has been our experience that by using these readings with Beach's text it is possible to provide students with a rigorous introduction to psychology while at the same time maintaining their interest throughout the course.

Many of the readings are controversial and can provide the bases for spirited class discussions, for example: George Miller's and B. F. Skinner's differing views on psychology's proper role in modern society; Martin Seligman's indictment of learning theory and related research; Earl Hunt's and Clifford Lunneborg's critical examination of the concept of IQ and IQ tests; Lionel Tiger's ideas about the possible evolutionary origins of human sex role differentiation; the articles on the language development of the deaf and that on black dialect and its relationship to educational achievement; Mervyn Cadwallader's observations about marriage as a wretched institution;

and the articles on marijuana. If these fail to stimulate discussion, the students should be checked closely for signs of *rigor mortis*.

We would like to thank the many authors and publishers who have permitted us to use their articles and who have permitted us rather wide latitude in editing their work in order to meet our space limitations. We are also grateful to our colleagues, particularly Robert Bolles, Phillip Dale, Lawrence Halpern, Earl Hunt, David Rosenhan, Richard Roth, and Ronald Smith, and some 3000 introductory psychology students for their suggestions, criticisms, and patience.

Finally, we especially thank our wives, Elizabeth Sjursen and Barbara Beach, for their help in finding appropriate articles, aid in securing permission to use those articles, and for occasionally assuring us that someday we would have it all done.

Seattle, Washington   F. H. S.
January 1973   L. R. B.

Contents

Readings in Psychology

Core Concepts and Special Topics

1 Psychology's Potential

There is a great deal of disagreement among psychologists and non-psychologists alike about what the proper goals of psychology ought to be. Some think that the endeavor merely ought to produce knowledge about the basic nature of human beings, knowledge which they think will inevitably have a strong influence upon people's views of themselves and upon the approaches that are taken to solve the personal and social problems that continually plague them. Others think that more tangible products are in order, primary among which ought to be methods of controlling human behavior so that it is acceptable both to the individuals involved and to society as a whole. As we shall see in the two articles that follow, persons who hold the first view are often alarmed by the possibility that a psychological tyranny could result from focusing solely on methods of behavioral control. On the other hand, persons who hold the second view often see no alternative to such methods if the human condition is to be improved. Dr. George Miller's article, *Psychology as a Means of Promoting Human Welfare* is representative of the first view and Dr. B. F. Skinner's article, *Freedom and the Control of Men* represents the second. Note, however, that even in the midst of their disagreement, both sides are united in the opinion that a science of human behavior can improve on the "common sense" methods that presently dictate the way in which people are treated by government, the military, employers, educational institutions, and by each other.

PSYCHOLOGY AS A MEANS OF PROMOTING HUMAN WELFARE

George A. Miller

REVOLUTIONARY POTENTIAL OF PSYCHOLOGY

I will begin by stating publicly something that I think psychologists all feel, but seldom talk about. In my opinion, scientific psychology is potentially one of the most revolutionary intellectual enterprises ever conceived by the mind of man. If we were ever to achieve substantial progress toward our stated aim—toward the understanding, prediction, and control of mental and behavioral phenomena—the implications for every aspect of society would make brave men tremble.

Responsible spokesmen for psychology seldom emphasize this revolutionary possibility. One reason is that the general public is all too ready to believe it, and public resistence to psychology would be all too easy to mobilize. Faced with the possibility that revolutionary pronouncements might easily do more harm than good, a prudent spokesman finds other drums to march to.

Regardless of whether we agree that prudence is always the best policy, I believe there is another reason for our public modesty. Anyone who claims that psychology is a revolutionary enterprise will face a demand from his scientific colleagues to put up or shut up. Nothing that psychology has done so far, they will say, is very revolutionary. They will admit that psychometric tests, psychoanalysis, conditioned reflexes, sensory thresholds, implanted electrodes, and factor analysis are all quite admirable, but they can scarcely be compared to gunpowder, the steam engine, organic chemistry, radio-telephony, computers, atom bombs, or genetic surgery in their revolutionary consequences for society. Our enthusiastic spokesman would have to retire in confused embarrassment.

Since I know that rash statements about the revolutionary potential of psychology may lead to public rejection and scientific ridicule, why do I take such risks on this occasion? My reason is that I do not believe the psychological revolution is still pie in the sky. It has already begun.

One reason the psychological revolution is not more obvious may be that we have been looking for it in the wrong place. We have assumed that psychology should provide new technological options, and that a psychological revolution will not occur until someone in authority exercises those options to attain socially desirable goals. One reason for this assumption, perhaps, is that it follows the model we have inherited from previous applications of science to practical problems. An applied scientist is supposed to provide instrumentalities for modifying the environment—instru-

From the *American Psychologist*, 1969, *24*, 1063–1075. Copyright 1969 by the American Psychological Association, and reproduced by permission.

mentalities that can then, under public regulation, be used by wealthy and powerful interests to achieve certain goals. The psychological revolution, when it comes, may follow a very different course, at least in its initial stages. . . .

. . . I believe that the real impact of psychology will be felt, not through the technological products it places in the hands of powerful men, but through its effects on the public at large, through a new and different public conception of what is humanly possible and what is humanly desirable.

I believe that any broad and successful application of psychological knowledge to human problems will necessarily entail a change in our conception of ourselves and of how we live and love and work together. Instead of inventing some new technique for modifying the environment, or some new product for society to adapt itself to however it can, we are proposing to tamper with the adaptive process itself. Such an innovation is quite different from a "technological fix." I see little reason to believe that the traditional model for scientific revolutions should be appropriate.

Consider, for example, the effect that Freudian psychology has already had on Western society. It is obvious that its effects, though limited to certain segments of society, have been profound, yet I do not believe that one can argue that those effects were achieved by providing new instrumentalities for achieving goals socially agreed upon. As a method of therapy, psychoanalysis has had limited success even for those who can afford it. It has been more successful as a method of investigation, perhaps, but even there it has been only one of several available methods. The impact of Freud's thought has been due far less to the instrumentalities he provided than to the changed conception of ourselves that he inspired. The wider range of psychological problems that Freud opened up for professional psychologists is only part of his contribution. More important in the scale of history has been his effect on the broader intellectual community and, through it, on the public at large. Today we are much more aware of the irrational components of human nature and much better able to accept the reality of our unconscious impulses. The importance of Freudian psychology derives far less from its scientific validity than from the effects it has had on our shared image of man himself.

I realize that one might argue that changes in man's conception of himself under the impact of advances in scientific knowledge are neither novel nor revolutionary. For example, Darwin's theory changed our conception of ourselves, but not until the past decade has it been possible to mount a truly scientific revolution based on biological science. One might argue that we are now only at the Darwinian stage in psychology, and that the real psychological revolution is still a century or more in the future. I do not find this analogy appropriate, however.

To discover that we are not at the center of the universe, or that our remote ancestors lived in a tree, does indeed change our conception of man and society, but such new conceptions can have little effect on the way we behave in our daily affairs and in our institutional contexts. A new conception of man based on psychology, however, would have immediate implications for the most intimate details of our social and personal lives. This fact is unprecedented in any earlier stage of the Industrial Revolution.

The heart of the psychological revolution will be a new and scientifically based conception of man as an individual and as a social creature. When I say that the psychological revolution is already upon us, what I mean is that we have already begun to change man's self-conception. If we want to further that revolution, not only must we strengthen its scientific base, but we must also try to communicate it to our students and to the public. It is not the industrialist or the politician who should exploit it, but Everyman, every day.

The enrichment of public psychology by scientific psychology constitutes the most direct and important application of our science to the promotion of human welfare. Instead of trying to foresee new psychological products that might disrupt our existing social arrangements, therefore, we should be self-consciously analyzing the general effect that our scientific psychology may have on popular psychology. As I try to perform this analysis for myself, I must confess that I am not altogether pleased with the results.

I would like now to consider briefly some of the effects we are having and where, in my view, our influence is leading at the present time. Let me begin with a thumbnail sketch of one major message that many scientific psychologists are trying to communicate to the public.

CONTROL OF BEHAVIOR

One of the most admired truisms of modern psychology is that some stimuli can serve to reinforce the behavior that produces them. The practical significance of this familiar principle arises from the implication that if you can control the occurrence of these reinforcing stimuli, then you can control the occurrence of adaptive behavior intended to achieve or avoid them. This contingency between behavior and its consequences has been demonstrated in many studies of animal behavior, where environmental conditions can be controlled, or at least specified, and where the results can be measured with some precision.

Something similar holds for the human animal, of course, although it is complicated by man's symbolic proclivities and by the fact that the disparity between experimenter and subject changes when the subject is also a man. Between men, reinforcement is usually a mutual relation and each person controls the other to some extent. This relation of mutual reinforcement, which man's genius for symbols has generalized in terms of money or the promise of money, provides the psychological basis for our economic system of change. Psychologists did not create this economic system for controlling behavior, of course. What we have tried to do is to describe its psychological basis and its limits in terms sufficiently general to hold across different species, and to suggest how the technique might be extended to educational, rehabilitative, therapeutic, or even political situations in which economic rewards and punishments would not normally be appropriate. Once a problem of behavior control has been phrased in these terms, we may then try to discover the most effective schedule of reinforcements.

My present concern has nothing to do with the validity of these ideas. I am concerned with their effect on the public at large, for it is there, if I am right, that we are most likely to achieve a psychological revolution.

In the public view, I suspect, all this talk about controlling behavior comes across as unpleasant, if not actually threatening. Freud has already established in the public mind a general belief that all behavior is motivated. The current message says that psychologists now know how to use this motivation to control what people will do. When they hear this, of course, our scientific colleagues are likely to accuse us of pseudoscientific claims; less scientific segments of the public are likely to resent what they perceive as a threat to their personal freedom. Neither reaction is completely just, but neither is completely unjustifiable.

I believe these critics see an important truth, one that a myopic concentration on techniques of behavior control may cause us to overlook. At best, control is but one component in any program for personal improvement or social reform. Changing behavior is pointless in the absence of any coherent plan for how it should be changed. It is our plan for using control that the public wants to know about. Too often, I fear, psychologists have implied that acceptable uses for behavior control are either self-evident or can be safely left to the wisdom and benevolence of powerful men. Psychologists must not surrender the planning function so easily. Humane applications of behavior control must be based on intelligent diagnosis of the personal and social problems we are trying to solve. Psychology has at least as much, probably more, to contribute to the diagnosis of personal and social problems as it has to the control of behavior.

Regardless of whether we have actually achieved new scientific techniques of behavior control that are effective with human beings, and regardless of whether control is of any value in the absence of diagnosis and planning for its use, the simple fact that so many psychologists keep talking about control is having an effect on public psychology. The average citizen is predisposed to believe it. Control has been the practical payoff from the other sciences. Control must be what psychologists are after, too. Moreover, since science is notoriously successful, behavior control must be inevitable. Thus the layman forms an impression that control is the name of the road we are traveling, and that the experts are simply quibbling about how far down that road we have managed to go.

Closely related to this emphasis on control is the frequently repeated claim that living organisms are nothing but machines. A scientist recognizes, of course, that this claim says far more about our rapidly evolving conception of machines than it says about living organisms, but this interpretation is usually lost when the message reaches public ears. The public idea of a machine is something like an automobile, a mechanical device controlled by its operator. If people are machines, they can be driven like automobiles. The analogy is absurd, of course, but it illustrates the kind of distortion that can occur.

If the assumption that behavior control is feasible in some precise scientific sense becomes firmly rooted in public psychology, it could have unfortunate consequences, particularly if it is coupled with an assumption that control should be exercised by an industrial or bureaucratic elite. Psychologists must always respect and advocate the principle of *habeas mentem*—the right of a man to his own mind (Sanford, 1955). If we really did have a new scientific way to control human behavior, it would be highly immoral to let it fall into the hands of some small group of men, even if they were psychologists.

Perhaps a historical analogy would be appropriate. When the evolution of species was a new and exciting idea in biology, various social theorists took it up and interpreted it to mean that capitalistic competition, like the competition between species, was the source of all progress, so the great wealth of the new industrialists was a scientifically necessary consequence of the law of the survival of the fittest. This argument, called "social Darwinism," had unfortunate consequences, both for social science and for society generally (Hofstadter, 1944).

If the notion should now be accepted that it is a scientifically necessary consequence of the law of reinforcement that industrialists or bureaucrats must be allowed the same control over people that an experimenter has over his laboratory animals, I fear that a similar period of intolerable exploitation might ensue—if, indeed, it has not already begun.

The dangers that accompany a science of behavior control have been pointed out many times. Psychologists who study motivation scientifically are usually puzzled by this widespread apprehension that they might be successful. Control is not something invented by psychologists. Everyone is "controlled" all the time by something or other. All we want is to discover how the controls work. Once we understand that, society can use the knowledge in whatever manner seems socially advantageous. Our critics, on the other hand, want to know who will diagnose our problems, who will set our social goals, and who will administer the rewards and punishments.

All that I have tried to add to this familiar dialogue is the observation that the social dangers involved need not await the success of the scientific enterprise. Behavior control could easily become a self-fulfilling prophecy. If people generally should come to believe in the scientific control of behavior, proponents of coercive social programs would surely exploit that belief by dressing their proposals in scientific costumes. If our new public conception of human nature is that man's behavior can be scientifically controlled by those in positions of power, governments will quickly conform to that conception. Thus, when I try to discern what direction our psychological revolution has been taking, some aspects of it disturb me deeply and lead me to question whether in the long run these developments will really promote human welfare.

This is a serious charge. If there is any truth to it, we should ask whether any other approaches are open to us.

Personally, I believe there is a better way to advertise psychology and to relate it to social problems. Reinforcement is only one of many important ideas that we have to offer. Instead of repeating constantly that reinforcement leads to control, I would prefer to emphasize that reinforcement can lead to satisfaction and competence. And I would prefer to speak of understanding and prediction as our major scientific goals.

In the space remaining, therefore, I want to try to make the case that understanding and prediction are better goals for psychology than is control—better both for psychology and for the promotion of human welfare—because they lead us to think, not in terms of coercion by a powerful elite, but in terms of the diagnosis of problems and the development of programs that can enrich the lives of every citizen.

PUBLIC PSYCHOLOGY: TWO PARADIGMS

It should be obvious by now that I have somewhere in the back of my mind two alternative images of what the popular conception of human nature might become under the impact of scientific advances in psychology. One of these images is unfortunate, even threatening; the other is vaguer, but full of promise. Let me try to make these ideas more concrete.

The first image is the one I have been describing. It has great appeal to an authoritarian mind, and fits well with our traditional competitive ideology based on coercion, punishment, and retribution. The fact that it represents a serious distortion of scientific psychology is exactly my point. In my opinion, we have made a mistake by trying to apply our ideas to social problems and to gain acceptance for our science within the framework of this ideology.

The second image rests on the same psychological foundation, but reflects it more accurately; it allows no compromise with our traditional social ideology. It is assumed, vaguely but optimistically, that this ideology can be modified so as to be more receptive to a truer conception of human nature. How this modification can be achieved is one of the problems we face; I believe it will not be achieved if we continue to advertise the control of behavior through reinforcement as our major contribution to the solution of social problems. I would not wish to give anyone the impression that I have formulated a well-defined social alternative, but I would at least like to open a discussion and make some suggestions. . . .

Varela (1970, in press) contrasts two conceptions of the social nature of man. Following Kuhn's (1962) discussion of scientific revolutions, he refers to these two conceptions as "paradigms." The first paradigm is a set of assumptions on which our social institutions are presently based. The second is a contrasting paradigm based on psychological research. Let me outline them for you very briefly.

Our current social paradigm is characterized as follows: All men are created equal. Most behavior is motivated by economic competition, and conflict is inevitable. One truth underlies all controversy, and unreasonableness is best countered by facts and logic. When something goes wrong, someone is to blame, and every effort must be made to establish his guilt so that he can be punished. The guilty person is responsible for his own misbehavior and for his own rehabilitation. His teachers and supervisors are too busy to become experts in social science; their role is to devise solutions and see to it that their students or subordinates do what they are told.

For comparison, Varela offers a paradigm based on psychological research: There are large individual differences among people, both in ability and personality. Human motivation is complex and no one ever acts as he does for any single reason, but, in general, positive incentives are more effective than threats or punishments. Conflict is no more inevitable than disease and can be resolved or, still better, prevented. Time and resources for resolving social problems are strictly limited. When something goes wrong, how a person perceives the situation is more important to him than the "true facts," and he cannot reason about the situation until his irrational feelings have been toned down. Social problems are solved by correcting causes, not symptoms, and this can be done more effectively in groups than individually. Teachers and supervisors must be experts in social science because they are responsible for the cooperation and individual improvement of their students or subordinates. . . .

Here, then, is the real challenge: How can we foster a social climate in which some such new public conception of man based on psychology can take root and flourish? In my opinion, this is the proper translation of our more familiar question about how psychology might contribute to the promotion of human welfare.

I cannot pretend to have an answer to this question, even in its translated form, but I believe that part of the answer is that psychology must be practiced by nonpsychologists. We are not physicians; the secrets of our trade need not be reserved for highly trained specialists. Psychological facts should be passed out freely to all who need and can use them. And from successful applications of psychological principles the public may gain a better appreciation for the power of the new conception of man that is emerging from our science. . . .

Of course, everyone practices psychology, just as everyone who cooks is a chemist, everyone who reads a clock is an astronomer, everyone who drives a car is an engineer. I am not suggesting any radical departure when I say that nonpsychologists must practice psychology. I am simply proposing that we should teach them to practice it better, to make use self-consciously of what we believe to be scientifically valid principles.

Our responsibility is less to assume the role of experts and try to apply psychology ourselves than to give it away to the people who really need it—and that includes everyone. The practice of valid psychology by non-psychologists will inevitably change people's conception of themselves and what they can do. When we have accomplished that, we will really have caused a psychological revolution. . . .

REFERENCES

Hofstadter, R. *Social Darwinism in American thought*. Philadelphia: University of Pennsylvania Press, 1944.

Kuhn, T., *The structure of scientific revolutions*. Chicago: University of Chicago Press, 1962.

Sanford, F. II. Creative health and the principle of *habeas mentem*. *American Psychologist*, 1955, **10**, 829–835.

Varela, J. A. *Introduction to social science technology*. New York: Academic Press, 1970, in press.

FREEDOM AND THE CONTROL OF MEN

B. F. Skinner

The second half of the twentieth century may be remembered for its solution of a curious problem. Although Western democracy created the conditions responsible for the rise of modern science, it is now evident that it may never fully profit from that achievement. The so-called "democratic philosophy" of human behavior to which it also gave rise is increasingly in conflict with the application of the methods of science to human affairs. Unless this conflict is somehow resolved, the ultimate goals of democracy may be long deferred.

I

Just as biographers and critics look for external influences to account for the traits and achievements of the men they study, so science ultimately explains behavior in terms of "causes" or conditions which lie beyond the individual himself. As more and more causal relations are demonstrated, a practical corollary becomes difficult to resist: it should be possible to

Reprinted from *The American Scholar*, Winter, 1955–1956, 25, 47–65. By permission of Dr. B. F. Skinner.

produce behavior according to plan simply by arranging the proper conditions. Now, among the specifications which might reasonably be submitted to a behavioral technology are these: Let men be happy, informed, skillful, well behaved and productive.

This immediate practical implication of a science of behavior has a familiar ring, for it recalls the doctrine of human perfectibility of eighteenth- and nineteenth-century humanism. A science of man shares the optimism of that philosophy and supplies striking support for the working faith that men can build a better world and, through it, better men. The support comes just in time, for there has been little optimism of late among those who speak from the traditional point of view. Democracy has become "realistic," and it is only with some embarrassment that one admits today to perfectionistic or utopian thinking.

The earlier temper is worth considering, however. History records many foolish and unworkable schemes for human betterment, but almost all the great changes in our culture which we now regard as worthwile can be traced to perfectionistic philosophies. Governmental, religious, educational, economic and social reforms follow a common pattern. Someone believes that a change in a cultural practice—for example, in the rules of evidence in a court of law, in the characterization of man's relation to God, in the way children are taught to read and write, in permitted rates of interest, or in minimal housing standards—will improve the condition of men: by promoting justice, permitting men to seek salvation more effectively, increasing the literacy of a people, checking an inflationary trend, or improving public health and family relations, respectively. The underlying hypothesis is always the same: that a different physical or cultural environment will make a different and better man.

The scientific study of behavior not only justifies the general pattern of such proposals; it promises new and better hypotheses. The earliest cultural practices must have originated in sheer accidents. Those which strengthened the group survived with the group in a sort of natural selection. As soon as men began to propose and carry out changes in practice for the sake of possible consequences, the evolutionary process must have accelerated. The simple practice of making changes must have had survival value. A further acceleration is now to be expected. As laws of behavior are more precisely stated, the changes in the environment required to bring about a given effect may be more clearly specified. Conditions which have been neglected because their effects were slight or unlooked for may be shown to be relevant. New conditions may actually be created, as in the discovery and synthesis of drugs which affect behavior.

This is no time, then, to abandon notions of progress, improvement or, indeed, human perfectibility. The simple fact is that man is able, and now as never before, to lift himself by his own bootstraps. In achieving control of the world of which he is a part, he may learn at last to control himself.

II

Timeworn objections to the planned improvement of cultural practices are already losing much of their force. Marcus Aurelius was probably right in advising his readers to be content with a haphazard amelioration of mankind. "Never hope to realize Plato's republic," he sighed, ". . . for who can change the opinions of men? And without a change of sentiments what can you make but reluctant slaves and hypocrites?" He was thinking, no doubt, of contemporary patterns of control based upon punishment or the threat of punishment which, as he correctly observed, breed only reluctant slaves of those who submit and hypocrites of those who discover modes of evasion. But we need not share his pessimism, for the opinions of men can be changed. The techniques of indoctrination which were being devised by the early Christian Church at the very time Marcus Aurelius was writing are relevant, as are some of the techniques of psychotherapy and of advertising and public relations. Other methods suggested by recent scientific analyses leave little doubt of the matter.

The study of human behavior also answers the cynical complaint that there is a plain "cussedness" in man which will always thwart efforts to improve him. We are often told that men do not want to be changed, even for the better. Try to help them, and they will outwit you and remain happily wretched. Dostoevsky claimed to see some plan in it. "Out of sheer ingratitude," he complained, or possibly boasted, "man will play you a dirty trick, just to prove that men are still men and not the keys of a piano. . . . And even if you could prove that a man is only a piano key, he would still do something out of sheer perversity—he would create destruction and chaos—just to gain his point. . . . And if all this could in turn be analyzed and prevented by predicting that it would occur, then man would deliberately go mad to prove his point." This is a conceivable neurotic reaction to inept control. A few men may have shown it, and many have enjoyed Dostoevsky's statement because they tend to show it. But that such perversity is a fundamental reaction of the human organism to controlling conditions is sheer nonsense.

So is the objection that we have no way of knowing what changes to make even though we have the necessary techniques. That is one of the great hoaxes of the century—a sort of booby trap left behind in the retreat before the advancing front of science. Scientists themselves have unsuspectingly agreed that there are two kinds of useful propositions about nature—facts and value judgments—and that science must confine itself to "what is," leaving "what ought to be" to others. But with what special sort of wisdom is the non-scientist endowed? Science is only effective knowing, no matter who engages in it. Verbal behavior proves upon analysis to be composed of many different types of utterances, from poetry and exhortation to logic and factual description, but these are not all equally useful in talking about cultural practices. We may classify useful propositions according to the degrees of confidence with which they may be asserted. Sentences about nature range from highly probable "facts" to sheer guesses. In general, future events are less likely to be correctly described than past. When a scientist talks about a projected experiment, for example, he must often resort to statements having only a moderate likelihood of being correct; he calls them hypotheses.

Designing a new cultural pattern is in many ways like designing an experiment. In drawing up a new constitution, outlining a new educational program, modifying a religious doctrine, or setting up a new fiscal policy, many statements must be quite tentative. We cannot be sure that the practices we specify will have the consequences we predict, or that the consequences will reward our efforts. This is in the nature of such proposals. They are not value judgments—they are guesses. To confuse and delay the improvement of cultural practices by quibbling about the word *improve* is itself not a useful practice. Let us agree, to start with, that health is better than illness, wisdom better than ignorance, love better than hate, and productive energy better than neurotic sloth.

Another familiar objection is the "political problem." Though we know what changes to make and how to make them, we still need to control certain relevant conditions, but these have long since fallen into the hands of selfish men who are not going to relinquish them for such purposes. Possibly we shall be permitted to develop areas which at the moment seem unimportant, but at the first signs of success the strong men will move in. This, it is said, has happened to Christianity, democracy and communism. There will always be men who are fundamentally selfish and evil, and in the long run innocent goodness cannot have its way. The only evidence here is historical, and it may be misleading. Because of the way in which physical science developed, history could until very recently have "proved" that the unleashing of the energy of the atom was quite unlikely, if not impossible. Similarly, because of the order in which processes in human behavior have become available for purposes of control, history may seem to prove that power will probably be appropriated for selfish purposes. The first techniques to be discovered fell almost always to strong, selfish men. History led Lord Acton to believe that power corrupts, but he had probably never encountered absolute power, certainly not in all its forms, and had no way of predicting its effect.

An optimistic historian could defend a different conclusion. The principle that if there are not enough men of good will in the world the first step is to create more seems to be gaining recognition. The Marshall Plan (as originally conceived), Point Four, the offer of atomic materials to power-starved countries—these may or may not be wholly new in the history of international relations, but they suggest an increasing awareness of the power of governmental good will. They are proposals to make certain changes in the environments of men for the sake of consequences which should be rewarding for all concerned. They do not exemplify a disinterested generosity, but an interest which is the interest of everyone. We have not yet seen Plato's philosopher-king, and may not want to, but the gap between real and utopian government is closing.

III

But we are not yet in the clear, for a new and unexpected obstacle has arisen. With a world of their own making almost within reach, men of good will have been seized with distaste for their achievement. They have uneasily rejected opportunities to apply the techniques and findings of science in the service of men, and as the import of effective cultural design has come to be understood, many of them have voiced an outright refusal to have any part in it. Science has been challenged before when it has encroached upon institutions already engaged in the control of human behavior; but what are we to make of benevolent men, with no special interests of their own to defend, who nevertheless turn against the very means of reaching long-dreamed-of goals?

What is being rejected, of course, is the scientific conception of man and his place in nature. So long as the findings and methods of science are applied to human affairs only in a sort of remedial patchwork, we may continue to hold any view of human nature we like. But as the use of science increases, we are forced to accept the theoretical structure with which science represents its facts. The difficulty is that this structure is clearly at odds with the traditional democratic conception of man. Every discovery of an event which has a part in shaping a man's behavior seems to leave so much the less to be credited to the man himself; and as such explanations become more and more comprehensive, the contribution which may be claimed by the individual himself appears to approach zero. Man's vaunted creative powers, his original accomplishments in art, science and morals, his capacity to choose and our right to hold him responsible for the consequences of his choice—none of these is conspicuous in this new self-portrait. Man, we once believed, was free to express himself in art, music and literature, to inquire into nature, to seek salvation in his own way. He could initiate action and make spontaneous and capricious changes of course. Under the most extreme duress some sort of choice remained to him. He could resist any effort to control him, though it might cost him his life. But science insists that action is initiated by forces impinging upon the individual, and that caprice is only another name for behavior for which we have not yet found a cause.

In attempting to reconcile these views it is important to note that the traditional democratic conception was not designed as a description in the scientific sense but as a philosophy to be used in setting up and maintaining a governmental process. It arose under historical circumstances and served political purposes apart from which it cannot be properly understood. In rallying men against tyranny it was necessary that the individual be strengthened, that he be taught that he had rights and could govern himself. To give the common man a new conception of his worth, his dignity, and his power to save himself, both here and hereafter, was often the only resource of the revolutionist. When democratic principles were put into practice, the same doctrines were used as a working formula. This is exemplified by the notion of personal responsibility in Anglo-American law. All governments make certain forms of punishment contingent upon certain kinds of acts. In democratic countries these contingencies are expressed by the notion of responsible choice. But the notion may have no meaning under governmental practices formulated in other ways and would certainly have no place in systems which did not use punishment.

The democratic philosophy of human nature is determined by certain political exigencies and techniques, not by the goals of democracy. But exigencies and techniques change; and a conception which is not supported for its accuracy as a likeness—is not, indeed, rooted in fact at all—may be expected to change too. No matter how effective we judge current democratic practices to be, how highly we value them or how long we expect them to survive, they are almost certainly not the *final* form of government. The philosophy of human nature which has been useful in implementing them is also almost certainly not the last word. The ultimate achievement of democracy may be long deferred unless we emphasize the real aims rather than the verbal devices of democratic thinking. A philosophy which has been appropriate to one set of political exingencies will defeat its purpose if, under other circumstances, it prevents us from applying to human affairs the science of man which probably nothing but democracy itself could have produced.

IV

Perhaps the most crucial part of our democratic philosophy to be reconsidered is our attitude toward freedom—or its reciprocal, the control of human behavior. We do not oppose all forms of control because it is "human nature" to do so. The reaction is not characteristic of all men under all conditions of life. It is an attitude which has been carefully engineered, in large part by what we call the "literature" of democracy. With respect to some methods of control (for example, the threat of force), very little engineering is needed, for the techniques or their immediate consequences are objectionable. Society has suppressed these methods by branding them "wrong," "illegal" or "sinful." But to encourage these attitudes toward objectionable forms of control, it has been necessary to disguise the real nature of certain indispensable techniques, the commonest examples of which are education, moral discourse, and persuasion. The actual procedures appear harmless enough. They consist of supplying information, presenting opportunities for action, pointing out logical relationships, appealing to reason or "enlightened understanding," and so on. Through a masterful piece of misrepresentation, the illusion is fostered that these procedures do not involve the control of behavior; at most, they are simply ways of "getting someone to change his mind." But analysis not only reveals the presence of well-defined behavioral processes, it demonstrates a kind of control no less inexorable, though in some ways more acceptable, than the bully's threat of force.

Let us suppose that someone in whom we are interested is acting unwisely—he is careless in the way he deals with his friends, he drives too fast, or he holds his golf club the wrong way. We could probably help him by issuing a series of commands: don't nag, don't drive over sixty, don't hold your club that way. Much less objectionable would be "an appeal to reason." We could show him how people are affected by his treatment of them, how accident rates rise sharply at higher speeds, how a particular grip on the club alters the way the ball is struck and corrects a slice. In doing so we resort to verbal mediating devices which emphasize and support certain "contingencies of reinforcement"—that is, certain relations between behavior and its consequences—which strengthen the behavior we wish to set up. The same consequences would possibly set up the behavior without our help, and they eventually take control no matter which form of help we give. The appeal to reason has certain advantages over the authoritative command. A threat of punishment, no matter how subtle, generates emotional reactions and tendencies to escape or revolt. Perhaps the controllee merely "feels resentment" at being made to act in a given way, but even that is to be avoided. When we "appeal to reason," he "feels freer to do as he pleases." The fact is that we have exerted *less* control than in using a threat; since other conditions may contribute to the result, the effect may be delayed or, possibly in a given instance, lacking. But if we have worked a change in his behavior at all, it is because we have altered relevant environmental conditions, and the processes we have set in motion are just as real and just as inexorable, if not as comprehensive, as in the most authoritative coercion.

"Arranging an opportunity for action" is another example of disguised control. The power of the negative form has already been exposed in the analysis of censorship. Restriction of opportunity is recognized as far from harmless. As Ralph Barton Perry said in an article which appeared in the Spring, 1953, *Pacific Spectator*, "Whoever determines what alternatives shall be made known to man controls what that man shall choose *from*. He is deprived of freedom in proportion as he is denied access to *any* ideas, or is confined to any range of ideas short of the totality of relevant possibilities." But there is a positive side as well. When we present a relevant state of affairs, we increase the likelihood that a given form of behavior will be emitted. To the extent that the probability of action has changed, we have made a definite contribution. The teacher of history controls a student's behavior (or, if the reader prefers, "deprives him of freedom") just as much in *presenting* historical facts as in suppressing them. Other conditions will no doubt affect the student, but the contribution made to his behavior by the presentation of material is fixed and, within its range, irresistible.

The methods of education, moral discourse, and persuasion are acceptable not because they recognize the freedom of the individual or his right to dissent, but because they make only *partial* contributions to the control of his behavior. The freedom they recognize is freedom from a more coercive form of control. The dissent which they tolerate is the possible effect of other determiners of action. Since these sanctioned methods are frequently ineffective, we have been able to convince ourselves that they do not represent control at all. When they show too much strength to permit disguise, we give them other names and suppress them as energetically as we suppress the use of force. Education grown too powerful is rejected as propaganda or "brain-washing," while really effective persuasion is decried as "undue influence," "demagoguery," "seduction," and so on.

If we are not to rely solely upon accident for the innovations which give rise to cultural evolution, we must accept the fact that some kind of control of human behavior is inevitable. We cannot use good sense in human affairs unless someone engages in the design and construction of environmental conditions which affect the behavior of men. Environmental changes have always been the condition for the improvement of cultural patterns, and we can hardly use the more effective methods of science without making changes on a grander scale. We are all controlled by the world in which we live, and part of that world has been and will be constructed by men. The question is this: Are we to be controlled by accident, by tyrants, or by ourselves in effective cultural design?

The danger of the misuse of power is possibly greater than ever. It is not allayed by disguising the facts. We cannot make wise decisions if we continue to pretend that human behavior is not controlled, or if we refuse to engage in control when valuable results might be forthcoming. Such measures weaken only ourselves, leaving the strength of science to others. The first step in a defense against tyranny is the fullest possible exposure of controlling techniques. A second step has already been taken successfully in restricting the use of physical force. Slowly, and as yet imperfectly, we have worked out an ethical and governmental design in which the strong man is not allowed to use the power deriving from his strength to control his fellow men. He is restrained by a superior force created for that purpose—the ethical pressure of the group, or more explicit religious and governmental measures. We tend to distrust superior forces, as we currently hesitate to relinquish sovereignty in order to set up an international police force. But it is only through such counter-control that we have achieved what we call peace—a condition in which men are not permitted to control each other through force. In other words, control itself must be controlled.

Science has turned up dangerous processes and materials before. To use the facts and techniques of a science of man to the fullest extent without making some monstrous mistake will be difficult and obviously perilous. It is no time for self-deception, emotional indulgence, or the assumption of attitudes which are no longer useful. Man is facing a difficult test. He must keep his head now, or he must start again—a long way back.

V

Those who reject the scientific conception of man must, to be logical, oppose the methods of science as well. The position is often supported by predicting a series of dire consequences which are to follow if science is not checked. A recent book by Joseph Wood Krutch, *The Measure of Man*, is in this vein. Mr. Krutch sees in the growing science of man the threat of an unexampled tyranny over men's minds. If science is permitted to have its way, he insists, "we may never be able really to think again." A controlled culture will, for example, lack some virtue inherent in disorder. We have emerged from chaos through a series of happy accidents, but in an engineered culture it will be "impossible for the unplanned to erupt again." But there is no virtue in the accidental character of an accident, and the diversity which arises from disorder can not only be duplicated by design but vastly extended. The experimental method is superior to simple observation just because it multiplies "accidents" in a systematic coverage of the possibilities. Technology offers many familiar examples. We no longer wait for immunity to disease to develop from a series of accidental exposures, nor do we wait for natural mutations in sheep and cotton to produce better fibers; but we continue to make use of such accidents when they occur, and we certainly do not prevent them. Many of the things we value have emerged from the clash of ignorant armies on darkling plains, but it is not therefore wise to encourage ignorance and darkness.

It is not always disorder itself which we are told we shall miss but certain admirable qualities in men which flourish only in the presence of disorder. A man rises above an unpropitious childhood to a position of eminence, and since we cannot give a plausible account of the action of so complex an environment, we attribute the achievement to some admirable faculty in the man himself. But such "faculties" are suspiciously like the explanatory fictions against which the history of science warns us. We admire Lincoln for rising above a deficient school system, but it was not necessarily something *in him* which permitted him to become an educated man in spite of it. His educational environment was certainly unplanned, but it could nevertheless have made a full contribution to his mature behavior. He was a rare man, but the circumstances of his childhood were rare too. We do not give Franklin Delano Roosevelt the same credit for becoming an educated man with the help of Groton and Harvard, although the same behavioral processes may have been involved. The founding of Groton and Harvard somewhat reduced the possibility that fortuitous combinations of circumstances would erupt to produce other Lincolns. Yet the founders can hardly be condemned for attacking an admirable human quality.

Another predicted consequence of a science of man is an excessive uniformity. We are told that effective control—whether governmental, religious, educational, economic or social—will produce a race of men who differ from each other only through relatively refractory genetic differences. That would probably be bad design, but we must admit that we are not now pursuing another course from choice. In a modern school, for example, there is usually a syllabus which specifies what every student is to learn by the end of each year. This would be flagrant regimentation if anyone expected every student to comply. But some will be poor in particular subjects, others will not study, others will not remember what they have been taught, and diversity is assured. Suppose, however, that we someday possess such effective educational techniques that every student will in fact be put in possession of all the behavior specified in a syllabus. At the end of the year, all students will correctly answer all questions on the final examination and "must all have prizes." Should we reject such a system on the grounds that in making all students excellent it has made them all alike? Advocates of the theory of a special faculty might contend that an important advantage of the present system is that the good student learns *in spite of* a system which is so defective that it is currently producing bad students as well. But if really effective techniques are available, we cannot avoid the problem of design simply by preferring the status quo. At what point should education be deliberately inefficient?

Such predictions of the havoc to be wreaked by the application of science to human affairs are usually made with surprising confidence. They not only show a faith in the orderliness of human behavior; they presuppose an established body of knowledge with the help of which it can be positively asserted that the changes which scientists propose to make will have quite specific results—albeit not the results they foresee. But the predictions made by the critics of science must be held to be equally fallible and subject also to empirical test. We may be sure that many steps in the scientific design of cultural patterns will produce unforeseen consequences. But there is only one way to find out. And the test must be made, for if we cannot advance in the design of cultural patterns with absolute certainty, neither can we rest completely confident of the superiority of the status quo. . . .

CORE CONCEPTS OF PSYCHOLOGY

2 Sensation and Perception

In the past it has been tempting to think of sensation and perception as consisting of simple, mechanistic processes; the sense organ is stimulated, a message goes to the brain, and whatever caused the initial stimulation is perceived. Recently, however, this "passive recorder" view has had to be rejected. The major reasons for rejecting it are outlined in the first of the next two articles, *The Development of Perception as an Adaptive Process* by Dr. Eleanor J. Gibson, in which perception is seen as a process of extracting information from stimulation. That is, animals and human beings actively search for information that will enable them to adapt to varying environmental conditions. One of the things that makes this viewpoint appealing is the novel way it treats perceptual learning; it rejects the traditional learning approach in favor of an information processing approach.

Even though our sensory and perceptual systems serve us admirably, they still have their limits. This is demonstrated in the second article, *High Intensity Sounds in the Recreational Environment*, in which Dr. David M. Lipscomb shows that excessively loud sounds (rock 'n roll music for example) can mechanically "drive" the auditory system to the point of producing marked physiological damage and impaired hearing.

THE DEVELOPMENT OF PERCEPTION AS AN ADAPTIVE PROCESS

Eleanor J. Gibson

To tell you how I see perceptual development as a mark of adaptiveness, I must explain first what I think perception is and what perceptual learning is. . . .

Perception is extracting information from stimulation (Gibson 1966). Stimulation emanates from the objects and surfaces and events in the world around us and it *carries information about* them; though different from them, it *specifies* them. If we were to consider stimulation only as individual rays of light or vibrations in the air, this specification would not be intelligible, because information about objects and layout of the world around us lies in relations, like edges between things; it is not punctate, but structured over space and time. Not only is there information about things in stimulation; there is rich information, far more, potentially, than we utilize.

Let me give an example. Some animals, especially bats and dolphins, locate food and find their way around by means of echolocation. The dolphin emits clicking sounds at varying rates from one per second to bursts of 500 or more. These clicks are thought to be used for food-finding and navigation. To quote a dolphin expert, "The click trains, or sonar, search the seascape in front of a dolphin in much the same way that the cone of light from a miner's headlamp shows his way through a mine. In the presence of reflected light, we see where we look. In the presence of reflected sound, or the echoes of their own clicks, dolphins hear where they point their beam of sound. The click-echoes returned from the environment before the moving dolphin are information-bearing. The echoes contain information about the size, shape, location, movement if any, and texture of the living and nonliving things in the water" (McVay 1967, p. 8). It has in fact been demonstrated that dolphins can differentiate in this way objects of different sizes and shape and even different metallic substances, and can swim an obstacle course without collision. Three points emerge from this: one, that potential stimulus information about features of the environment is vast; second, that the information accurately specifies the layout of the world and the objects in it; and third, that perception is an active process, a search for the relevant information that specifies the path an animal needs to travel, the obstacles to be avoided, the mate or the food to be approached.

So perception, functionally speaking, is extracting information about the world from stimulation, a highly adaptive process since the animal must somehow discover where to go, what to seize, and what to avoid. What kind

From the *American Scientist*, 1970, 58, 98–107. Reprinted by permission, *American Scientist*, journal of The Society of the Sigma Xi, and author.

of world is there to perceive? We can describe it in several ways. I choose a classification that refers to properties of the environment. These include properties of the *spatial layout* (surfaces, edges, drop-offs); properties of *events* (motion, occlusion, appearance, disappearance, and reappearance); and properties of *objects* that make them distinguishable and identifiable. For man at least we can include another class; man-made symbols—*coded items* that stand for objects and events, such as speech and writing. . . .

How do animals *learn* to perceive the permanent distinguishable properties of the world in the changing flux of stimulation? Not, I believe, by association, but by a process of extracting the invariant information from the variable flux. I think several processes are involved, all attentional ones. (See Gibson 1969 for a detailed statement of the theory of perceptual learning.) One is perceptual abstraction. . . . Another is filtering of the irrelevant, an attenuation in the perceiving of random, varying, noninformative aspects of stimulation. A third is active, exploratory search. The dolphin beaming his clicking sounds is an example of the latter. . . .

With respect to the search process in perceptual learning, a very important question is what terminates the search and thus selects what is learned. For many years no one questioned the proposition that external reinforcement (e.g. food or shock) is the selective principle for learning things like bar-pressing or choosing one arm of a maze rather than another. But is a distinctive feature selected as relevant because it wins a reward or avoids punishment? Is this the way that higher-order structural relations are detected? Although this might happen in a teaching situation, I do not think it is the true principle of perceptual learning. So much of it goes on very early in life and is necessarily self-regulated. No experimenter is on hand to deliver reinforcement; probably not even a parent could provide it deliberately, since he seldom has any way of knowing just what the child is perceiving.

I think the reinforcement is internal—the *reduction of uncertainty*. Stimulation is not only full of potential information; there is too much of it. There is a limit to what can be processed, and variable, random, irrelevant stimulation leads only to perception of confusion—what someone has referred to as cognitive clutter as opposed to cognitive order. But distinctive features, invariants, and higher-order structure serve the function of reducing uncertainty, taking order and continuity out of chaos and flux. The search for invariants, both low-level contrastive features and high-level order, is the task of perception, while detection of them at once reduces uncertainty and is reinforcing.

PERCEPTUAL DEVELOPMENT IN SPECIES AND INDIVIDUALS

. . . Is there perceptual development, in the animal series and in the individual, and is it adaptive? Are there trends in what is responded to? . . . In order to give some specific answers, I shall compare two modes of perceiving and give evidence, in both cases, of species differences and of development within the life span.

The two modes are perception of *space and events in space* and the perception of *objects and permanent items*, like written letters, that can be approached and examined closely. I have chosen to contrast these because there is reason to think that in their phylogenetic development there is a considerable difference between them. Localizing oneself in the spatial layout or monitoring events going on in the space around one seem to develop earlier and to be neurologically more primitive than fine-grain identification of objects and outline figures such as letters. . . .

PERCEPTION OF SPACE

Consider, first, development of the perception of space and of events in space. Is there phylogenetic continuity here within the vertebrate phylum? Indeed there is. The similarities between species are far greater than their differences in this respect. We can adduce evidence for this in three important cases—perception of imminent collision (called "looming"); perception of depth-downward; and perceived constancy of the sizes of things.

Looming can be defined as accelerated magnification of the form of an approaching object. It is an optical event over time. It specifies a future collision (Schiff, Caviness, and Gibson 1962). If a vehicle or even a small object such as a baseball is perceived as coming directly toward him by a human adult, he ducks or dodges out of the way. Is the perception of imminent collision together with its avoidance instinctive? If so, in what species, and how early? Schiff (1965) constructed an artificial looming situation in which nothing actually approached the animal observer but there was abstract optical information for something approaching.

In Schiff's experiments, a shadow was projected by a shadow-casting device on a large translucent screen in front of the animal. The screen was large enough to fill a wide visual angle. The projected shadow could be made to undergo continuously accelerated magnification until it filled the screen or, on the other hand, continuously decelerating minification. Magnification resulted in a visual impression of an object approaching at a uniform speed. Minification gave a visual impression of an object receding into the distance. The projected silhouette could be varied in form, so as to compare, for instance, jagged contours with smooth ones, or silhouettes of meaningful objects with meaningless ones. Subjects studied included fiddler crabs, frogs, chicks, kittens, monkeys, and humans.

The crabs responded to magnification (but not to minification) by running backwards, flinching, or flattening out. Frogs jumped away from the ghostly approaching object. Chicks responded more often to magnification than minification by running, crouching, and hopping. Kittens (28 days old) tended to respond to magnification with struggle and head movements, but the kittens were restrained in holders and well-differentiated avoidance behavior did not show up clearly. Rhesus monkeys (including infants five to eight months of age) were observed in the situation under four conditions (magnification, minification, lightening of the screen, and darkening of the screen). Both young and adult animals withdrew rapidly in response to the approach display, leaping to the rear of the cage. Alarm cries frequently accompanied retreat in the younger animals. The receding display brought responses which might be described as curiosity, but never retreat. The lightening and darkening of the screen had no effect, and this served as a control, that is, a change of mere stimulation as compared with change of magnification. . . .

What about a human subject? Schiff measured the galvanic skin reflex in adult human subjects in the looming situation. There was decrease of skin resistance in the majority of subjects for magnification but not for minification. Human infants, Burton White found (1969), began to blink at a rapidly approaching object (with air currents controlled) at about three weeks of age. The reliability of the response increased for another 10 or 12 weeks. Perhaps sensitivity to visual approach of a missile takes this long to mature or be learned in the human infant; but perhaps another indicator response would show that it is picked up even earlier. Some observers claim that attempted head withdrawal to visual looming occurs as early as two weeks in human infants. . . .

Now let me give you some phylogenetic comparisons for avoidance of a falling-off place, that is, a drop-off of the ground. Depth downwards is specified in the light to the animal's eye. Does this information by itself cause the animal to avoid it? Some years ago, Dr. Richard Walk and I constructed an apparatus for answering this question (Gibson and Walk 1960). We called it a "visual cliff." "Cliff," because there was a simulated drop-off downward, and "visual" because we attempted to eliminate all other information for the drop-off. Figure 1 shows an apparatus constructed for testing small animals, such as a rat or a chick. The animal is placed on a center board. A checkerboard floor extends out from the center board on one side, an inch or two below it. A similar floor is 10 inches or more below on the other side. A sheet of glass extends from the center board, above the floor, an inch or two below the board, so that tactual information for the cliff is eliminated, and air currents and echoes are equated.

What is the visual information? . . . The best information, our experiments suggested, was the motion perspective produced by the animal's own movements—especially head movements—as the cliff edge is observed in comparison to the shallow edge. Differences in texture density were eliminated and a monocular animal was used to make this observation.

Many animal species have been tested on the visual cliff: rodents, birds, turtles, cats (including lions, tigers, and snow leopards), sheep and goats, dogs, and of course primates (Walk and Gibson 1961; Routtenberg and Glickman 1964). All these species, save flying ones or swimming ones, avoided the cliff edge of the apparatus and chose the safe, shallow edge on

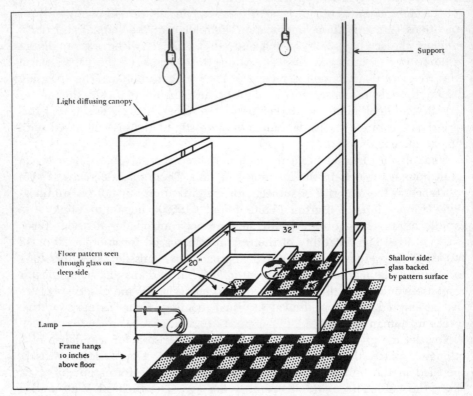

Figure 1. Drawing of a visual cliff (from Walk and Gibson 1961; copyright by American Psychological Association and reproduced by permission).

the basis of visual information alone. Texture must be present on the ground under the animal, however, for a safe surface of support to be perceived. The animal will not walk out upon a homogeneous, untextured surface—he demands "optical support" as well as felt support. This surely has value for survival.

Avoidance of a drop-off and dependence upon optical support must be developmentally primitive. This conclusion is suggested not only by the continuity of the behavior within the vertebrate phylum, but also by ablation experiments and ontogenetic data. When the striate cortex of the cat is removed (Meyer 1963) pattern vision in the sense of identification goes, but a cat will still avoid a cliff, if he can move freely.

Ontogenetically, Walk and I found that cliff avoidance develops very early and, in some species, without any opportunity for learning. Precocial animals such as chicks and goats avoid a cliff a few hours after birth, as soon as they can be tested. Rats reared in the dark avoid a cliff as soon as they are brought out, with no opportunity for preliminary visual experience.

Primates cannot be tested at birth, but human infants avoid a cliff as early as they can crawl. Monkeys, like human infants, are carried by their mothers in early infancy. But monkeys placed on the untextured glass without optical support at three days of age (Rosenblum and Cross 1963) showed indications of emotional disturbance (crouching, vocalization, self-clasping, and rocking), whereas there was no disturbance when they were placed on the glass with a texture just below it.

We may conclude that perception of a safe surface in contrast to a drop-off appears early in evolution and early in life, and that little learning may be required for its appearance. It is modified by biased circumstances, such as prolonged dark rearing, but terrestrial animals do not generally have to be taught this useful adaptation.

Now consider my third case: perceived constancy of the sizes of things. Information for size constancy is given normally by motion; motion of the object toward or away from a stationary observer, or movement of the observer toward the object. Since information for constant size—the rule relating size and distance—is given in motion, it should belong with my "primitive" mode of perceiving. Let us see if it does, if there is continuity over species and early development without any marked dependence on learning with external reinforcement.

As for continuity among animal species, size constancy has been demonstrated in the chimpanzee, by Köhler (1915); in the monkey by Klüver (1933) and by Locke (1937); in the cat by Gunter (1951) and by Freeman (1968); in the weanling rat (Heller 1968); in the duckling (Pastore 1958); and in fish (Herter 1953). It is no surprise to the thoughtful biologist that animals other than man exhibit size constancy. How indeed could they locomote or seize things accurately if the apparent sizes of things around them were constantly shrinking or expanding as distance changed with the target's movement or the observer's position?

Is learning involved in perceiving things as constant in size? It might well be, since the conditions for extracting the invariant depend on motion of an object or of the observer in relation to it. The mother's face approaches the baby as she bends to pick it up; the baby moves his hand toward and away from his eyes and moves them together and apart, for hours at a time. These are guaranteed opportunities for presenting him with appropriately structured stimulation. But such learning would have to take place very early, for Bower (1966) has found evidence of size constancy as young as two months in the human infant. He used the method of operant conditioning, the response being a leftward turning of the head. The infant was trained to respond thus to a 30-cm. white cube placed one meter from his eyes. The reinforcement for the head-turning response was an experimenter popping up and "peek-a-booing" at the infant and then disappearing again (an ingenious and, it turns out, remarkably effective reinforcement. The infant learns to do something to *get a perception*). After training, three new stimuli were introduced for generalization tests. These were the 30-cm. cube placed 3 meters away; a 90-cm. cube placed 1 meter away; and the 90-cm. cube placed 3 meters away. . . .

The conditioned stimulus situation would be expected to elicit the most head-turnings, and the one appearing to the infant most like it, the next most. If the infant has size constancy, one would expect the cube identical with the training one to evoke the next most responses, even when it is farther away (test stimulus 1). If size constancy hasn't been attained, one might expect the cube projecting the same-sized retinal image (test stimulus 3) to elicit most response. The infants, in practice, responded to test stimulus 1 next most often after the training situation, evidence that they perceived the cube in its true, objective size. Next most often came the larger cube placed at the same distance as the training cube; and last of all, the large cube placed at 3 meters where it projected the identical-sized retinal image.

Does this result mean that *no* learning is involved in the development of size constancy? Definitely not, since even eight weeks gives a lot of opportunity for visual experience. But it means that any learning could not have involved association with specific motor acts, such as reaching a certain distance or walking so many paces. But perceived motion of an object could provide an opportunity for discovery of the rule relating projective size of object to nearness of the object. Dark-reared rats (Heller 1968) did not exhibit size constancy when first brought into the light, despite normal performance on the visual cliff. Some visual experiences with objects moving in space may be necessary, therefore, for size constancy to develop, but it does so very early. Later changes, appearing when judgmental methods are used (Piaget 1961), probably indicate development of a more analytical attitude toward perceiving objects rather than the mere localizing of things in their true sizes.

PERCEPTION OF OBJECTS

Now, let me turn to my other class of perceptions—the fine-grain identification of objects, and the use of coded stimuli to substitute for them. Is there continuity over species and early appearance as there is with the spatial perceptions?

There is continuity, yes, but in this instance there is a good case for a striking evolutionary change, and also for a long course of perceptual learning in the individual. The human child must learn the distinctive features of the objects, representations, and symbolic items that human life requires him to differentiate.

What about the *phylogeny* of object identification? Certainly animals identify some objects at quite an early age. The herring gull chick identifies by a spot of red the beak of its parent hovering over it. This information is referred to by the ethologists as an "innate releaser." Releasers seem in many cases to be very simple unlearned signals for the discharging of a fixed unlearned pattern of responses, like the chemical signal that releases attack behavior in some species of snake. A mere trace of the chemical in a box will bring the attack. Sometimes the effective stimulus pattern is more complex, as is the visual pattern that constitutes "owlness" and releases mobbing behavior in the chaffinch, or the quite complex and informative song patterns of many birds, but the role of learning is still minimal in these cases.

Do we have studies of learned object identification in any animals but primates? Of course, the studies of imprinting in precocial animals come to mind. Certain properties of an object like high brightness contrast and motion release in the newborn animal a following response, and following the moving object serves, presumably, to "impress" its features on the "mind" of the subject so that he will later discriminate it from other objects and approach it rather than others. Here, in a manner insuring that the precocial animal will take to his parent or at least to his species, is a very immediate kind of learning that seems to contain the rudiments of perceptual learning. It is not a matter of association of stimulus and response; the response is ready to go at once and, besides, recognition can be measured by other responses than following. There is no external reinforcement; the mother can butt an infant goat away and he will follow her just the same. What is learned is typical of perceptual learning: an increased specificity of response to visual and auditory stimulation characteristic of the releasing object. To what extent there is increased differentiation we really don't know, for early imprinting is quickly followed by opportunities for learning to discriminate feature-contrasts that insure more precise differentiation.

We can study this latter process most easily in the young human animal, so I shall trace some of the steps in his learning to differentiate complex objects in his environment. Does he begin, like the precocial animal, with innate attention to high-contrast visual stimulation and to motion? Some people think so and like to compare the turning of the eyes or head toward a voice or a shiny moving thing to imprinting. One of the first and most prominent objects in an infant's world is the face of his caretaker. Studies of development of recognition of a human face tell us much (Gibson 1969, Ch. 16). At first, it appears to be motion of the head (like a nod) that is compelling, but very shortly the eyes emerge as a prominent feature—the dominant feature for a discriminative response. They are bright, and they move. After a time, the facial contour, the contours of brow and nose around the eyes, and later the mouth (especially in motion) differentiate as critical features. But not until nearly four months must these features be present in an invariant and "face-like" relation for the recognition response to occur. At four months, a "realistic" face is smiled at more. Not until six months are individual faces differentiated, and not until much later still are facial expressions. We know little as yet about how this learning goes on, but it is perceptual learning; there is increasing differentiation of more and more specific stimulus information. Motor responses play little or no role, nor does reinforcement.

"Learning-to-learn" about objects was demonstrated in a long-term experiment with infants 6 to 12 months old by Ling (1941). She presented infants with a pair of solid wooden objects, differently shaped. Both were colored bright yellow and were of a graspable size. They were presented to the infant on a board within reaching distance. One was fastened to the board. The other was removable and was furthermore sweet to taste, having been dipped in a saccharine solution. The infant learned over a period of days to reach at once for the shape that was sweetened. Then five series of problems were presented to him. The first series had four problems: circle vs. cross, circle vs. triangle, circle vs. square, and circle vs. oval. After successive mastery of these, the child progressed to a series in which one of the forms was rotated; then a series in which sizes were transformed; a fourth, in which the number of "wrong" blocks was increased; and a fifth, in which the positive and negative shapes were reversed. There was evidence of more and more rapid learning as the series continued, as well as transfer of discriminations with rotation and change of size. What were the babies learning that transferred? Distinctive features of the shapes they were comparing, to be sure, but something more general too, Ling thought. They learned search strategies of systematic observation and comparison, "attention to form differences, rather than improvement in form discrimination *per se*." Compared with control babies of the same age, they made a more immediate and minute examination of the stimulus patterns and inhibited extraneous bodily movement.

Now I want to finish with the top-level achievement of fine-grain identification—the identification of written symbols. Only man does this and only a well-grown, well-tutored man at that. Monkeys can indeed learn to discriminate a pair of fairly small line drawings from one another, but they are much slower at this task and make many more errors than human children of four or five (Hicks and Hunton 1964; Hunton and Hicks 1965). Both phylogenetically and ontogenetically, this is the peak of perceptual achievement. Here we find that education is most essential. How is one letter discriminated from another? I think by learning the distinctive features for the set of letters. There is evidence to show that this is the way letters really are discriminated, that there is a set of distinctive features, not idiosyncratic to an individual perceiver or to a given graphic character but characterizing the set and permitting each letter to be distinguished by its unique pattern of features within the set. . . .

CONCLUSION

Is the development of perception an adaptive process? It is as much so as the development of locomotion. Nature seems to have insured first the means of detecting the information needed for getting around and avoiding such dangers as obstacles, pitfalls, and missiles. Discrimination of objects by simple signs based on single physical characteristics of high vividness is primitive too. But fine-grain differentiation of multidimensional complex sets of objects is high in the evolutionary scheme and in development, a process where adaptation is achieved only through education.

REFERENCES

Bower, T. G. R. 1966. The visual world of infants. *Scient. Amer.* 215:80–92.

Freeman, R. B. 1968. Perspective determinants of visual size-constancy in binocular and monocular cats. *Amer. J. Psychol.* 81:67–73.

Gibson, E. J., and R. D. Walk. 1960. The "visual cliff." *Scient. Amer.* 202:64–71.

Gibson, J. J. 1966. *The senses considered as perceptual systems.* Boston: Houghton-Mifflin.

Gunter, R. 1951. Visual size constancy in the cat. *Brit. J. Psychol.* 42:288–93.

Heller, D. P. 1968. Absence of size constancy in visually deprived rats. *J. Comp. Physiol. Psychol.* 65:336–39.

Herter, K. 1953. *Die Fischdressuere und ihre sinnes physiologischen Grundlagen.* Berlin: Akademie-Verlag.

Hicks, L. H., and V. D. Hunton. 1964. The relative dominance of form and orientation in discrimination learning by monkeys and children. *Psychon. Sci.* 1:411–12.

Hunton, V. D., and L. H. Hicks. 1965. Discrimination of figural orientation by monkeys and children. *Percept. Mot. Skills* 21:55–59.

Klüver, H. 1933. *Behavior mechanisms in monkeys.* Chicago: Univ. Chicago Press.

Köhler, W. 1915. Untersuchungen am Schimpansen und am Haushuhn. *Abh. preuss. Akad. Wiss.* (phys.-math.) No. 3, 1–70.

Ling, B. C. 1941. Form discrimination as a learning cue in infants. *Comp. Psychol. Monogr.* 17, Whole No. 86.

McVay, S. 1967. How hears the dolphin? *Princeton Alumni Weekly*, October, pp. 6–9.

Meyer, P. M. 1963. Analysis of visual behavior in cats with extensive neocortical ablations. *J. Comp. Physiol. Psychol.* 56:397–401.

Pastore, N. 1958. Form perception and size constancy in the duckling. *J. Psychol.* 45:259–61.

Piaget, J. 1961. *Les mécanismes perceptifs.* Paris: Presses Universitaires de France.

Rosenblum, L. A., and H. A. Cross. 1963. Performance of neonatal monkeys on the visual cliff situation. *Amer. J. Psychol.* 76:318–20.

Routtenberg, A., and S. E. Glickman. 1964. Visual cliff behavior in undomesticated rodents, land and aquatic turtles, and cats (panthera). *J. comp. physiol. Psychol.* 58:143–46.

Schiff, W. 1965. The perception of impending collision: A study of visually directed avoidant behavior. *Psychol. Monogr.* 79, Whole No. 604.

Schiff, W., J. A. Caviness, and J. J. Gibson. 1962. Persistent fear responses in rhesus monkeys to the optical stimulus of "looming." *Science* 136:982–83.

Walk, R. D., and E. J. Gibson. 1961. A comparative and analytical study of visual depth perception. *Psychol. Monogr.* 75, No. 15.

White, B. L. In press, 1969. Child development research: An edifice without a foundation. *Merrill-Palmer Quarterly.*

HIGH INTENSITY SOUNDS IN
THE RECREATIONAL ENVIRONMENT

David M. Lipscomb

The causes of hearing impairment in children are myriad. Pediatricians are constantly required to recognize these disorders and either render or seek out the proper treatment. Conductive hearing loss is a manifestation of some obstructive condition which reduces the capability of the transmission system of the middle ear to conduct sound vibrations to the cochlea. In some children with impaired hearing the outer and middle ears are intact but the lesion lies in the cochlea. Such a sensori-neural disorder may be caused by high fever, drug toxicity, congenital maldevelopment, hereditary factors, or (more recently recognized) sustained loud noise.

Noise-Induced Hearing Loss

Once considered a rare phenomenon, the incidence of noise-induced hearing impairment in children from exposure to high intensity sounds in their play and recreation environment is now not only common, but increasing at an alarming rate. For example, when Weber *et al.*[1] in 1967 audiometrically tested 1,000 school-age Colorado children they found high frequency hearing impairment (HFI) more frequent in older than in younger children. Significantly more boys than girls had HFI.

Last year, in a survey which I and my associates conducted in Knoxville Public Schools, we tested the hearing of 3,000 children, 1,000 each from grades six, nine and 12. . . . A relatively small number of sixth-graders (3.8%) had HFI, whereas a dramatic increase (11%) was found among ninth-graders. High school seniors showed an . . . incidence of HFI (10.6%). . . . We also found HFI to be more common among boys than girls. While we had expected some increase in the incidence of HFI as a function of age, we did not anticipate such a marked rise.

We concluded from this survey that young people may be losing some hearing because of the high-intensity sound environment to which they subject themselves. A common source of such high intensity sound is rock 'n roll music. . . .

Experimental Stimulation

For these reasons we set up an experiment to measure the extent of anatomic damage of the hearing mechanism which might be brought about

Reprinted from *Clinical Pediatrics*, 1969, 8, 63–68. By permission of J. B. Lippincott Company and author.

The assistance of Jack Ferrell, Thomas Davidson, Michael Crum, Christine Owen and Judy Yeiser is gratefully acknowledged.

[1] Weber, H. J., McGovern, F. J. and Zink, D.: An evaluation of 1000 children with hearing loss. *Journal of Speech and Hearing Disorders* 32: 343, 1967.

by intense sound stimulation. We used guinea pigs to evaluate the histologic changes in the auditory sensory receptors.

The guinea pigs were subjected to rock 'n roll music adjusted to sound levels approximating those measured in dance halls. . . .

Prior to stimulation, each animal was lightly anesthetized and an Audilin plug was inserted into the left ear to provide protection from the sound. The protected ear was an experimental control.

Stimulation schedules were varied to approximate the random exposure by teenagers listening to high intensity music. Twenty-seven stimulation periods were used in 58 days, the duration of each exposure varying from a low of 35 minutes to a maximum of 227 minutes per session. After 65 hours of total exposure each animal's protective plug was removed, allowing 23 hours of bilateral sound exposure for the remaining time. Upon completion of the stimulus schedule, each guinea pig had sustained a total of 88 hours and six minutes exposure to the high intensity music.

Analysis of Specimens

Cochlear tissue preparations from each test animal were made by the surface preparation technic, to examine microscopically longitudinal segments of the Organ of Corti.

All structures and cells in this area appear normal, and no cell destruction was noted in any of the tissues removed from . . . [the protected ear]. . . . The cells one and one-half turns from the base of the unprotected . . . cochlea show[ed] widespread damage. Several inner hair cells . . . [were] obliterated or misshapen, and numerous outer hair cells . . . [were] collapsed and appear to be missing. . . .

Discussion

Most alarming is the widespread irreversible damage in the cochlea of an experimental animal exposed to sound comparable in intensity to that which many young persons expose themselves every day. . . .

Caution must be exercised, of course, when relating observations from experimental animals to humans. The inference is clear, however, that the typical discotheque sound environment is sufficiently intense to be extremely hazardous to the health and well-being of sensory cells in the cochlea.

The erratic pattern of damage shown by the cochleogram precludes the assumption, however, that discrete frequency pure-tone audiometric studies can provide evidence of cochlear damage. Unfortunately, pure-tone audiometry cannot delineate early signs of damage resulting from sound trauma, unless the cochlear injury is specifically located in one of the sensory regions tested by the pure tone stimulus. . . . Thus, it is entirely possible that the damaged cells could be located so as not to affect hearing acuity for any of the discrete frequencies usually tested by audiometry. . . .

Conclusions and Recommendations

1. Exposure to 88 hours of high intensity rock 'n roll music over a two-month period resulted in marked sensory cell damage in the cochlea of an experimental animal.
2. Persons who expose themselves to high intensity "rock" music for a total exposure time exceeding 23 hours in a two-month period may suffer irreversible damage to cochlear sensory cells.
3. A program of hearing conservation must be initiated. The dangers of exposure to high intensity recreation environment sounds must be made clear to those participating in such activities. Pediatricians are in a position to spearhead such a program and we sincerely hope that they will initiate such action.
4. We would encourage the use of ear protective devices. With the use of imagination, these could be made quite attractive and stylish, perhaps to the extent that their use might become a fad among young persons.
5. Conventional audiometric procedures are inadequate for discovering early cochlear damage resulting from high intensity sound exposure.

3 Memory and Rules

Discussions of human thinking usually focus on three major areas—memory, learning, and intellectual functioning. The four articles that follow are selected to give you an up-to-date view of psychologists' current ideas about these areas.

The first article, Dr. Gordon H. Bower's *Analysis of a Mnemonic Device*, describes the properties of methods that are designed to help people remember more accurately. Many such mnemonic methods have been devised and a folklore, of sorts, has developed about what are and what are not necessary properties of successful methods. Dr. Bower's experiments serve to dispel the inaccuracies in the folklore. Indeed, you may find that if you follow the advice in this article, you may be able to improve your own ability to remember things, names and the like.

The second article, Dr. Martin E. P. Seligman's *On the Generality of the Laws of Learning*, is a critical examination of the area of learning. The investigation of learning has been the principle occupation of a good number of psychologists for a good number of years. Many people regard the findings of these investigations as the closest thing to scientific laws that psychology has to offer. Others, however, regard these same investigations as tedious and repetitious elaborations of a few simpleminded laboratory experiments, the results of which have little or nothing to do with how learning takes place in the real world. Dr. Seligman takes a middle path between these two extremes, but still, the experiments he discusses call some of the traditional views of learning into question and require that these views be modified accordingly.

The third article, by Benjamin Franklin, is an example of the effects of positive reinforcement on behavior. We include it because it is both instructive and humorous. The fourth article concerns an area that has a unique and highly controversial place in psychology—intelligence and intelligence testing. *On Intelligence*, by Drs. Earl B. Hunt and Clifford E. Lunneborg, gives the history of IQ tests and the background of the concept of intelligence. It then looks at the question of whether intelligence fundamentally is biologically (that is, genetically) determined or whether it is wholly or in part determined by the breadth and richness of a person's past experience. This leads to a discussion of some of the hotly debated issues regarding intelligence, especially the question of whether there are racial differences in intelligence.

ANALYSIS OF A MNEMONIC DEVICE

Gordon H. Bower

It is in the nature of the mind to forget and in the nature of man to worry over his forgetfulness. Forgetfulness is the constant thorn in the side of the scholar and the scientist, the bane of every student's existence. Stories about such total memory catastrophes as amnesia, loss of personal identity, dissociated or multiple personalities have such a gut-level appeal and fascination for us that we will pay to see them dramatized. . . .

Since time immemorial men have searched for various incantations, rituals, tricks, gimmicks, artifice, and methods to improve their memories. Incantations and prayer aside, the latter efforts have been partly successful, and by now a very few highly specific and reasonably successful methods are known. Collections of these mnemonic tricks are sold in commercial memory courses, which are usually advertized in the back pages of newspapers and pulp magazines. These typically lurid advertisements proclaim how success in life, love, school, and business is the sure-fire sequel of the super-powered memory that will issue from the reader's signing up and paying for the course. Although such hard-sell tactics are somewhat repugnant to respectable scholars (who view their grant proposals and fund-raising speeches in a different light), we should not be deterred by these commercial trappings from investigating scientifically some of the mnemonic devices. In this paper I will discuss one of these mnemonic devices, show how it works, begin some experimental analyses of its principal components, and show how these lead into scientific questions about the mind and language that are at the current frontiers of psychological research.

From the *American Scientist*, 1970, 58(5), 496–510. Reprinted by permission, *American Scientist*, journal of The Society of the Sigma Xi, and author.

THE MNEMONIC AND ITS HISTORY

The particular mnemonic to be studied, called the "method of loci," has been known in Western civilization since ancient Greek times. Cicero (in *De Oratore*) claimed that the method originated in an observation by a Greek poet, Simonides, about whom he told the following story: Simonides was commissioned to compose a lyric poem praising a Roman nobleman and to recite this panegyric at a banquet in his honor attended by a multitude of guests. Following his oration before the assembled guests, Simonides was briefly called outside the banqueting hall by a messenger of the gods Castor and Pollux, whom he had also praised in his poem; while he was absent, the roof of the hall collapsed, killing all the celebrants. So mangled were the corpses that relatives were unable to identify them.

But Simonides stepped forward and named each of the many corpses on the basis of where they were located in the huge banquet hall. This feat of total recall is said to have convinced Simonides of a basic prescription for remembering—to use an orderly arrangement of locations into which one could place the images of things or people that are to be remembered.

Cicero relates this story about Simonides in connection with his discussion of memory regarded as one of the phases of rhetoric. In ancient times rhetoric teachers provided memory instruction because, in those days before inexpensive paper and writing implements, public speakers had to memorize an entire speech, or at least the sequence of main topics. For this reason most references to the method of loci come down to us from treatises on rhetoric, such as Cicero's *De Oratore*, the anonymous *Rhetorica ad Herennium*, and Quintilian's *Institutio oratoria*. Frances Yates tells the historical story in fascinating detail in *The Art of Memory* and provides a detailed description of how the method of loci was used in ancient times:

> It is not difficult to get hold of the general principles of the mnemonic. The first step was to imprint on the memory a series of loci or places. The commonest, though not only, type of mnemonic place system used was the architectual type. The clearest description of the process is that given by Quintilian. In order to form a series of places in memory, he says, a building is to be remembered, as spacious and varied a one as possible, the Forecourt, the living room, bedrooms, and parlours, not omitting statues and other ornaments with which the rooms are decorated. The images by which the speech is to be remembered . . . are then placed in imagination on the places which have been memorized in the building. This done, as soon as the memory of the facts requires to be revived, all these places are visited in turn and the various deposits demanded of their custodians. We have to think of the ancient orator as moving in imagination through his memory building whilst he is making his speech, drawing from the memorized places the images he has placed on them. The method ensures that the points are remembered in the right order, since the order is fixed by the sequence of places in the building [Yates 1966, p. 3].

To summarize, the prescription for memorizing a series of items is (a) first to memorize a list of "memory snapshots" of locations arranged in a familiar order; (b) to make up a vivid image representing, symbolizing, or suggesting each of the items of information that is to be remembered; and (c) to take the items in the sequence they are to be learned and to associate them one by one with the corresponding imaginary locations in memory. The associations are to be established by "mentally visualizing" the image of the items placed into the imaginary context of the locational snapshots. The same loci are used over and over for memorizing any new set of items. Without this feature—if an entire new set of loci had to be learned for each new list—the use of the method would be uneconomical.

To illustrate, the modern home dweller might have a series of loci, such as "my driveway," "interior of my garage," "front door," "upper shelf of coat closet," and "kitchen sink." The list is easily memorized because the places and their order in nature are familiar to the person. If he were to use these loci to remember a grocery shopping list—say, hot dogs, cat food, tomatoes, bananas, and whiskey—then he would try to imagine vivid mental pictures of the items at the respective loci. Examples, . . . might be "giant *hot dogs* rolling down the *driveway*," "a *cat eating* noisily in the *garage*," "ripe *tomatoes* splattered over the *front door*," "bunches of *bananas* swinging from the *closet shelf*," and "a bottle of *whiskey* gurgling down the *kitchen sink*. The images may be elaborated in as much detail as desired, with movement and color, in unusual sizes and shapes, in any form to arouse interest. Then, when the person wishes to remember the shopping list, he need only walk mentally through his list of loci asking himself, in effect, "What did I put in the *driveway*? What in the *garage*?" and so on. The loci on the list are well learned and are easily called to mind. Recall of the scene constructed at each locus enables him to recognize and name the other main object in it, thus appearing to recall the items in their correct order.

DOES THE SYSTEM WORK?

The mnemonic system appears on the surface to be fantastic legerdemain, constructed by elves, and reasonable people are likely to believe that magical and occult power of mentation are required to use the system effectively. Similar systems have also been associated in modern times with showmanship and magicians, and psychologists have tended to be rightly skeptical about the authenticity of spectacular memory performances. Is there any acceptable scientific evidence that such mnemonic systems are not simply elaborate systems for self-deception? Do they in fact really improve anyone's memory?

There is much anecdotal evidence that the system does work. A recent case is recorded by A. R. Luria in his charming account, *The Mind of a Mnemonist*. The man, S., had a truly fantastic memory. Luria, who studied him periodically over a span of many years found that S. could remember volumes of information of all sorts rapidly and without effort and could retain it for years in some cases. He relied extensively on diverse idiosyncratic associations and ruses for converting most materials into visual images, and he seemed to have discovered for himself the method of loci. The following quotation relates one of his methods:

> When S. read through a long series of words, each word would elicit a graphic image. And since the series was fairly long, he had to find some way of distributing these images in a mental row or sequence. Most often (and this habit persisted throughout his life), he would "distribute" them along some roadway or street he visualized in his mind. . . . Frequently he would take a mental walk along that street . . . and slowly make his way down, "distributing" his images at houses, gates, and in store windows. . . . This technique of converting a series of words into a series of graphic images explains why S. could so readily reproduce a series from start to finish or in reverse order; how he could rapidly name the word that preceded or followed one I'd selected from the series. To do this he would simply begin his walk, either from the beginning or end of the street, find the image of the object I had named, and "take a look at" whatever happened to be situated on either side of it [Luria 1968, pp. 31–33].

In recent years such personal anecdotes have been supplemented and amplified by controlled laboratory experiments testing mnemonic devices on "normal" intelligent adults (typically college students). A typical experiment might compare recall by subjects using the method of loci to recall by other subjects instructed to learn by their usual means, and the two groups might be compared on memory for lists of related or unrelated items, objects, events, persons, or words. The results are often striking and dramatic, the subjects using loci frequently recalling two to seven *times* as much as control subjects. This figure represents genuine improvement; the control subjects are not shamming. In fact, they are trying very hard to remember, but are using the hit-or-miss procedures college students have developed over the years (which, one would have supposed, should be fairly efficient learning strategies). . . .

COMPONENTIAL ANALYSIS OF THE MNEMONIC

The next step after a few such demonstrations is to begin more careful analyses of the components of the mnemonic device, so that one may better understand the method, decide which components are essential and which are inconsequential, and perhaps understand how memory works more generally. The method of loci contains a number of distinct components. The more salient ones are:

1. There is a known list of "cues."
2. The cues are memory images of geographic locations.

3. Cues and items on the list to be learned are to be associated during input of the list items.
4. Associations are to be made in one-to-one pairings.
5. Associations are to be effected through imaginal elaboration, specifically by use of visual imagery.
6. The imaginal construction should be unusual, bizarre, striking.
7. If the list items are studied a second time, the same items should be placed at the same loci; even if ordered output is not required, constant ordered input is desirable.
8. At the time of recall the person must cue his recall of the list items.
9. The recall cues must be the same as or similar to those he thought of while studying the items.

Recent research provides information about each of these factors and its contribution to the overall mnemonic effect. I will briefly discuss the factors in turn.

1. A known list of "cues." What is important is that the cues (loci) be available to the person at the time the list items are studied and at the time recall is attempted. The cues, in fact, could be actual pictures of locations, or objects, or unrelated words for that matter, shown by the experimenter as he reads the critical list words to the subject.

2. The cues are memory images of locations. Neither memory images nor locations are crucial for the mnemonic effect. First, presentation of external stimuli, such as pictures, by the experimenter can substitute for the person's cuing himself with memory images. Second, the cues need not be images or pictures of geographical locations. Such loci have the advantage of being concrete, easily visualized, and already learned in a natural serial order; but various experimental comparisons suggest that any readily visualized object or context would supply as good a cue as do scenes of geographic locations (which, after all, are just coherent collections of objects). This conclusion is suggested by the equally good recall produced by the "numeric pegword" system.

The numeric pegword system is similar to the method of loci except that the memory pegs or pigeonholes are images of unrelated concrete objects associated in one-to-one fashion with the first twenty or more integers. Typical pegwords . . . are concrete nouns that rhyme with the numbers—like "one is a bun, two is a shoe, three is a tree," and so on. To learn a new list of items, "one-bun" is used in the same way as the first location in the method of loci, "two-shoe" is used like the second location, and so forth. That is, the person is to visualize the first object in some interaction with a bun, visualize the second object interacting with a shoe, and so on. The pegword and loci methods are identical except for the nature of the cues and for the fact that the pegword system provides *direct* access to numerical-order information. For instance, a person learning by the pegword system can directly recall in isolation that the seventeenth item was *car*; he can also say, retrieving in the reverse direction, that *car* was the seventeenth item; in contrast, the "loci" learner can only reconstruct such numeric information by counting from the beginning or end of his chain of cues.

3. Cues and list items are to be associated during list input. Formation of such associations is critically necessary for the mnemonic effect. If the person is taught the locations or pegwords but is not told how and when to use them, there is no memory improvement whatever. A similar absence of effect arises if the person is exposed to external cues such as pictures while he is hearing the list items but does not attempt to connect them. Such external or imaginal cues become effective memory "retrieval cues" only if the person tries to associate or relate them to the list items at the time the items are studied.

4. One-to-one pairings of cue and item. Pairing appears to be an irrelevant and immaterial part of the method. Multiple items can be hooked onto the same pegword or can be imagined clustered together in the same location. No appreciable loss in recall occurs *if* the items hooked to a given pegword arrive simultaneously or in close succession and *if* the person elaborates one grand imaginal scene depicting some unitary interactions among the several items and the peg or location cue (see Bower, in press). Having the several items that are being associated to a given pegword *simultaneously in mind* seems to be the crucial matter. Without such cognitive simultaneity, retention of earlier items is disrupted somewhat by the learning of later items (see Fig. 1). By using the simultaneous method, therefore, a list of 40 items can be stored equally well as one-to-one pairings with 40 loci or as four-to-one pairings with 10 loci. What may be lost in the four-to-one pairings is information concerning the serial order of the items within the successive quartets of the list; that information may not be preserved in the simultaneous composite scene the person constructs for each quartet.

5. Use imaginal elaboration, especially visual imagery. Imaginal elaboration of the items—seeking out and depicting interacting relationships between the referents—appears to be critically important in producing the large effects typically observed. The imagery has to be of concrete objects or referents of the words, not of words themselves. (In fact, imagery of verbal symbols—words, digits, number arrays—is generally very poor.) Since construction of verbal relationships between cue and item can sometimes produce just as high recall as mental imagery of object interrelations (see Wood 1967), the specific claims for imagery require closer examination. But it is clear that various kinds of cognitive elaboration or construction of relationships lead to greater acquisition of associations (between cue and item) than does rote rehearsal or verbal repetition.

6. Unusual, bizarre imagery. The evidence for the prescription to use odd, bizarre imagery is, to date, entirely negative. That is, four laboratory experiments that have studied this variable have not demonstrated that "bizarreness of imagery" produces a consistent, significant effect on remembering. Subjects instructed to concoct bizarre associative scenes re-

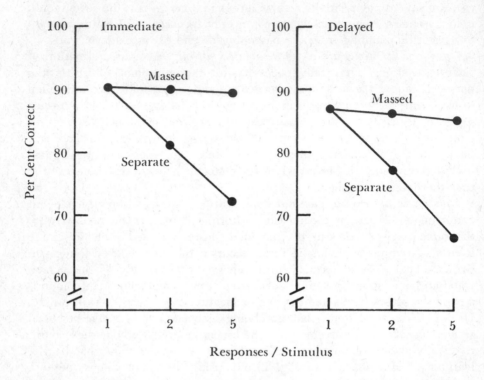

Figure 1. Immediate and 30-minute delayed retention of 1, 2, or 5 items associated to each cue, when studied all together (massed) or individually at separate times. (Reprinted by permission, American Scientist, *journal of The Society of the Sigma Xi.)*

member the cue-to-item associations no better than do others instructed to compose familiar, regular, sensible associative scenes. Differential effects are similarly absent when subjects study pictures of associative scenes that are bizarre versus regular as rated by other people (K. Wollen, personal communication, 1970). Little thought is required to see that bizarreness is itself a poorly defined dimension; any effect such prescriptions might have in naturalistic settings is probably due to incidental factors (for example, arousing or maintaining interest in learning by the novel association).

7. *Repeating each item on the same locus.* When the person receives two or more study trials on the same set of words, it is important to repeat each item on the same locus. If the items do not have to be recalled in a special serial order, then the training agent (teacher, experimenter) may vary the order of presenting the items from one trial to the next. If the subject automatically assigns each reordering of the items to his string of pegwords from start to finish, several items will be hooked to a given peg (with relatively long intervals between successive "hookings"), and a given item will be hooked to several pegs. Along this way lie trouble and poor performance. First, hooking item C to the same cue (A) to which B was previously hooked may produce something like "unhooking" or unlearning of the prior association between the cue A and the item B. This is more likely if during A–C learning the person does not implicitly revive B and associate the simultaneous complex A–B–C (refer back to Fig. 1 and its associated text).

Further, if an item becomes hooked to several different pegs, the person has the problem of monitoring for and inhibiting repetitions of this item in his recall. During oral recall, as he goes through his pegs, he continually must be asking himself, "Is this an item I've already recalled on this trial?" Such discriminations require that a separate kind of occurrence information be stored in a working short-term memory; the discriminatory decisions based on that monitor memory may be mistaken, and the person may suppress his recall of some correct items, thus lowering his performance scores. For such reasons the subject will be much better off if he places a given item on the same peg at each trial (see Bower, Lesgold, and Tieman 1969).

8. At recall the person must cue himself. If the person associates items with a set of cues, those cues must be made available to him by some means if they are to aid his recall. The pegword and loci methods prescribe that the person should generate or present himself with his own cues by running through his well-known list. But if the cues are external, and manipulated by the experimenter, their presence vs. absence will produce effects similar to presence vs. absence of the imaginal cues.

9. Recall cues must be similar to those studied. If cue A has been associated at input with item B, then any effective cue A' for retrieving B from memory must be "similar" to A. The main and significant dimensions of similarity are that cues A and A' be close in semantic meaning (for example, synonymous) or consist of images of neighboring regions in space or belong to common perceptual categories.

An important sort of similarity for practical reasons is that between imagining a situation (A) and actually being in that situation (A'). This similarity is traded on whenever we establish in imagination associations that we wish to have activated later in real life. One example is the "systematic desensitization" treatment for specific phobias, in which a patient in therapy learns to replace his anxiety reaction (aroused by the phobic object or situation) by calm relaxation (see Wolpe 1958). The breaking and replacement of the old object-to-anxiety association is all done in imagination, by visualization, in the therapist's office, but the changed association transfers and occurs in real-life contacts with the formerly phobic object.

A second example is a recommended and effective way to remember future intentions, as when we think to ourselves, "Tomorrow morning when I leave home for the office, I must remember to bring that book for Sam," or "After my class tomorrow I have to telephone the service station." The best way to remember such future intentions is to visualize vividly some specific act usually done in the cue situation (for example, eating breakfast, gathering up lecture notes) and in imagination link performance of that cuing act to thinking about and performing the required act.

To summarize the discussion of the method of loci, the important ingredients appear to be formation of imaginal associations between known cues and previously unknown list items at input, and use of these cues for recall. The control subject, exposed to the same list of items to remember but not using the method of loci, is in what psychologists call a "free recall" experiment. His problem is that he does not know how or where to search in memory for the items just presented to him. For instance, he might know that they were words, but since he knows many thousands of words, how is he to begin searching for the ones he has tagged as having been on the list just presented? The magnitude of his problem would be similar to that of trying to retrieve a few specific books in the Library of Congress after all the books and documents had been dumped haphazardly and randomly in one enormous unsorted pile. The method of loci or pegword mnemonic solves this search problem by providing the learner with a known bank of pigeonholes or file cabinets in which he stores the list items. At recall, the person knows where to start his recall and how to proceed from one unit to the next; he has a way to monitor the adequacy of his recall; he knows when he has forgotten an item; and he knows when he has finished his recall. All of these are the good fruits of the retrieval scheme, and they mainly account for its effectiveness. . . .

REFERENCES

Bower, G. H., A. Lesgold, and D. Tieman. 1969. Grouping operations in free recall. *J. Verb. Learn. Verb. Behav.* 8:481–93.

Luria, A. R. 1968. *The mind of a mnemonist.* New York: Basic Books.

Wolpe, J. 1958. *Psychotherapy by reciprocal inhibition.* Stanford, Calif.: Stanford University Press.

Wood, G. 1967. Mnemonic systems in recall. *J. Educ. Psychol.* 58:1–27.

Yates, F. A. 1966. *The art of memory.* Chicago: University of Chicago Press.

ON THE GENERALITY OF THE LAWS OF LEARNING

Martin E. P. Seligman

Sometimes we forget why psychologists ever trained white rats to press bars for little pellets of flour or sounded metronomes followed by meat powder

From the *Psychological Review*, 1970, 77, 406–418. Copyright 1970 by the American Psychological Association, and reproduced by permission.

The preparation of this manuscript was supported in part by National Institute of Mental Health Grant MH 16546-01 to the author. The author gratefully acknowledges the helpful comments of R. Bolles, P. Cabe, S. Emlen, J. Garcia, E. Lenneberg, R. MacLeod, H. Rachlin, D. Regan, R. Rosinski, P. Rozin, T. A. Ryan, R. Solomon, and F. Stollnitz.

for domestic dogs. After all, when in the real world do rats encounter levers which they learn to press in order to eat, and when do our pet dogs ever come across metronomes whose clicking signals meat powder? It may be useful now to remind ourselves about a basic premise which gave rise to such bizarre endeavors, and to see if we still have reason to believe this premise.

The General Process View of Learning

It was hoped that in the simple, controlled world of levers and mechanical feeders, of metronomes and salivation, something quite general would emerge. If we took such an arbitrary behavior as pressing a lever and such an arbitrary organism as an albino rat, and set it to work pressing the lever for food, then *by virtue* of the very arbitrariness of the environment, we would find features of the rat's behavior general to real-life instrumental learning. Similarly, if we took a dog, undistracted by extraneous noises and sights, and paired a metronome's clicking with meat, what we found about the salivation of the dog might reveal characteristics of associations in general. For instance, when Pavlov found that salivation stopped occurring to a clicking that used to signal meat powder, but no longer did, he hoped that this was an instance of a *law*, "experimental extinction," which would have application beyond clicking metronomes, meat powder, and salivation. What captured the interest of the psychological world was the possibility that such laws might describe the general characteristics of the behavior acquired as the result of pairing one event with another. When Thorndike found that cats learned only gradually to pull strings to escape from puzzle boxes, the intriguing hypothesis was that animal learning in general was by trial and error. In both of these situations, the very arbitrariness and unnaturalness of the experiment was assumed to guarantee generality, since the situation would be uncontaminated by past experience the organism might have had or by special biological propensities he might bring to it.

The basic premise can be stated specifically: In classical conditioning, the choice of CS, US,[1] and response is a matter of relative indifference; that is, any CS and US can be associated with approximately equal facility, and a set of general laws exist which describe the acquisition, extinction, inhibition, delay of reinforcement, spontaneous recovery, etc., for all CSs and USs. In instrumental learning, the choice of response and reinforcer is a matter of relative indifference; that is, any emitted response and any reinforcer can be associated with approximately equal facility, and a set of general laws exist which describe acquisition extinction, discriminative control, generalization, etc., for all responses and reinforcers. I call

---

[1] CS=Conditioned stimulus; US=Unconditioned stimulus and CR=Conditioned Response [Editors' note].

this premise the assumption of equivalence of associability, and I suggest that it lies at the heart of general process learning theory.

This is not a straw man. Here are some quotes from three major learning theorists to document this assumption:

> It is obvious that the reflex activity of any effector organ can be chosen for the purpose of investigation, since signalling stimuli can get linked up with any of the inborn reflexes [Pavlov, 1927, p. 17].
>
> any natural phenomenon chosen at will may be converted into a conditional stimulus . . . any visual stimulus, any desired sound, any odor, and the stimulation of any part of the skin [Pavlov, 1928, p. 86].
>
> All stimulus elements are equally likely to be sampled and the probability of a response at any time is equal to the proportion of elements in S' that are connected to it. . . . On any acquisition trial all stimulus elements sampled by the organism become connected to the response reinforced on that trial [Estes, 1959, p. 399].
>
> The general topography of operant behavior is not important, because most if not all specific operants are conditioned. I suggest that the dynamic properties of operant behavior may be studied with a single reflex [Skinner, 1938, pp. 45–46].

A Reexamination of Equivalence of Associability

The premise of equivalence places a special premium on the investigations of arbitrarily related, as opposed to naturally occurring, events. Such events, since they are supposedly uncontaminated by past experience or by special propensities the organism brings to the situation, provide paradigms for the investigations of general laws of learning. More than 60 years of research in both the instrumental and classical conditioning traditions have yielded considerable data suggesting that similar laws hold over a wide range of arbitrarily chosen events: the shape of generalization gradients is pretty much the same for galvanic skin responses classically conditioned to tones when shock is the US (Hovland, 1937), and for salivating to being touched at different points on the back when food is the US (Pavlov, 1927). Partial reinforcement causes greater resistance to extinction than continuous reinforcement regardless of whether rats are bar pressing for water or running down alleyways for food. Examples of analogous generality of laws could be multiplied at great length.

Inherent in the emphasis on arbitrary events, however, is a danger: *that the laws so found will not be general, but peculiar to arbitrary events.*

The Dimension of Preparedness

It is a truism that an organism brings to any experiment certain equipment and predispositions more or less appropriate to that situation. It brings specialized sensory and receptor apparatus with a long evolutionary history which has modified it into its present appropriateness or inappropriateness for the experiment. In addition to sensory-motor capacity, the organism brings associative apparatus, which likewise has a long and specialized evolutionary history. For example, when an organism is placed in a classical conditioning experiment, not only may the CS be more or less perceptible and the US more or less evocative of a response, *but also the CS and US may be more or less associable.* The organism may be more or less prepared by the evolution of its species to associate a given CS and US or a given response with an outcome. If evolution has affected the associability of specific events, then it is possible, even likely, that the very *laws* of learning might vary with the preparedness of the organism from one class of situations to another. If this is so, investigators influenced by the general process view may have discovered only a subset of the laws of learning: the laws of learning about arbitrarily concatenated events, those associations which happen in fact to be equivalent.

We can define a continuum of preparedness operationally. Confront an organism with a CS paired with US or with a response which produces an outcome. Depending on the specifics, the organism can be either prepared, unprepared, or contraprepared for learning about the events. *The relative preparedness of an organism for learning about a situation is defined by the amount of input* (e.g., numbers of trials, pairings, bits of information, etc.) *which must occur before that output* (responses, acts, repertoire, etc.), *which is construed as evidence of acquisition, reliably occurs.* It does not matter how input or output are specified, as long as that specification can be used consistently for all points on the continuum. Thus, using the preparedness dimension is independent of whether one happens to be an S-R theorist, a cognitive theorist, an information processing theorist, an ethologist, or what have you. Let me illustrate how one can place an experimental situation at various points on the continuum for classical conditioning. If the organism makes the indicant response consistently from the very first presentation of the CS on, such "learning" represents a clear case of instinctive responding, the extreme of the prepared end of the dimension. If the organism makes the response consistently after only a few pairings, it is somewhat prepared. If the response emerges only after many pairings (extensive input), the organism is unprepared. If acquisition occurs only after very many pairings or does not occur at all, the organism is said to be contraprepared. The number of pairings is the measure that makes the dimension a continuum, and implicit in this dimension is the notion that "learning" and "instinct" are continuous. Typically ethologists have examined situations in the prepared side of the dimension, while general process learning theorists have largely restricted themselves to the unprepared region. The contraprepared part of the dimension has been largely uninvestigated, or at least unpublished.

The dimension of preparedness should not be confused with the notion of operant level. The frequency with which a response is made in a given situation is not necessarily related to the associability of that response with a given outcome. As will be seen later, frequent responses may not be acquired when they are reinforced as readily as infrequent responses. Indeed, some theorists (e.g., Turner & Solomon, 1962) have argued that high-probability, fast-latency responding may actually antagonize operant rein-forceability.

The first empirical question with which this paper is concerned is whether sufficient evidence exists to challenge the equivalence of associability. For many years, ethologists and others (for an excellent example, see Breland & Breland, 1966) have gathered a wealth of evidence to challenge the general process view of learning. Curiously, however, these data have had little impact on the general process camp, and while not totally ignored, they have not been theoretically incorporated. In view of differences in method-ology, this is perhaps understandable. I do not expect that presenting these lines of evidence here would have any more effect than it has already had. More persuasive to the general process theorist should be the findings which have sprung up within his own tradition. Within traditional conditioning and training paradigms, a considerable body of evidence now exists which challenges the premise. In reviewing this evidence, we shall find the di-mension of preparedness to be a useful integrative device. It is not the intent of this article to review exhaustively the growing number of studies which challenge the premise. Rather, we shall look within each of the major paradigms which general process learning theorists have used and discuss one or two clear examples. The theme of these examples is that all events are not equivalent in their associability: that although the organism may have the necessary receptor and effector apparatus to deal with events, there is much variation in its ability to learn about relations between events.

CLASSICAL CONDITIONING

The investigation of classical aversive conditioning has been largely con-fined to the unconditioned response of pain caused by the stimulus of electric shock (cf. Campbell & Church, 1969), and the "laws" of classical conditioning are based largely on these findings along with those from salivary conditioning. Recently, Garcia and his collaborators (Garcia, Ervin, & Koelling, 1966; Garcia, Ervin, Yorke, & Koelling, 1967; Garcia & Koelling, 1966; Garcia, McGowan, Ervin, & Koelling, 1968), and Rozin and his col-laborators (Rodgers & Rozin, 1966; Rozin, 1967, 1968, 1969) have used illness as an unconditioned response and reported some intriguing findings. In the paradigm experiment (Garcia & Koelling, 1966), rats received "bright-noisy, saccharin-tasting water." What this meant was that whenever the rat licked a drinking tube containing saccharine-flavored water, lights flashed and a noise source sounded. During these sessions the rats were X-irradiated. X-irradiation makes rats sick, but it should be noted that the illness does not set in for an hour or so following X-raying. Later the rats were tested for acquired aversions to the elements of the compound CS. The rats had acquired a strong aversion to the taste of saccharine, *but had not acquired an aversion to the "bright-noise."* The rats had "associated" the taste with their illness, but not the exteroceptive noise-light stimuli. So that it could not be argued that saccharin is such a salient event that it masked the noise and light, Garcia and Koelling ran the complementary experiment: "Bright and noisy saccharin-tasting water" was again used as a CS, but this time electric shock to the feet was the US. The rats were then tested for aversion to the elements of the CS. In this case, the bright noise became aversive, but the saccharin-tasting water did not. This showed that the bright noise was clearly perceptible; but the rats associated only the bright noise with the exteroceptive US of footshock, and not the taste of saccharin in spite of its also being paired with shock.

In the experiment, we see both ends as well as the middle of the preparedness continuum. Rats are prepared, by virtue of their evolutionary history, to associate tastes with malaise. For in spite of a several-hour delay of reinforcement, and the presence of other perceptible CSs, only the taste was associated with nausea, and light and noise were not. Further, rats are contraprepared to associate exteroceptive events with nausea and contraprepared to associate tastes with footshock. Finally, the association of footshock with light and sound is probably someplace in the unprepared region. The survival advantage of this preparedness seems obvious: organisms who are poisoned by a distinctive food and survive, do well not to eat it again. Selective advantage should accrue, moreover, to those rats whose associative apparatus could bridge a very long CS-US interval and who could ignore contiguous, as well as interpolated, exteroceptive CSs in the case of taste and nausea.

Does such prepared and contraprepared acquisition reflect the evolutionary results of selective pressure or does it result from experience? It is possible that Garcia's rats may have previously learned that tastes were uncorrelated with peripheral pain and that tastes were highly correlated with alimentary consequences. Such an argument involves an unorthodox premise: that rats' capacities for learning set and transfer are considerably broader than previously demonstrated. The difference between a position that invokes selective pressure (post hoc) and the experiential set position is testable: Would mating those rats who were most proficient at learning the taste–footshock association produce offspring more capable of such learning than an unselected population? Conversely, would interbreeding refractory rats select out the facility with which the taste–nausea association is made?

Supporting evidence for preparedness in classical conditioning has come from other recent experiments on specific hungers and poisoning. Rodgers and Rozin (1966) and Rozin (1967, 1968) have demonstrated that at least part of the mechanism of specific hungers (other than sodium) involves conditioned aversion to the taste of the diet the rats were eating as they became sick. Deficient rats spill the old diet and will not eat it, even after they have recovered. The association of the old taste with malaise seems to be made in spite of the long delay between taste of the diet and gradual onset of illness. The place and the container in which the old diet was set, moreover, do not become aversive. The remarkable ability of wild rats who recover from being poisoned by a novel food, and thereafter avoid new tastes (Barnett, 1963; Rozin, 1968), also seems to result from classical conditioning. Note that the wild rat must be prepared to associate the taste with an illness which does not appear for several hours in only one trial; note also that it must be contraprepared to associate some contiguous CSs surrounding the illness with malaise.

Do these findings really show that rats can associate tastes and illness when an interval of many minutes or even hours intervenes or are they merely a subtle instance of contiguity? Peripheral cues coming either from long-lasting aftertastes or from regurgitation might bring the CS and US into contiguity. Rozin (1969) reported evidence against aftertaste mediation: rats received a high concentration of saccharin paired with apomorphine poisoning. Later, the rats were given a choice between the high concentration and a low concentration. The rats preferred the low concentration, even though the aftertaste that was purportedly contiguous with malaise should be more similar to the low concentration (since it had been diluted by saliva) than the high concentration.

Not only do rats acquire an aversion for the old diet, on which they got sick, but they also learn to prefer the taste of a new diet containing the needed substance. This mechanism also seems to involve prepared conditioning of taste to an internal state. Garcia et al. (1967) paired the taste of saccharin with thiamine injections given to thiamine deficient rats, and the rats acquired a preference for saccharin. So both the rejection of old foods and acceptance of new foods in specific hungers can be explained by prepared conditioning of tastes to internal state.

INSTRUMENTAL LEARNING

E. L. Thorndike, the founder of the instrumental learning tradition, was by no means oblivious to the possibility of preparedness in instrumental learning, as we shall see below. He also hinted at the importance of preparedness in one of his discussions of classical conditioning (Thorndike, 1935, p. 192–197): one of his students (Bregman, 1934) attempted to replicate the results of Watson and Rayner (1920), who found that little Albert became afraid of a white rat, rabbit, and a dog which had been paired with a startling noise. Bregman was unable to show any fear conditioning when she paired more conventional CSs, such as blocks of wood and cloth curtains, with startling noise. Thorndike speculated that infants at the age of locomotion were more disposed to manifest fear to objects that wiggle and contort themselves than to motionless CSs.

Thorndike's parallel views on instrumental learning rose from his original studies of cats in puzzle boxes. As every psychologist knows, he put cats in large boxes and investigated the course of learning to pull strings to escape. What is less widely known is that he put his cats in not just one puzzle box, but in a whole series of different ones. . . .

In one box the cats had to pull a string to get out, in another a button had to be pushed, in another a lever had to be depressed, etc. One of his boxes—Box Z—was curious: it was merely a large box with nothing but a door that the experimenter could open. Thorndike opened the door in Box Z whenever cats licked themselves or scratched themselves. The cat is known to use both of these frequently occurring responses instrumentally: it scratches itself to turn off itches, and licks itself to remove dirt. In addition, Thorndike had established that getting out of a puzzle box was a sufficient reward for reinforcing the acts of string pulling, button pushing, and lever clawing. In spite of this, Thorndike's cats seemed to have a good deal of trouble learning to scratch themselves or lick themselves to get out of the boxes.

A reanalysis of the individual learning curves presented by Thorndike (1964) for each of the seven cats who had experience in Box Z documents the impression: of the 28 learning curves presented for these seven cats in the boxes other than Z, 22 showed faster learning than in Z, three showed approximately equal learning, and only three showed slower learning. While all of the cats eventually showed improved speeds of licking or scratching for escape, such learning was difficult and irregular. Thorndike noted another unusual property of licking and scratching:

> There is in all these cases a noticeable tendency . . . to diminish the act until it becomes a mere vestige of a lick or scratch . . . the licking degenerated into a mere quick turn of the head with one or two motions up and down with tongue extended. Instead of a hearty scratch, the cat waves its paw up and down rapidly for an instant. Moreover, if sometimes you do not let the cat out after the feeble reaction, it does not at once repeat the movement, as it would do if it depressed a thumb piece, for instance, without success in getting the door open [Thorndike, 1964, p. 48].

Contemporary investigators have reported related findings. Konorski (1967, pp. 463–467) attempted to train "reflex" movements, such as anus licking, scratching, and yawning, with food reinforcement. While reporting success with scratching and anus licking, like Thorndike, he observed spontaneous simplification and arhythmia in the responses. More importantly, he reported that reinforcement of "true yawning" with food is very difficult, if not impossible. Bolles and Seelbach (1964) reported that rearing could be reinforced by noise offset, but not punished by noise onset, exploration could be modified by both, and grooming by neither. This difference could not be accounted for by difference in operant level, which is substantial for all these behaviors of the rat.

Thorndike (1964) speculated that there may be some acts which the organism is not neurally prepared to connect to some sense impressions:

If the associations in general were simply between situation and impulse to act, one would suppose that the situation would be associated with the impulse to lick or scratch as readily as with the impulse to turn a button or claw a string. Such is not the case. By comparing the curves for Z on pages 57–58 with the others, one sees that for so simple an act it takes a long time to form the association. This is not the final reason, for lack of attention, a slight increase in the time taken to open the door after the act was done, or *an absence of preparation in the nervous system for connections between these particular acts and definite sense impressions* [italics added] may very well have been the cause of the difficulty in forming the associations [p. 113].

This speculation seems reasonable: after all, in the natural history of cats, only behavior such as manipulating objects which maximized chances for escaping traps would be selected, and licking is not in the repertoire which maximizes escape. At minimum, Thorndike demonstrated that the emission of licking paired with an event which could reinforce other emitted acts was not sufficient to reinforce licking equally well. In the present terms, Thorndike had discovered a particular instrumental training situation for which cats are relatively contraprepared.

Brown and Jenkins (1968, Experiment 6) have reported findings which appear to come from the opposite end of the dimension. Pigeons were exposed to a lighted key which was paired with grain delivered in a lighted food hopper below the key. But unlike the typical key-pecking situation, the pigeons' pecking the key did not produce food. Food was contingent only on the key's being lit, not on pecking the key. In spite of this, all pigeons began pecking the key after exposure to the lighted key, followed by grain. Moreover, key pecking was maintained even though it had no effect on food. One can conclude from these "autoshaping" results that the pigeon is highly prepared for associating the pecking of a lighted key with grain.

There is another curiosity in the history of the instrumental learning literature which is usefully viewed with the preparedness dimension: the question of why a reinforcer is reinforcing. For over 20 years, disputes raged about what monolithic principle described the necessary and sufficient conditions for learning. Hull (1943) claimed that tissue-need reduction must occur for learning to take place, while Miller (1951) held that drive reduction was necessary and sufficient. Later, Sheffield, Roby, and Campbell (1954) suggested that a consummatory response was the necessary condition. More recently, it has become clear that learning can occur in the absence of any of these (e.g., Berlyne, 1960). I suggest that when CSs or responses are followed by such biologically important events as need reducers, drive reducers, or consummatory responses, learning should take place readily because natural selection has prepared organisms for such relationships. The relative preparedness of organisms for these events accounts for the saliency of such learning and hence the appeal of each of the monolithic principles. But organisms *can* learn about bar pressing paired with light onset, etc.; they are merely less prepared to do so, and hence, the now abundant evidence against the earlier principles was more difficult to gather.

Thus, we find that in instrumental learning paradigms, there are situations which lie on either side of the rat's bar pressing for food on the preparedness dimension. A typical rat will ordinarily learn to bar press for food after a few dozen exposures to the bar press—food contingency. But cats, who can use scratching and licking as instrumental acts in some situations, have trouble using these acts to get out of puzzle boxes, and dogs do not learn to yawn for food even after many exposures to the contingency. On the other hand, pigeons acquire a key peck in a lighted key–grain situation, even when there is no contingency at all between key pecking and grain. These three instrumental situations represent unprepared, contraprepared, and prepared contingencies, respectively. Later we shall discuss the possibility that they obey different laws as a function of different preparedness.

TWO FAILURES OF GENERAL PROCESS LEARNING THEORY: LANGUAGE AND THE FUNCTIONAL AUTONOMY OF MOTIVES

The interest of psychologists in animal learning theory is on the wane. Although the reasons are many, a prominent one is that such theories have failed to capture and bring into the laboratory phenomena which provide fertile models of complex human learning. This failure may be due in part to the equivalence premise. By concentrating on events for which organisms have been relatively unprepared, the laws and models which general process learning theories have produced may not be applicable beyond the realm of arbitrary events, arbitrarily connected. This would not be an obstacle if all of human learning consisted of learning about arbitrary events. But it does not. *Homo sapiens* has an evolutionary history and a biological makeup which has made it relatively prepared to learn some things and relatively contraprepared to learn others. If learning varies with preparedness, it should not be surprising that the laws for unprepared association between events have not explained such phenomena as the learning of language or the acquisition of motives.

Lenneberg (1967) has recently provided an analysis of language, the minimal conclusion of which is that children do not learn language the way rats learn to press a lever for food. Put more strongly, the set of laws which describe language learning are not much illuminated by the laws of the acquisition of arbitrary associations between events, as Skinner (1957) has argued. Unlike such unprepared contingencies as bar pressing for food, language does not require careful training or shaping for its acquisition. We do not need to arrange sets of linguistic contingencies carefully to get children to speak and understand English. Programmed training of speech is relatively ineffective, for under all but the most impoverished linguistic environments, human beings learn to speak and understand. Children of the deaf make as much noise and have the same sequence and age of onset for cooing as children of hearing parents. Development of language seems roughly the same across cultures which presumably differ widely in the arrangement of reinforcement contingencies, and language skill is not predicted by chronological age but by motor skill (see Lenneberg, 1967, especially pp. 125–158, for a fuller discussion).

The acquisition of language, not unlike pecking a lighted key for grain in the pigeon and the acquisition of birdsong (Petrinovich, 1970), is prepared. The operational criterion for the prepared side of the dimension is that minimal input should produce acquisition. One characteristic of language acquisition which separates it from the bar press is just this: elaborate training is not required for its production. From the point of view of this paper, it is not surprising that the traditional analyses of instrumental and classical conditioning are not adequate for analysis of language. This is not because language is a phenomenon *sui generis*, but because the laws of instrumental and classical conditioning were developed to explain unprepared situations and not to account for learning in prepared situations. This is not to assert that the laws which govern language acquisition will necessarily be the same as those governing the Garcia phenomenon, birdsong, or the key peck, but to say that species-specific, biological analysis might be fruitfully made of these phenomena.

It is interesting to note in this context the recent success that Gardner and Gardner (1970) have had in teaching American sign language to a chimpanzee. The Gardners reasoned that earlier failures to teach spoken English to chimpanzees (Hayes & Hayes, 1952; Kellogg & Kellogg, 1933) did not result from cognitive deficiencies on the part of the subjects, but from the contraprepared nature of vocalization as a trainable response. The great manual dexterity of the chimpanzee, however, suggested sign language as a more trainable vehicle. Hayes (1968) has recently reanalyzed the data from Vicki (the Hayes' chimp) and confirmed the suggestion that chimpanzees' difficulty in using exhalation instrumentally may have caused earlier failures.

Language is not the only example of human learning that has eluded general process theory. The extraordinary persistence of acquired human motives has not been captured in ordinary laboratory situations. People, objects, and endeavors which were once unmotivating to an individual acquire and maintain strongly motivating properties. Fondness for the objects of sexual learning long after sexual desire is gone is a clear example. Acquisition of motives is not difficult to bring into the laboratory, and the extensive literature on acquired drives has often been taken as an analysis of acquired human motivation. A rat, originally unafraid of a tone, is shocked while the tone is played. Thereafter, the rat is afraid of the tone. But the analogy breaks down here; for once the tone is presented several times without shock, the tone loses its fear-inducing properties (Little & Brimer, 1968; Wagner, Siegel, & Fein, 1967). (The low resistance to extinction of the conditioned emotional response should not be confused with the high resistance to extinction of the avoidance response. This inextinguishability probably stems from the failure of the organism to stay around in the presence of the CS long enough to be exposed to the fact that shock no longer follows the CS, rather than a failure of fear of the CS to extinguish.) Yet, acquired motivators for humans retain their properties long after the primary motivation with which they were originally paired is absent. Allport (1937) raised the problem for general process theory as the "functional autonomy of motives." But in the 30 years since the problem was posed, the failure of acquired human motives to extinguish remains unanalyzed experimentally. . . .

PREPAREDNESS AND THE LAWS OF LEARNING

The primary empirical question has been answered affirmatively: The premise of equivalence of associability does not hold, *even in the traditional paradigms for which it was first assumed.* But does this matter? Do the same laws which describe the learning of unprepared events hold for prepared, unprepared, and contraprepared events? Given that an organism is prepared, and therefore learns with minimal input, does such learning have different properties from those unprepared associations that the organism acquires more painstakingly? Are the same mechanisms responsible for learning in prepared, unprepared, and relatively contraprepared situations?

We can barely give a tentative answer to this question, since it has been largely uninvestigated. Only a few pieces of evidence have been gathered to suggest that once a relatively prepared or contraprepared association has been acquired, it may not display the same family of extinction curves, values for delay of reinforcement, punishment effects, etc., as the lever press for food in the rat. Consider again the Garcia and Koelling (1966) findings: the association of tastes with illness is made with very different delays of reinforcement from ordinary Pavlovian associations. Unlike salivating to sounds, the association will be acquired with delays of up to one hour and more. Detailed studies which compare directly the delay of reinforcement gradients, extinction functions, etc., for prepared versus unprepared associations are needed. It would be interesting to find that the extinction and inhibition functions for prepared associations were different than for unprepared associations. If preparation underlies the observations of functional autonomy, prepared associations might be highly resistant to extinction, punishment, and other changes in instrumental contingencies. Breland and Breland (1966) reported that many of the "prepared" behaviors that the organisms they worked with acquired would persist even under counterproductive instrumental contingencies. To what extent would the autoshaped key pecking responses of Brown and Jenkins (1968) be weakened by extinction or punishment, as bar pressing for food is weakened? Williams and Williams (1969) reported that autoshaped key-pecking responses persist even when they actually "cost" the pigeon reinforcement.

Does contraprepared behavior, after being acquired, obey the same laws as unprepared behavior? Thorndike (1964) reported that when he finally trained licking for escape, the response no longer looked like the natural response, but was a pale, mechanical imitation of the natural response. Would the properties of the response differentiation and shaping of such behavior be like those of unprepared responses? The answer to this range of questions is presently unknown.

Preparedness has been operationally defined, and it is possible that different laws of learning may vary with the dimension. How can the dimension be anchored more firmly? Might different cognitive and physiological mechanisms covary with dimension?

Acquired aversions to tastes following illness is commonplace in humans. These Garcia phenomena are not easily modified by cognition in contrast to other classically conditioned responses in humans (e.g., Spence & Platt, 1967). The knowledge that the illness was caused by the stomach flu and not the Sauce Bearnaise does not prevent the sauce from tasting bad in the future. Garcia, Kovner, and Green (1970) reported that distinctive tastes can be used by rats as a cue for shock avoidance in a shuttlebox; but the preference for the taste in the home cage is unchanged. When the taste is paired with illness, however, the preference is reduced in the home cage. Such evidence suggests that prepared associations may not be cognitively mediated, and it is tempting to speculate that cognitive mechanisms (expectation, attention, etc.) come into play with more unprepared or contraprepared situations. If this is so, it is ironic that the "blind" connections which both Thorndike and Pavlov wanted to study lie in the prepared realm and not in the unprepared paradigms they investigated.

We might also ask if different neural structures underlie differently prepared learning. Does elaborate prewiring mediate prepared associations such as taste and nausea, while more plastic structures mediate unprepared and contraprepared associations?

We have defined the dimension of preparedness and given examples of it. To anchor the dimension we need to know the answers to three questions about what covaries with it: (a) Do different laws of learning (families of functions) hold along the dimension? (b) Do different cognitive mechanisms covary with it? (c) Do different physiological mechanisms also covary with preparedness?

PREPARATION AND THE GENERAL PROCESS VIEW OF LEARNING

If the premise of equivalence of associability is false, then we have reason to suspect that the laws of learning discovered using lever pressing and salivation may not hold for any more than other simple, unprepared associations. If the laws of learning for unprepared association do not hold for prepared or contraprepared associations, is the general process view salvageable in any form? This is an empirical question. Its answer depends on whether *differences* in learning vary systematically along the dimension of preparedness; the question reduces to whether the preparedness continuum is a nomological continuum. For example, if one finds that the families of extinction functions vary systematically with the dimension, then one might be able to formulate *general* laws of extinction. Thus, if prepared CRs extinguished very slowly, unprepared CRs extinguished gradually, and contraprepared CRs extinguished precipitously, such a systematic, continuous difference in *laws* would be a truly general law of extinction. But before such general laws can be achieved, we must first investigate what the laws of prepared and contraprepared associations actually are. If this were done, then the possibility of general laws of learning would be again alive.

REFERENCES

Allport, G. The functional autonomy of motives. *American Journal of Psychology*, 1937, **50**, 141–156.

Barnett, S. *The rat: A study in behavior*. London: Methuen, 1963.

Berlyne, D. E. *Conflict, arousal, and curiosity*. McGraw-Hill: New York, 1960.

Bolles, R., & Seelbach, S. Punishing and reinforcing effects of noise onset and termination for different responses. *Journal of Comparative and Physiological Psychology*, 1964, **58**, 127–132.

Bregman, E. An attempt to modify the emotional attitude of infants by the conditioned response technique. *Journal of Genetic Psychology*, 1934, **45**, 169–198.

Breland, K., & Breland, M. *Animal behavior*. New York: Macmillan, 1966.

Brown, P., & Jenkins, H. Autoshaping of the pigeon's key-peck. *Journal of the Experimental Analysis of Behavior*, 1968, **11**, 1–8.

Campbell, F. A., & Church, R. M. *Punishment and aversive behavior*. New York: Appleton-Century-Crofts, 1969.

Estes, W. K. The statistical approach to learning theory. In S. Koch (Ed.), *Psychology: A study of a science*. Vol. 2. New York: McGraw-Hill, 1959.

Garcia, J., Ervin, F., & Koelling, R. Learning with prolonged delay of reinforcement. *Psychonomic Science*, 1966, **5**, 121–122.

Garcia, J., Ervin, F., Yorke, C., & Koelling, R. Conditioning with delayed vitamin injections. *Science*, 1967, **155**, 716–718.

Garcia, J., Kovner, R., & Green, K. F. Cue properties versus palatability of flavors in avoidance learning. *Psychonomic Science*, 1970, in press.

Garcia, J., & Koelling, R. Relation of cue to consequence in avoidance learning. *Psychonomic Science*, 1966, **4**, 123–124.

Garcia, J., McGowan, B., Ervin, F., & Koelling, R. Cues: Their relative effectiveness as a function of the reinforcer. *Science*, 1968, **160**, 794–795.

Gardner, B., & Gardner, A. Two-way communication with an infant chimpanzee. In A. Schrier & F. Stollnitz (Eds.), *Behavior of nonhuman primates*. Vol. 3. New York: Academic Press, 1970, in press.

Hayes, K. J. Spoken and gestural language learning in chimpanzees. Paper presented at the meeting of the Psychonomic Society, St. Louis, October 1968.

Hayes, K. J., & Hayes, C. Imitation in a home-raised chimpanzee. *Journal of Comparative and Physiological Psychology*, 1952, **45**, 450–459.

Hovland, C. The generalization of conditioned responses. I. The sensory generalization of conditioned responses with varying frequencies of tone. *Journal of Genetic Psychology*, 1937, **17**, 279–291.

Hull, C. L. *Principles of behavior.* New York: Appleton-Century-Crofts, 1943.

Kellogg, W. N., & Kellogg, L. A. *The ape and the child.* New York: McGraw-Hill, 1933.

Konorski, J. *Integrative activity of the brain.* Chicago: University of Chicago Press, 1967.

Lenneberg, E. *The biological foundations of language.* New York: Wiley, 1967.

Little, J., & Brimer, C. Shock density and conditioned suppression. Paper presented at the meeting of the Eastern Psychological Association, Washington, D. C., April 1968.

Miller, N. E. Learnable drives and rewards. In S. S. Stevens (Ed.), *Handbook of experimental psychology.* New York: Wiley, 1951.

Pavlov, I. P. *Conditioned reflexes.* New York: Dover, 1927.

Pavlov, I. P. *Lectures on conditioned reflexes.* New York: International Publishers, 1928.

Petrinovich, L. Psychobiological mechanisms in language development. In G. Newton & A. R. Riesen (Eds.), *Advances in psychobiology.* New York: Wiley, 1970, in press.

Rodgers, W., & Rozin, P. Novel food preferences in thiamine-deficient rats. *Journal of Comparative and Physiological Psychology*, 1966, **61**, 1–4.

Rozin, P. Specific aversions as a component in specific hungers. *Journal of Comparative and Physiological Psychology*, 1967, **63**, 421–428.

Rozin, P. Specific aversions and neophobia resulting from vitamin deficiency or poisoning in half wild and domestic rats. *Journal of Comparative and Physiological Psychology*, 1968, **66**, 82–88.

Rozin, P. Central or peripheral mediation of learning with long CS-US intervals in the feeding system. *Journal of Comparative and Physiological Psychology*, 1969, **67**, 421–429.

Sheffield, F. D., Roby, T. B., & Campbell, B. A. Drive reduction versus consummatory behavior as determinants of reinforcement. *Journal of Comparative and Physiological Psychology*, 1954, **47**, 349–354.

Skinner, B. F. *The behavior of organisms.* New York: Appleton-Century-Crofts, 1938.

Skinner, B. F. *Verbal behavior.* New York: Appleton-Century-Crofts, 1957.

Spence, K. W., & Platt, J. R. Effects of partial reinforcement on acquisition and extinction of the conditioned eye blink in a masking situation. *Journal of Experimental Psychology*, 1967, **74**, 259–263.

Thorndike, E. L. *Animal intelligence.* New York: Hafner, 1964. (Originally published: New York: Macmillan, 1911.)

Thorndike, E. L. *The psychology of wants, interests, and attitudes.* New York: Appleton-Century, 1935.

Turner, L., & Solomon, R. L. Human traumatic avoidance learning: Theory and experiments on the operant-respondent distinction and failures to learn. *Psychological Monographs*, 1962, **76** (40, Whole No. 559).

Wagner, A., Siegel, L., & Fein, G. Extinction of conditioned fear as a function of the percentage of reinforcement. *Journal of Comparative and Physiological Psychology*, 1967, **63**, 160–164.

Watson, J. B., & Rayner, R. Conditioned emotional reactions. *Journal of Experimental Psychology*, 1920, **3**, 1–14.

Williams, D. R., & Williams, H. Auto-maintenance in the pigeon: Sustained pecking despite contingent non-reinforcement. *Journal of the Experimental Analysis of Behavior*, 1969, **12**, 511–520.

OPERANT REINFORCEMENT OF PRAYER

Benjamin Franklin

We had for our chaplain a zealous Presbyterian minister, Mr. Beatty, who complained to me that the men did not generally attend his prayers and exhortations. When they enlisted, they were promised, besides pay and provisions, a gill of rum a day, which was punctually serv'd out to them, half in the morning, and the other half in the evening; and I observ'd they were as punctual in attending to receive it; upon which I said to Mr. Beatty:

> "It is, perhaps, below the dignity of your profession to act as steward of the rum, but if you were to deal it out and only just after prayers, you would have them all about you." He liked the tho't, undertook the office, and, with the help of a few hands to measure out the liquor, executed it to satisfaction, and never were prayers more generally and more punctually attended; so that I thought this method preferable to the punishment inflicted by some military laws for non-attendance on divine service.

ON INTELLIGENCE

Earl B. Hunt and Clifford E. Lunneborg

What is intelligence? Stories of wise men and fools have been with us since antiquity. The word itself dates from Roman times. Science, itself, is much younger and the idea that the scientific method could be applied to human behavior is quite recent. Before trying to describe what Psychology has to say about mental power, let us first look at a bit of history.

This article was especially written for this book of readings.

Three things had to happen before intelligence could be studied scientifically. First, the mind and mental functioning had to be rescued from the mystical realm in which they had been set apart from the physical body, and the mind's activities had to be recognized as suitable topics for empirical observation. Second, scientists had to be interested in individual differences[1] in mental functioning as well as universal laws. Third, techniques had to become available to deal with the mathematical and statistical problems that analysis of individual differences posed. It was not until late in the nineteenth century that all these things happened. By the mid-1800s German physiologists and philosophers lead by Wilhelm Wundt had convinced the learned men of the day that mental activity was a fit topic for experimental as well as armchair study. At about the same time, in England and elsewhere, Darwinism was focussing attention on the importance of individual differences in shaping the evolution of a species by natural selection. Finally, a number of French, Italian, and Belgian mathematicians were setting out the pieces of a branch of mathematics known as probability and statistics, which permitted the systematic study of variability in the frequency of events.

SIR FRANCIS GALTON

All these forces converged on a remarkable English gentleman, Sir Francis Galton. Galton was a first cousin of Charles Darwin, and, like his cousin, a well-traveled man. He was an African explorer, mathematician, and climatologist as well as a naturalist. Besides establishing the study of individual differences and thus becoming the intellectual ancestor of much of modern psychology, Galton first developed the ideas behind fingerprinting, eugenics, and twentieth-century mathematical statistics. Were he to take an intelligence test today, he would have scored in the upper range. We are interested in him for five ideas, all tightly woven together, that have left their mark on the study of intelligence. The ideas are: variability, measurement, generality, heritability, and correlation.

In his book, *Classification of Men according to Their Natural Gifts*, Galton observed that "the very curious law of deviation from the average" which had been developed by the Astronomer Royal of Belgium, Quetelet, applied to the distribution of intellectual gifts among Englishmen. That "very curious law," which today we call the normal distribution, states that if you are measuring something which is produced from many different causes, then most of your measures will fall close to the average value, and that as you consider values progressively smaller (or larger) than this average, you will encounter progressively fewer observations. For Quetelet the law well explained the distributions of heights among French draftees

---

[1] "Individual differences" is a short-hand term meaning the differences which exist among individual persons [Editors' note].

and of chest circumferences among Scottish soldiery. Most were average, but there were a few short and a few tall Frenchmen, and a few very thin and a few very stocky Scots. Galton believed that this was a natural law applying to all measurements of human quality, including intelligence.

To test this theory Galton needed measurements of intellect. There were none available, so Galton proceeded to write the first psychological questionnaire and to assemble the first battery of tests to assess individual differences. The questionnaire assessed visual imagery and was circulated among Galton's acquaintances. The test battery was assembled for Galton's laboratory, where (for a fee) he measured visitors to the London exhibition of 1884. The test seems strange to us today. Among its measures were: the ability to detect slight differences between weights and between colors, breathing capacity, speed of striking a blow, visual accuracy, hand steadiness, and memory for visual forms. We shall explain the reason for these measures shortly. What is more important here is the way Galton went about his task. Galton had introduced testing intended specifically to determine individual differences. Even more important, he reported the results of his measurements (on over 9000 visitors to his laboratory) in a *normative form.* What this means is that he reported scores relative to the average, rather than on an absolute basis. High and low performance became high and low relative to the average. This, we shall see, established a very strong tradition in intellectual assessment.

Now let us look at why Galton chose the measurements he did. The answer is that Galton believed in a generalized concept of fitness or vigor. The superior man was expected to be superior in everything. Thus speed in striking a punching bag, accuracy of vision, and tests of the extent of memory were all tests of vigor, and a man might as easily demonstrate his genius in wrestling and rowing as in mathematics or jurisprudence. (If this seems naive to us today, remember that only a few hundred years before Galton, James II maintained, with widespread support, that certain families had a divine right, ordained by God, for political leadership.) Empiricist that he was, Galton's belief in general vigor was shaken by two of his observations. One was that vividness in visual imagery, as he measured it, was actually less in Galton's undoubtedly gifted intellectual circle than it was in the public at large. The other was that he found it impossible to distinguish England's eminent scientists from her other citizens on the basis of the size of their heads! Nevertheless, until the day he died, Galton maintained a belief in generalized vigor. Today we have distinguished separate physical and intellectual capacities, but the question of whether there is a generalized intellectual power, or a number of special ones, is still open.

Like most Englishmen of his day, Galton was strongly influenced by the ideas of his cousin, Darwin. He believed that intelligence was basically inherited and that the function of education was to permit "vigor" to be expressed in a recognized form. As usual, Galton did not rely on argument to prove his case. He conducted a large study of family histories and, although we may be inclined to a different interpretation today, there is no disguising his finding that the sons of jurists were uncommonly well rewarded at the bar or that the grandsons of generals were decorated on the field. To this day the extent to which intelligence is inherited is a matter of controversy. It was not an argument to Galton. He bequeathed his considerable fortune to the establishment of an institute for eugenics, to improve the human species (or at least the English part of it) through genetics.

While Galton's conclusions about human genetics may be disputed, there is no dispute about the value of his fifth and final contribution to the study of individual differences. Francis Galton invented the correlation coefficient. While to the student who has had a course in statistics this may seem little reason for joy, its development was one of the most important steps in scientific thinking since the rejection of appeals to Divine Providence. Let us explain why, since this has importance quite beyond the study of intelligence. Science was dominated, perhaps still is, in the popular mind, by a simple physical model of "what causes what," by a search for general laws of causation. Galton found this model inadequate for his studies, both in the genetics of sweet peas and in the consideration of human individual differences. He realized that science had to consider "partial causality," that is, to allow that A might influence B without completely controlling B. The idea can be illustrated by considering height. Galton knew that tall fathers tend to have tall sons, but he could find no equation which would exactly predict the height of a son from the height of his father. He concluded, correctly, that father's height was a partial cause of son's height. If an outcome had several partial causes—mother's height, child's diet, encouragement at exercise, and so forth, might be other determinants of a boy's stature—science needed a way of assessing the relative importance of each determiner. Mother's and father's heights might be equally important, for example, and diet a lesser contributor.

Galton and his assistant, the famous statistician Karl Pearson, developed a measure suitable for defining the strength of association between imperfectly related variables. It was called the coefficient of correlation, and is usually symbolized by r. Suppose one takes *two* sets of measures on a group of people (for example, height and weight). The coefficient of correlation is a number between -1.0 and $+1.0$ which indicates the strength of the relationship between the two measures. A negative correlation means that small values on one measure tend to go together with large numbers on the other—for example, the number of men employed in constructing a building should be negatively correlated with the time required to complete the building. A positive correlation indicates that high values on the two scales are associated—as, for example, are height and weight. The closer the correlation approaches 1.0 (or -1.0) the stronger the relationship. A zero correlation indicates no relation. Sadly for Galton, the correlation between head size and intelligence is zero. There are more interesting correlations in intelligence. For instance, the correlation between the tested intelligence of mothers and their natural children has been found to be .50, while the correlation between the intelligence of foster mothers and foster children is .20. There is a stronger relationship in the first than in the second case.

We need to make two additional comments while we are on the topic of correlation. First, despite its origins, correlation does not necessarily imply causation. In his own work, for instance, Galton found a correlation between height and length of the middle finger of .70. He did not argue, nor would we, that one caused the other, that growing a long finger was even a partial cause of growing taller. Rather, the sensible interpretation of this and many other correlations is that it tells us the extent to which the two measures, height and finger length, are influenced by the same factors. Secondly, it needs to be kept in mind that the correlation is a statement not about the measures or scores on any individual but about the relationship between two measures in a population. This is a very important notion. *Unless the correlation is 1 or —1 exactly* individuals may vary in the strength of their own associations. For instance, most heavy people are above average height, but some are not. On the average, intelligent fathers and mothers have intelligent children, but there are exceptions. The student must keep this in mind when we discuss empirical findings.

To close our discussion of Galton, we state one fact. Virtually all theories of intelligence since his time have rested on an interpretation of correlations. That is how important his contribution was.

ALFRED BINET

In spite of his impeccable scientific approach, Galton's tests were not closely associated with anything of social interest. We think, today, that the reason for this was that he mixed up tests of physical and mental functioning, and that his idea of generalized vigor was wrong. Be that as it may, Galton's work had little practical value, which brings us to the second great contributor to intelligence testing. At the turn of the century, Alfred Binet, a French lawyer and physician, accepted the assignment of developing a test which would predict which Parisian children would, or would not, be able to benefit from ordinary schooling. Note that the goal was a pragmatic, technological one—to get a test that works. Unlike Galton, Binet was not pursuing a scientific inquiry. Binet was aware of Galton's work, and had even done similar research of his own. As a result Binet accepted Galton's stress on measurement and correlation, but questioned the advisability of Galton's particular measures. Binet took a quite different approach to test construction. He collected a very large number of questions which seemed, on pragmatic grounds, to require intelligence to answer.

Many of the questions were solicited from "experts," usually teachers, and were taken directly from the school curriculum. He then used statistical analysis to find out which questions distinguished bright, normal, and retarded school children at different ages. Questions which were useful were assembled into a single test which, when published in 1905, immediately gave good results. He, and others, refined the test many times. In 1916 the test was introduced into the United States by the Stanford University psychologist, L. M. Terman, and the "Stanford-Binet" English version rapidly became the predominant intelligence test in the English speaking world. To this day the single most important question one can ask about a new test is "How well does it correlate with the Stanford-Binet?" There is a very good argument that our pragmatic definition of intelligence has become "whatever it is that the Stanford-Binet test measures." It behooves us, then, to look closely at this test and at the explicit and implicit judgments behind it.

Binet agreed with Galton that there was a generalized thing called intelligence. Binet tests produce a single score, computed by lumping together performance in a number of quite different tasks. A second assumption is that the concept of intelligence is to be tied to school performance. This is quite reasonable *given Binet's original goal* which was to provide a way of locating children who needed special schooling. The problem arises when one imputes a meaning to the score beyond the fact that it can be used to predict school performance. There is a fine but important distinction between the proposition that more intelligent children ought to do better in school than less intelligent children—predicting school performance from intelligence—and the similar sounding proposition that the better performers in school are the more intelligent—defining intelligence in terms of school success. Whatever our conception of intelligence, we would probably expect it to affect school performance but not to be synonymous with it. In the construction and validation of a test it is very easy to stray over the line.

A third point, linked to the second, is that the Binet scales and their successors have placed the emphasis on what the person tested can do, rather than on how he does whatever he does. The result of this has been an atheoretic[2] bias to intelligence assessment. Intelligence tests, by and large, tell us more about what intelligent people *can do* (and less intelligent cannot) than about what intelligence *is*.

Finally, like Galton, Binet and his successors sidestepped the question of an absolute scale of intelligence. Because Binet was concerned with children, for whom it is reasonable to assume that intelligence has a growth aspect—six year olds on the average are more intelligent than three year olds—he selected tasks or questions for inclusion in the intelligence scales

[2] "Atheoretic" means that no theory has been created to aid in understanding and extending some set of observations or research results [Editors' note].

on the basis of their ability to differentiate normal children of one age from normal children of other ages. As a result, Binet's tests and, indeed, most IQ-type tests give only age-related scores. One's IQ is a statement about the level of one's global cognitive performance relative to others of the same age.

The IQ was originally defined as a ratio. The tested subject's mental age (MA)—defined by the age level of the items he or she could correctly answer—was divided by the subject's chronological age (CA) and then multiplied by 100 to eliminate any decimal numbers. Thus, if a child of eight years could correctly answer items at the sixth and earlier year levels but not at the seventh or older year levels the IQ would be given by $IQ = (MA/CA) \times 100 = (6/8) \times 100 = 75$. Because intelligence was found not to grow at the same rate over the life span—indeed, for some time psychologists accepted the idea that intelligence did not grow at all after about age sixteen—this ratio IQ had some limitations and has largely been replaced by a deviation IQ. This deviation IQ results from mathematically transforming the score earned on an intelligence test so that, for people of any given age, the average transformed score will be 100, and the spread or variability of scores will be the same. For the reader with some understanding of statistics this can be summarized by saying that, for the modern Stanford-Binet test, deviation IQs at each age have a mean of 100 and a standard deviation of 16 (for other tests the standard deviation is 15). Clearly, a six-year-old girl with IQ of 120 does not have the same problem solving capability, judgment, or store of information as a 26-year-old woman with the same IQ. Because of the relative constancy of the IQ over much of the life span, however, the child's IQ may be a good predictor of later intellectual performance. This relativistic approach further contributes to an atheoretic view of intelligence.

COMPONENTS OF INTELLIGENCE

We now come to a very important but, unfortunately, very technical problem. Both Binet and Galton espoused the view that there was a general thing called intelligence. If this is true, then there should be a substantial positive correlation between all tasks—for example, reading, mathematics, problem solving—which require intelligence. The problem is that the correlations are not quite right. People who do well on reading do not, *on the average*, do quite as well as they should in mathematics, and performances in some intellectual tasks, such as art or music, do not correlate at all well with other tasks. These facts led to an intensive study by a number of British educational psychologists, led by Charles Spearman. They concluded that indeed there was a "general intelligence" but that there were also aptitudes for specific areas. Thus your performance in, say, mathematics, would be due both to your general intelligence and your mathematical aptitude.

That view has been effectively challenged, we believe, by more recent work. Particularly in the United States there is general agreement that there are several, perhaps a great many, aspects to intelligence and that they can be separately measured. Work in this area has depended largely upon a statistical technique called *factor analysis* which is a way of summarizing the correlations between large numbers of tests. The intent of factor analysis is to identify, from the pattern of correlations, a small number of basic factors which will explain the observed relations. In one of the better known series of factor analytic studies, L. L. Thurstone identified a set of primary mental abilities—number ability, verbal fluency, spatial visualization, memory, speed of perception, and reasoning—as explaining performance on a large number and wide variety of cognitive tasks.

The hope was that, once tests were constructed to tap each of these primary abilities, intelligence could be understood as expressed in a small number of independent cognitive abilities. Today most intelligence tests do this. At least three separate scores are used: verbal ability, quantitative ability, and the ability to understand spatial relations. Unfortunately, as psychologists have become more adept at constructing tests and at mathematically analyzing them, the number of independent abilities they have identified has mushroomed. Most recently, J. P. Guilford has postulated 120 separately measureable factors of intelligence, each a combination of some mental operation (recognizing, memorizing, associating to, evaluating) performed upon material (elements, groups of elements, relations among elements) from a particular content (figural, symbolic, behavioral) area. Other psychologists, however, have argued that there are perhaps only half a dozen "very important" factors.

A limitation of the factor analytic approach, however, is that in spite of the sophisticated mathematics, the basic data are still the correlations among tests. We still study the products of cognition rather than the processes themselves. Such analyses account for differences and similarities among test scores but have little to say about how people learn, think, or make decisions or about differences among people in the way they do these things. The factorial investigation of intelligence has proceeded without any theory about intelligent functioning, and, indeed, needs none; it is a summary of observations. Nonetheless, modern tests of mental performance have largely grown out of this approach.

WHAT DO WE KNOW ABOUT INTELLIGENCE?

Given this history, what do we know about intelligence? We shall now try to answer this question. The testing movement has produced two things: some facts and some controversies over what the facts mean. We urge the reader to keep in mind the difference between fact and controversy in following this discussion and in any further reading he may do in this field.

The first fact is that there are clearcut, stable, and practically significant differences in intellectual functioning among individuals. Furthermore, these differences can be revealed by tests lasting roughly three hours. It is easy to show that this is true. If a modern intelligence test is divided in half, randomly, and one half given to a group of people in April and the other half given to the same people in May, then the people who scored high on the April test will, *on the average*, do well on the May test and vice versa. (The correlation between different forms of the same intelligence test is usually greater than .90.) More importantly, the test scores will reflect real differences in how the people taking the test do in a number of real life situations. If school children are given an intelligence test at age 10, the scores on that test will be as good as any other measure in predicting their grades as seniors in high school six or seven years later. (Turning to statistics again, the correlation between an intelligence test score obtained at age 10 and high school grades six years later is about .60.) Intelligence test scores are also related to occupational success. Doctors and lawyers have IQs of about 130, clerks and mechanics IQs of about 109, and unskilled laborers IQs of 90, all, again, *on the average*. The interpretation of these facts is complex, since intelligence predicts school success, and one must succeed in school in order to get into many occupations, but there can be little doubt that intelligence does influence socio-economic success.

The influence of intelligence on life is even more striking when we examine the histories of the very bright and the rather dull.[3] In one of the most famous studies in Psychology, L. M. Terman and his coworkers identified slightly fewer than 1000 very bright students in the California school system in the 1920s. These people have been followed throughout their lives. Their average IQ was over 140. How did they do? By and large, they did very well. They became doctors, lawyers, businessmen, and scientists. Very few of them held "lower status" jobs, and even those who did usually did so with a flair. (The group included an army sergeant who was a successful fiction writer.) Terman's study gave *no* support to the idea of the wierd, sickly genius. The highly intelligent group was somewhat healthier than the general population, appeared to have more outside interests than the average man, had considerably more stable home lives, and in general found life quite satisfying.

About the same time as Terman began his work, another study was made of a "dull normal" group of California school children. This population consisted of individuals whose IQs were markedly below normal but who were not mentally incapacitated. The dull normals became unskilled laborers or service workers and were frequently on relief. Their home lives were less stable and they had a number of (usually minor) conflicts with

---

[3] We refer here to extremes within the "normal" range, that is, individuals who have sufficient intelligence to maintain themselves. Throughout we shall not discuss the case of individuals so grossly mentally defective that they must be cared for in an institution.

the law. Personality tests indicated that they were much less well adjusted to the world around them.

It is not trivial to say that the intelligence tests separates the bright from the dull. What we are saying is that in the space of a two or three hour interview a psychologist can obtain an accurate picture of a person's long-term mental capacity. We must never forget, however, that the picture is a good one "on the average." There will be mistakes, and society must allow an individual to recover from a bad prediction. On the other hand, citing the example of Little Ignatz, who became a physicist even though he had a low IQ in grade school, does not invalidate the idea of mental testing—so long as there are not too many Little Ignatzes.

The second fact seems silly upon first consideration. Intelligence is in the head. By this we mean that intelligence is a relatively stable feature of an adult's *biological* structure, and is not solely a function of the information he has acquired. We can illustrate this easily. The intelligence test is not terribly sensitive to the specific educational experiences of an individual, providing that he shares the same broad cultural background as the group for which the test was designed. Binet's original work included questions to French children about the distance from Paris to Orleans. In the United States Terman asked about the distance from New York to Chicago. The abilities to acquire information and to use the concept of distance are being tested, not the specific information acquired. Intelligence tests of roughly the same form, but with different content, produce similar results in virtually all Western European countries and in industrialized areas of Asia, such as urban Japan. A number of authorities have urged caution in applying the tests in non-Western, non-industrialized societies, but this hardly invalidates our point. Within Western European civilization, which includes an important segment of mankind, individuals possess a characteristic called intelligence which exists independently of the specific facts which the individual has acquired.

Our second argument for intelligence being in the head is that it is affected by biological variables. Gross damage to the brain due to injury, prolonged alcoholism, or the advanced stages of syphilis, encephalitis, or other disease attacking the central nervous system will cause deterioration in intelligence test performance. Indeed, deterioration in test performance is a diagnostic cue for the extent of the damage. Intelligence is also very much affected by nutritional factors during the period before birth and in early infancy. Convincing evidence has been obtained to show that certain vitamin deficiencies during the mother's pregnancy and during the first year of life can produce intellectual damage which may not show up until middle childhood. Finally, intelligence is to a substantial degree an inherited trait. Estimates of the extent to which intelligence is inherited in Western European civilizations range from 60 to 80 percent. (This does not mean that an individual inherits 60 to 80 percent of his intelligence; it means that 60 to 80 percent of the differences between individuals is inherited.) Two striking facts illustrate the inheritance factor. If identical twins are raised in different foster homes, their intellectual patterns will bear a closer resemblance to each other than to the foster brothers and sisters with whom they were raised. Furthermore, the intelligence scores of adopted children more closely resemble the scores of their biological parents than the scores of their social (foster) parents.

The fact that intelligence is based on biology does not mean that education is not important. A person's ability to do an intellectual task depends on his having the necessary information, the cognitive power to understand that information, and the will to use it. Information is acquired by education, cognitive power partly by education but mostly by biology, and "will" by a complex of biological and social factors which are as yet little understood.

Intellectual power develops gradually with increasing age. Current theories of human psychological development lead us to expect continued increases in brain power through adolescence. The *relative* pattern of intellectual growth, however, seems to be fairly well established by age seven or eight. During infancy and preschool, whether a child is at the top or the bottom of the class does not seem to tell us how the child will do as an adult. In the early school years, on the other hand, we seem to acquire a rather stable ordering of intellectual powers. Once adulthood is attained, intelligence is a remarkably stable trait. Assuming that a person has no major debilitating disease, such as those cited earlier, he or she can look forward to normal intellectual functioning to age 70 or beyond.[4] Indeed it has been estimated recently that the intellectual power of the average 70 year old is slightly in excess of the average person of 25. It should be noted, though, that the personality variables and specific knowledge acquired by different age groups may be quite different.

The last fact we wish to present is one we feel strongly about, since it is frequently overlooked. We have been referring to "intelligence" as if it were a single ability which could be measured by the IQ or some other score. *This is false.* Some people do very well at tasks requiring facility with words, others are good at problems involving mathematical reasoning, and others can visualize complex arrangements of supports, elements of a painting, or other useful things. Different people may arrive at the same IQ by employing a different combination of abilities. The particular combination of abilities (or lack of them) that one has probably makes a good deal of difference in how one adjusts to life. In our own research we have found that within a college population different patterns of intellectual ability are characteristic of students pursuing different lines

---

[4] Providing that the tasks involved do not require rapid responding. There does seem to be a loss of speed, but not accuracy, of mental functioning around age 45. On the other hand, recall that intellectual *power* is determined by knowledge as well as intelligence.

of study. We find people with high quantitative ability in engineering, and people with high verbal ability in English and law. Who is smarter? Who is to say? People differ in their cognitive profiles. In order to understand a person's mental functioning, you must understand how he employs his talents. This is not to deny that there are general factors in intelligence which are common to many tasks; there probably are. We do feel, however, that there has been too much discussion of intelligence as if it were a single thing summarized by the IQ.

THE CONTROVERSIES

Let us comment briefly on two current social controversies which are tied to the idea of mental measurement. The reader may realize that these controversies are a natural result of ideas that go all the way back to Galton.

American society at least pays lip service to the idea that everyone is created equal, and ought to "have a chance." It is demonstrably clear that certain racial and ethnic groups (notably Blacks) do not have equal opportunity. A great deal of effort was expended in the period from 1955 to 1970 toward the goal of bringing Black children's scholastic achievement up to the same level as that of Whites. By and large, this effort either did not succeed, or succeeded only for a few very expensive, small programs. Why? In an article in the *Harvard Education Review* in 1969, Professor Arthur Jensen of the University of California summarized the evidence, and offered the opinion that there were innate, genetic differences in intelligence between Black and White populations in the United States.[5] Jensen suggested that Blacks are less able than Whites, on the average, in abstract problem solving ability but that they are equal or superior to Whites in the ability to memorize by rote. Jensen did *not* propose an inferior role for Blacks in society, but he did propose specially designed educational programs tailored to the Black profile of intelligence. It is easy to see, however, that such a program could result in a channeling of Blacks and Whites into separate schools, and further socio-economic segregation.

Jensen's conclusions were based on two unassailable facts: that Blacks generally score below Whites on intelligence test measurements, even when socio-economic differences are accounted for, and that intelligence is largely hereditary. Jensen was met with criticism both of the studies he cited and the conclusions he drew from them. It was also charged that even though the facts were correct, the tests were suspect because they were "not ap-

[5] The idea of racial differences, which Jensen advocated, and racial superiority, which he did not, is, of course, not original with Jensen. Jensen's discussion is of interest because it is a scientific argument and, insofar as anyone can detect, is based on normal scientific reasoning and is not patently a product of political or social beliefs.

propriate for testing Blacks." We tend to agree with Jensen concerning the facts. We also point out that the tests *do* predict the scholastic achievement of Blacks in our present school system, and are appropriate when used for that purpose. The argument that the school system itself should be changed is a separate issue. We disagree with Jensen concerning the conclusions to be drawn from the facts.

Let us grant that *within* the White and Black populations intelligence is substantially a hereditary trait. It is still possible (and likely, considering the differences in social customs) that differences between the populations are in very large part not genetic. This could happen if there were systematic environmental differences that operate against Blacks. To illustrate by analogy, consider the case of height, which is almost completely inherited within a population. The sons and daughters of Japanese who have emigrated to the United States are substantially taller than their parents. This cannot be due to genetic factors, since the gene pool in the population is the same. (There was relatively little first-generation intermarriage between Japanese and the taller White population.) The difference is clearly due to dietary changes, i.e., to a systematic environmental difference between the populations. To conclude the analogy, the observation that intelligence or any other trait is hereditary *within* a population cannot, in itself, be used to assign a genetic cause to a difference between two populations.

There are many environmental factors which could work against full realization of intellectual potential in Black Americans. Why, then, do the special education programs not work? Tentatively, we suspect that it is because the programs in the 1960s were aimed at school children, and that by the time they had reached that age the environmental influences had already had a permanent effect. Recall that relative intelligence stabilizes by age 8, and many authorities would put the figure even lower. We stress again the importance of infancy and prenatal nutritional factors. If the very early childhood environment is what is doing the damage, a special educational program in the school years is likely to have little effect, whereas an effective infancy and early childhood program might be of great help. It is true that such a program could have strong influence on family-rearing patterns, and as such might be objectionable on moral and social grounds to both Whites and Blacks. On the other hand, we feel that there are many programs which could be initiated to improve prenatal care and infant nutrition and which would not be objected to on social grounds. These could be of great social benefit.

Incidentally, we do not maintain that there are no differences in intelligence between the various ethnic groups. There probably are, and there are probably sex differences as well. The differences seem to involve profiles, since some groups will score high on verbal tests and low on quantitative tests, other groups will do the reverse. In all cases there are very wide individual differences, so that knowing what sex or ethnic group a person falls into does not prove to be a very good predictor of that person's own cognitive power. We find no contradiction in knowing that the typical feminine pattern on intelligence tests is to have a higher verbal than mathematical score, and also knowing that one of the foremost mathematicians in the United States today, Mina Rees, is a woman. We personally feel that society should provide an opportunity for everyone to reach his maximum potential, without regard to whether he or she is following the typical pattern for their sex and ethnic group.[6]

The second great controversy about intelligence is also related to the heredity-environment issue. Science fiction writers sometimes picture a world in which a few superbrights control the machinery which does the work, while the dull normal majority are held in a state of somnolence. Is there such a trend? Professor Richard Hernstein of Harvard University believes there may be. He points out that a number of the institutions of our society influence us toward assortative mating for intelligence. What this means is that the brights marry the brights, and the dulls the dulls. Colleges are excellent examples of such institutions. Post adolescents of both sexes, selected for intellectual ability, have the opportunity to spend time together. The result is obvious. Carried to its extreme, this would produce two populations of people, bright ones and dull ones, since intelligence is heritable. Hernstein further worried about the social consequences, since he felt that in a technological society there might only be useful work and substantial economic rewards for those bright enough to manipulate the machinery.

The picture seems overdrawn for three reasons, only two of them psychological. The most important psychological and genetic fact is that the assortative mating devices which do operate for the very bright and for the dull are not nearly so rigid in the middle ranges of the population (IQ 85–115). This includes about two thirds of all people. Many of the bright and the dull come from movement both up and down from this middle group. A second psychological reason is that with improved instructional techniques, we ought to be able to bring less gifted individuals to a higher level of performance. This would lessen the pressure on educational institutions to be so selective on the basis of intelligence. To take a concrete example, consider medicine, a highly rewarded and important field. Our present training techniques enable us to turn out a satisfactory physician given that the entering student has an IQ of about 130. Better training techniques might lower the required intelligence to, say, 120. This does *not* mean the resulting physician would be less competent. In fact, there is every reason to believe that in most cases we are overly dependent upon intelligence as a way of selecting people for training of various kinds. In response to social pressures, we probably can afford to be much less assortative in our educational selectivity.

[6] May we point out that this is a political and not a scientific belief.

Finally, we would point out that it is not the case that advanced technology eliminates jobs for all but the very bright. In fact, the greatest economic demand in the future will be for people in the service jobs; barbers, beauticians, mechanics, and salespersons. It is easier to automate an accounting office than a janitorial crew.

Technology in society may produce some changes in educational selectivity and assortative mating. Indeed, such pressures have existed for a long time. Whether this is a good or bad thing depends on your social viewpoint. The available scientific data do not indicate that the degree of assortative mating for intelligence will accelerate markedly in the near future.

Finally, we would like to introduce a controversy which is one which bothers us, if not society. One of the greatest deficiencies of intelligence testing today is its lack of a theoretical basis. Since Binet, the tests have been selected because they worked and not because they were related to a theory of cognition. This is similar to a SCUBA diver using a depth gauge without knowing anything about pressure and density—it would work so long as he did not get into trouble. Much of the controversy over testing and intelligence today arises because we have been using measurement instruments without adequate thought about what is being measured. A major goal for future research will be the development of an intelligence test which is closely tied to our ideas of how the mind works. When such a test is developed we hope that many of the controversies over the meaning and proper use of intelligence tests will simply disappear.

SUMMARY

"Intelligence" refers to the mental power of an individual. It is a real quality which can be measured at little cost. Intelligence tests taken when a person is a child can be used to predict later success in school and, somewhat less accurately, success as an adult. Intellectual growth continues through adolescence and then, given good health, remains constant until advanced age. The pattern of one's growth, however, is predictable by age 7 or 8. Before this intelligence is more malleable. It is particularly affected by physiological factors before birth and in early childhood. Social and familial practices at this time may also be of a great deal of importance.

Intelligence is multifaceted. It cannot be summarized by stating a single IQ score, for this does not adequately describe an individual's cognition. Unfortunately, too little discussion is paid to the many factors of intelligence in social discussions of the concept. In spite of an impressive amount of work on definition of the different factors of intelligence, little work has been done to relate intelligence measurement to a theory of how the mind works. This is a major theoretical deficiency.

Intelligence is largely, but not completely, established by heredity. The extent to which intelligence varies between the sexes and the various racial groups is not clear. The fact of heritability of intelligence does not dictate that there must be either sexual or racial differences. It would be impossible to prove that such differences do not exist. It is a fact that different racial groups exhibit different *profiles* of intelligence. Certainly this is true for the sexes. Since both racial and sexual groups have markedly different environments, however, the cause of this difference cannot be assigned to biology or sociology. In any case, we must remember that within every large group there are wide individual differences on all measures of intelligence. The only sensible thing to do is to try to give each individual an opportunity to develop his or her own potential.

4 Social Interaction and Group Membership

The study of social interactions and groups is so vast and so interesting that it has been difficult to know just what to select for this section. After some consideration, we have elected to illustrate three areas that are currently receiving a great deal of attention. These are human territoriality, human aggressiveness, and the issue of "sexism."

The author of the first article, Dr. Robert Sommer, has devoted considerable effort to examining human territorial behavior. Several of his studies have revealed that slight modifications of environmental settings in schools, airports, mental hospitals, libraries, and so on exert either enhancing or inhibiting effects on social interactions. In his article, *The Ecology of Privacy*, Dr. Sommer shows how people intentionally use such environmental modifications to reduce social interactions in library reading rooms, thereby securing and maintaining their privacy. The next time you are in a library, keep this article in mind and you will be able to spot people using these very subtle, but often effective, offensive, and defensive measures; in fact, you will find that you use them yourself without being fully aware of doing so.

Aggression is an intense form of social interaction that often has unfortunate consequences. The second article, *Violence and Man's Struggle to Adapt*, by Drs. Marshall Gilula and David Daniels, examines aggressive behavior and attempts to answer many of the questions that commonly arise about it. For example, is aggressiveness an instinct? Can it be controlled and modified? What is the relationship between mental illness and aggressiveness? Does aggression in films and on television have any effect on aggressive behavior in children?

The Women's Liberation Movement has raised many questions in addition to the central issue of equality of rights and opportunities for women. Among these questions is whether there are any *innate* behavioral differences between women and men or whether the commonly observed differences in characteristic behaviors are purely a matter of culture and training. Efforts to answer this question in a reasoned, dispassioned way are complicated by the fact that many people are convinced that proof of the existence of innate differences would be proof that one sex is inferior to the other. This conclusion, of course, does not logically follow, but the emotions it generates makes discussion of the whole question a bit touchy. So, it is with some trepidation that we have included *Male Dominance? Yes, Alas. A Sexist Plot? No.* by Dr. Lionel Tiger, which contains the arguments for the hypothesis of innate differences. No matter where you stand now in regard to this question, read this article with care; it may be harmful to your prejudices.

THE ECOLOGY OF PRIVACY

Robert Sommer

Indispensable to many library patrons is a feeling of privacy, of being able to read and take notes without disturbing others or being disturbed by them. Few places make as strict a demand upon the physical setting to guarantee privacy as the library reading area. The library is one of the few public institutions in which interaction between people is actively discouraged. Museums, art galleries, and government buildings permit conversation which, in the view of many librarians, would prevent the concentration that readers require to get maximum benefit from library facilities. Undoubtedly there are some library patrons who prefer to chat as they read and students who prefer groups rather than individual studying. New libraries on university campuses often contain special rooms to satisfy the needs of more gregarious readers as well as to get them out of the way of students who prefer quiet and solitude while they study. Although silence and respect for others can be encouraged and maintained through official regulations, social disapproval, and staff surveillance, these tasks become much easier and sometimes unnecessary in the proper library environment. The purpose of this article is to discuss the part played by the library environment in regulating interaction between people. . . .

From *The Library Quarterly*, 1966, *36*, 234–248. Copyright 1966 by The University of Chicago Press. By permission of The University of Chicago Press and the author.

I am indebted to Nancy Felipe, Mary Juncker, Linda Larson, Faye Nixon, Pamela Pearce, and Melva Rush for their assistance. This study was supported in part by a grant from the U.S. Office of Education, HEW.

The present observations took place at the main library building of the University of California, Davis. The library contains approximately 400,000 volumes and serves a population of 8,000 students as well as faculty members. The library operates on the openstack plan, and access and circulation are controlled at two exit desks. We are concerned here primarily with three public reading areas—the periodical, reserve, and reference rooms. The pattern here follows that found elsewhere (cf. the Amherst, Dartmouth, and Michigan studies) in that the vast majority of students in these public reading areas is there to study and use materials brought with them rather than the collection. A library-staff member stated that probably 90 per cent or more of the readers in these areas were studying their own materials, and three years of direct observation of these areas tend to support this conclusion.

RESULTS

We began our observations in the library reserve room, a large room (twenty-nine by eighty-three feet) containing thirty-three small rectangular tables, each with four chairs, two per side. The observations took place at times when there was a choice of seats and were made by an undergraduate student, David Addicott. Of those students who entered the room alone, 64 per cent sat alone, 26 per cent sat diagonally across from another student, while only 10 per cent sat directly opposite or beside another student. These results, the opposite of findings in lounges and cafeterias where conversation was encouraged, led to an extended series of observations in this room and other study areas (Sommer 1965). These observations confirmed the hypothesis that people who came alone did indeed prefer to sit alone. When room density reached one per table, then the next preferred arrangement was diagonal seating. That is, two people occupied a table in such a way that neither sat alongside or opposite the other. In the periodical room, which contained four-chair and six-chair tables, we ranked the six-chair tables on a sociality continuum. At the top (see Fig. 1) is the most sociofugal [keeping people apart] arrangement, and at the bottom is the side-by-side arrangement which was the most sociopetal [bringing people together]. A majority of those pairs who sat side by side were observed to converse or otherwise interact during the brief observation period.

At this point we turned our attention to the largest study area in the building, the reference room. This is a very large high-ceilinged room containing eighteen large, heavy wooden tables (four by sixteen feet) each surrounded by twelve chairs, six to a side. . . .

To determine the patterns of occupation and succession in the reference room, an observer arrived at 8:00 A.M. when the room first opened and using a number sequence, recorded where each of the first occupants sat and the sex of each person. These observations ran from 8:00–8:45 A.M. on sixty-one week-day mornings. We found that approximately four-fifths

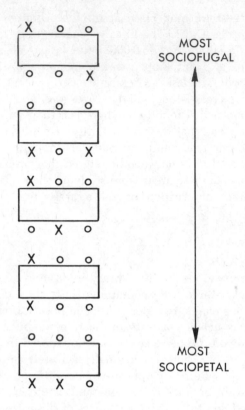

Figure 1. Sociality continuum for six-chair table. (By permission of the University of Chicago Press.)

of those students who were among the first ten occupants and came alone sat at empty tables. The same is true for the sixty-nine pairs, people who entered the room together, among the first ten occupants. Furthermore, there is a strong trend among the first individuals to gravitate to the end chairs at the table (see Fig. 2). The number in each circle refers to the number of times that place at a table was chosen by one of the first ten or second ten people during the duration of observations.

The situation at zero density is clear: the first occupants tend to sit one per table at an end chair if they come alone or two per table if both arrive together. We then examined our seating diagram to learn where the next person at the table would sit. There were 401 instances where a student sat at a table already occupied by a lone student. Figure 3 shows the seats protected when one person occupies a given location. Essentially this is where a stranger will not sit unless room density is very high. . . . Figure 3 shows that when one person occupied an end chair, the other person is likely to be found at the middle or far end of the table. When one individual occupies the B position, the other occupant is likely to be found

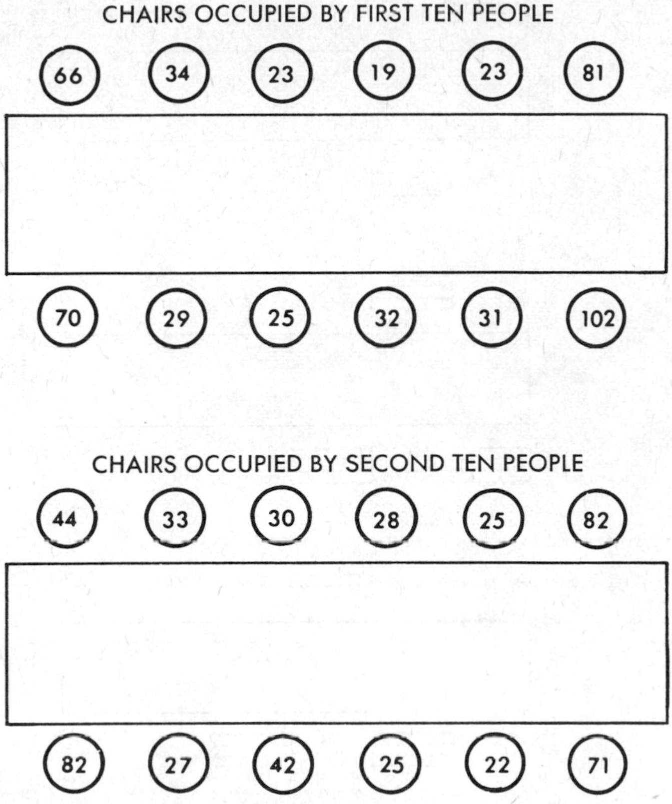

CHAIRS OCCUPIED BY FIRST TEN PEOPLE

(66) (34) (23) (19) (23) (81)

(70) (29) (25) (32) (31) (102)

CHAIRS OCCUPIED BY SECOND TEN PEOPLE

(44) (33) (30) (28) (25) (82)

(82) (27) (42) (25) (22) (71)

Figure 2. Seating of the first ten occupants at reference-room tables. (By permission of The University of Chicago Press.)

in a far end chair. When one occupant is found at C, the second person occupies *any* of the end chairs. Our diagrams also disclosed 113 pairs who conversed at one time or another (who were excluded from the preceding tabulations). Of this number of conversing pairs, 82 per cent were seated side by side, 12 per cent were seated directly across from one another, and 6 per cent were people alongside one another with an empty chair in between or catty-cornered across from one another. . . .

TERRITORIAL DEFENSE

Readers protect their privacy in many ways, some offensive and others defensive. The former are based on the notion that "the best defense is a good offense" and include both threat positions and threat postures. Position refers to an individual's location with reference to external coordinates; posture refers to his particular stance. Librarians are also familiar with the use of physical objects, such as coats, handbags, books, personal belongings,

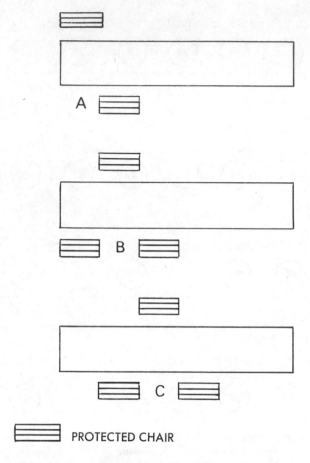

Figure 3. *Seats protected at each of three table locations.*
(By permission of The University of Chicago Press.)

which are used to mark out individual territories. A table space can be defended by position, posture, territorial markers, or some combination of the three. These are more than academic considerations as indicated by librarians' complaints about room capacity lowered by empty chairs "staked out" by students occupied elsewhere. Territorial possession is another reason why empty classrooms are not always successful as study halls during the evening hours. Conceivably the number of empty chairs in classrooms could accommodate all those students who wanted to study, but what happens in fact is that the first student in a room takes possession of it and subsequent students stay away. Stuart Stoke (1960) and his associates report that "the standard custom seems to award the whole classroom to the first student to take possession by squatter's rights. By looking sufficiently annoyed when other students try to study there, the first usually succeeds in maintaining his solitude. A classroom building which will take care of 800 students in classes may house only 23–50 in study." The effectiveness with which a student can keep intruders away depends upon population pressure on the room. We conducted a small experiment along these lines in a student soda fountain which contained ten small side rooms. We stationed a young girl who appeared to be studying at one of the three tables in the room. When the pressure for seats became heavy, she was unable to protect the entire room although she was able to defend successfully the three empty chairs at her particular table.

To learn something of the difference between two available methods of insuring privacy, offensive display and avoidance, a brief questionnaire was constructed which presented the student with table diagrams containing six, eight, and ten chairs respectively (see Fig. 4). There were two forms to the questionnaire which were distributed randomly within a class of forty-five students. Twenty-four students were given avoidance instruc-

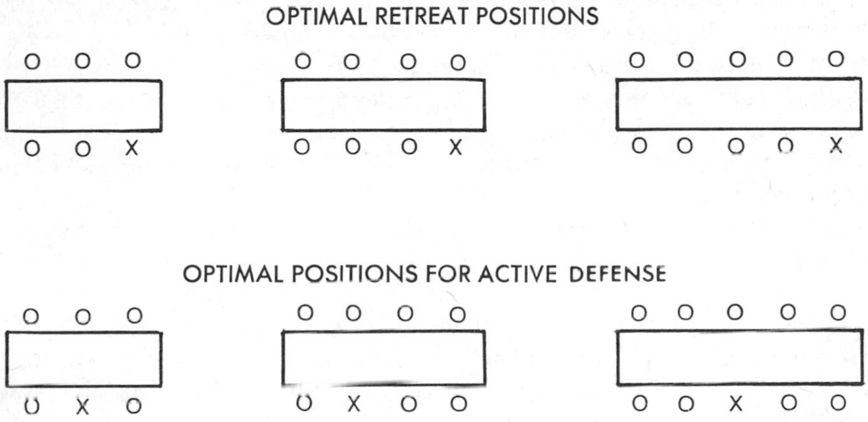

OPTIMAL RETREAT POSITIONS

OPTIMAL POSITIONS FOR ACTIVE DEFENSE

Figure 4. Optimal offensive and defensive positions. (By permission of The University of Chicago Press.)

tions: "If you wanted to be as far as possible from the distraction of other people, where would you sit at the table?" Twenty-one other students in the same class were shown the same diagrams and given the offensive-display instructions: "If you wanted to have the table to yourself, where would you sit to discourage anyone else from occupying it?"

Even though both sets of instructions were aimed at insuring privacy, the two tactics produced a striking difference in seats chosen. Those students who wanted to sit by themselves as far as possible from other people overwhelmingly chose the *end* chairs; those students who wanted to keep others away from the table almost unanimously chose the *middle* chair.

The utility of each tactic, offensive display or active retreat, depends in large measure on predictions of future room density. Occupying the middle seat at a table may keep people away when densities are low, but once the room begins to fill up, the man in the middle runs the risk of being completely surrounded. At high densities an end chair, which provides at least one side without people, is a more effective way of gaining privacy. The size of rooms and tables also has an effect; other things being equal it is easier to defend a small room or table than a large one. Privacy also can be increased by erecting barriers between areas. Studies in offices, army barracks, and dormitories have shown that barriers decrease communication between units while increasing it within units (Blake *et al.* 1956). Barriers also can be used to regulate room density. Partitions between reading areas at a table will insure that no more than, for example, six individuals occupy one side of a table. These barriers protect personal space and permit two people to sit side by side at very close distances without physical contact. By permitting greater physical closeness without psychological discomfort, barriers increase the upper limit of comfortable room density. Such barriers need not be ponderous or weighty objects. A small raised strip down the center of the table can effectively serve as a barrier and increase feelings of privacy by defining individual territories and preventing unnecessary conflict over "no man's land" in the center. A raised barrier can serve as a resting place for a reader's eyes when he looks away from his books. These "study breaks" are major sources of accidental intrusion. Barriers that are symbolic rather than physical impediments to movement also can regulate interaction. Subtle color changes or painted lines can define individual territories almost as well as raised partitions.

The finding described earlier, that the first occupants in the reference room gravitate to end chairs, can be interpreted in the light of our discussion of territorial defense. These data suggest that avoidance defensive positions are more widely used than offensive displays. Undoubtedly this has some connection with student's anticipation of future room density. If we studied a place where room density rarely exceeded one per table, we would predict more use of the central chairs by the first occupants. In the reference room a person's territory does not extend very far down the table. He has almost no influence over what happens at the opposite end of the table. For example, we have found that sexual segregation is a characteristic feature of campus life. If one observes students riding bicycles, eating in the cafeteria, or lolling on the grass, it is more common to see girls with girls and boys with boys than to see mixed groups. This is a function of the dormitory living arrangements as well as the special-interest groups on campus (home-economics majors are largely female, engineering majors are largely male, etc.). In the reserve room and periodical room with small four- and six-chair tables, there is sexual segregation in seating. When room density reaches approximately one per table, a newcomer in either room is twice as likely to sit with someone of his own sex than with someone of the opposite sex. However, when we look at the long tables in the reference room, a very different picture emerges. The second person at a long table, who typically sits at the opposite end, is equally likely to sit at a table occupied by someone of opposite sex as someone of his own sex. To use the term of the sociologists, the occupant so far away at the other end of the table is a "nonperson," and his sex or other personal characteristics are unimportant. . . .

SUMMARY

A series of observational, questionnaire, and experimental studies was undertaken to learn how readers found privacy in public reading areas of a university library. The first readers in the room gravitated to the end chairs at separate tables. The seats alongside a person or the seat directly across from him were rarely occupied except at times of high density. Individual readers marked out territories in various ways, using personal belongings and positioning of their own chair. Privacy can be obtained by offensive display or by avoidance procedures. In view of the large area that must be protected and the high population density at times, the majority of patrons used avoidance techniques. . . .

REFERENCES

Blake, R., Rhead, C. C., Wedge, B., & Mouton, J. S. Housing architecture and social interaction. *Sociometry*, 1956, **19**, 133–139.

Sommer, R. Further studies of group ecology. *Sociometry*, 1965, **28**, 337–348.

Stoke, S. M., et al., *Student reactions to study facilities*. Amherst, Mass.: Committee on Cooperation, 1960.

VIOLENCE AND MAN'S STRUGGLE TO ADAPT

Marshall F. Gilula and David N. Daniels

The need is not really for more brains, the need is now for a gentler, a more tolerant people than those who won for us against the ice, the tiger, and the bear (*1*).

Violence waits in the dusty sunlight of a tenement yard and in the shadows of a distraught mind. Violence draws nearer in the shouts of a protest march and in ghetto rumblings. Violence erupts from Mace-sprinkled billy clubs and a homemade Molotov cocktail. Violence of war explodes the peace it promises to bring. Hourly reports of violence bring numbness, shock, confusion, sorrow. We live in a violent world (*2*).

Violence surrounds us, and we must try to understand it in the hopes of finding alternatives that will meet today's demand for change. Do we benefit from violence? Or is violence losing whatever adaptive value it may once have had? We present two theses. (i) Violence can best be understood in

From *Science 164*: 396–405. Copyright 1969 by the American Association for the Advancement of Science. By permission of the American Association for the Advancement of Science and the authors.

the context of adaptation. Violence is part of a struggle to resolve stressful and threatening events—a struggle to adapt. (ii) Adaptive alternatives to violence are needed in this technological era because the survival value of violent aggression is diminishing rapidly.

The shock of Robert F. Kennedy's death prompted the formation of a committee on violence (3) in the Department of Psychiatry, Stanford University School of Medicine. We committee members reviewed the literature on violence and then interpreted this literature from the point of view of psychiatrists and psychologists. We discussed our readings in seminars and sought answers to our questions about violence. This article presents a synthesis of our group's findings and observations and reflects our view of adaptation theory as a unifying principle in human behavior. . . .

DEFINITION OF HUMAN ADAPTATION

Every culture prescribes the range of coping behaviors available to its people, but within this range individual adaptive behavior is forged and tested in times of stress. Stressful or new situations paradoxically offer us both the danger of failure and the opportunity for learning. Stress can be dangerous when it overwhelms the individual or group. Either the situation itself or unpleasant feelings about the situation (including massive anxiety) may block our usual resources and prevent problem solving, and aggressive reactions that are both indiscriminate and protective may occur. We may show primitive forms of behavior: passive adjustment, withdrawal, falsely blaming others, indiscriminate rage, violence, or confusion.

Alternately, stressful events provide a constructive challenge and expanded opportunity for learning. In a stressful situation that is not overwhelming, we seek information helpful in dealing with the situation and try to apply this information (7). From information seeking and subsequent exploratory behavior come not only greater use of information and eventual mastery of new situations but also a sense of heightened self-awareness, enhanced coping skills, and personal growth.

A number of commonly occurring stressful life situations that may challenge and develop our coping skills have been recognized (7). These are associated with the transitions in life and include adolescence, separation from parents, and marriage. Other challenging transitions involve cultural stresses, such as war and the threat of war; rapid technological change; and physical events, such as drought, earthquakes, and famine. These transition points in life are important because they provide opportunity for learning and developing more sophisticated ways of coping with problems.

We have marvelous adaptive abilities for coping with varying, even extreme, situations. These abilities result from cultural evolution interacting with our biological evolution. Culturally we survive through complex communal living. Through our living groups we obtain satisfaction, develop identity, and find meaning to life. Basic social values are of special cultural importance, for they determine the limits of acceptable behavior, especially during times of stress. Biologically we are uniquely endowed for complex communal living. Such biological characteristics as aggression, the upright posture, prehension, speech, prolonged infancy and maturation, and profound development of the brain—all favor and allow for rich, dynamic, and complex living. Development of the cerebral hemispheres has played an especially important role in adaptation, for the cerebrum constitutes the biological basis of higher intelligence, self-awareness, complex language, and flexibility (6).

Thus through the interaction of biological evolution and cultural evolution, we have the equipment for adapting to and molding diverse environments. But this ability to adapt by manipulating the environment is now our cause for greatest concern, for in changing the environment, man changes the conditions necessary for his survival. We now are seeing an unprecedented acceleration of various man-made changes which call for accompanying changes in man, changes which we are having difficulty in making. While biological change is extremely slow, cultural change theoretically occurs at least every generation, although some aspects of culture (such as technology) change faster than others (for example, beliefs and customs). The term "generation gap" not only describes how we today view the battle of the generations but also alludes to the speed of cultural change and how people have trouble keeping pace. Living in the electronic age, we watch televised accounts of preagricultural-age violence and feel our industrial-age mentality straining to cope with the environment.

Since survival results from the long-range adaptiveness of our behavior, knowledge of adaptive mechanisms is important for understanding the role of violence in human behavior and survival. In the section that follows we shall relate three theories of aggression to adaptation.

ADAPTATION AND THEORIES OF AGGRESSION

Aggression has helped man survive. Aggression in man—including behaviors that are assertive, intrusive, and dominant as well as violent—is fundamental and adaptive. Violence is not a result of aggression but simply a form of aggression. Nor is all violence necessarily motivated by destructive aggression. For instance, in the sadistic behavior of sexual assaults, violence is evoked in part by sexual motives. In other instances, violence can occur accidentally or without conscious intent, as in many auto accidents. Currently there are three main views of aggression—all involving adaptation—but each suggests a different solution to the problem of violent behavior. Broadly labeled, these theories are (i) the biological-instinctual theory, (ii) the frustration theory, and (iii) the social-learning theory.

1) *The biological-instinctual theory* (8–10) holds that aggressive behavior, including violence, is an intrinsic component of man resulting from natural selection: Man is naturally aggressive. It is hard to imagine the

survival of man without aggressiveness, namely because aggression is an element of all purposeful behavior and, in many cases, provides the drive for a particular action. This theory says that aggression includes a wide variety of behaviors, many of which are constructive and essential to an active existence. Stimulus-seeking behavior (for example, curiosity or the need to have something happen) is certainly at least as important a facet of human behavior as avoidance behavior and need-satisfaction. Seeking the novel and unexpected provides much of life's color and excitement. Aggression can supply much of the force and power for man's creative potential.

Psychiatric and psychoanalytic case studies are one source of evidence supporting this theory (*8–11*). Examples range from individuals with destructive antisocial behavior who express violent aggression directly and often impulsively, to cases of depression and suicide in which violent aggression is turned against the self, and to seriously inhibited persons for whom the expression of aggression, even in the form of assertion, is blocked almost entirely. Psychiatrists and other mental-health professionals describe many disordered behaviors as stemming from ramifications and distortions of the aggressive drive (*8*).

Animal studies (*4, 9, 12*) (including primate field studies), studies of brain-damaged humans, and male-female comparisons provide behavioral, anatomical, and hormonal data illustrating the human predisposition to aggression. Among nonhuman mammals, intraspecies violence occurs less frequently than with humans (*5*). When violent aggressive behaviors do occur among members of the same species, they serve the valuable functions of spacing the population over the available land and maintaining a dominance order among the group members. Uncontrolled aggression in animals generally occurs only under conditions of overcrowding. Aggression in humans, even in the form of violence, has had similar adaptive value historically.

The biological-instinctual theory suggests that since aggression is inevitable, effective controls upon its expression are necessary, and reduction of violence depends upon providing constructive channels for expressing aggression.

2) *The frustration theory* (*13*) states that aggressive behavior comes from interfering with ongoing purposeful activity. A person feels frustrated when a violation of his hopes or expectations occurs, and he then tries to solve the problem by behaving aggressively. Frustrations can take various forms: threats to life, thwarting of basic needs, and personal insults. This theory often equates aggression with destructive or damaging violent behavior. Major factors influencing aggressive responses to frustration are the nature of the frustration, previous experience, available alternatives for reaction (aggression is by no means the only response to frustration), the person's maturity, and the preceding events or feelings. Even boredom may provoke an aggressive response. As a response to frustration, aggres-

sion is often viewed as a learned rather than an innate behavior. According to this theory, frustration-evoked aggression aims at removing obstacles to our goals; hence the frustration theory also ties in with adaptation. The aggressive response to frustration often is a form of coping behavior that may have not only adjustive but also long-range consequences.

The frustration theory suggests that control or reduction of violence requires reducing existing frustrations as well as encouraging constructive redirection of aggressive responses to frustration. This reduction includes removing or improving frustrating environmental factors that stand between personal needs and environmental demands. Such factors include violation of human rights, economic deprivation, and various social stresses.

3) *The social-learning theory* (*14*) states that aggressive behavior results from child-rearing practices and other forms of socialization. Documentation comes from sociological and anthropological studies and from observing social learning in children. Aggressive behavior can be acquired merely by watching and learning—often by imitation—and does not require frustration. Aggressive behaviors rewarded by a particular culture or subculture usually reflect the basic values and adaptive behaviors of the group. In American culture, where achievement, self-reliance, and individual self-interest are valued highly, we also find a relatively high emphasis on military glory, a relatively high incidence of personal crime, and a society characterized by a relatively high degree of bellicosity. Similar patterns occur in other cultures. From this theory we infer that as long as a nation values and accepts violence as an effective coping strategy, violent behavior will continue.

The social-learning theory of aggression suggests that control and reduction of violence require changes in cultural traditions, child-rearing practices, and parental examples. Parents who violently punish children for violent acts are teaching their children how and in what circumstances violence can be performed with impunity. Other changes in cultural traditions would emphasize prevention rather than punishment of violent acts and, equally important, would emphasize human rights and group effort rather than excessive and isolated self-reliance. The first step toward making the changes that will reduce violence is to examine our values. We must decide which values foster violence and then begin the difficult job of altering basic values.

In reality, the three theories of aggression are interrelated. Proclivities for social learning and for frustration often have a biological determinant. For example, the biology of sex influences the learning of courting behavior. Regarding violence from these theories of aggression we see that the many expressions of violence include man's inherent aggression, aggressive responses to thwarted goals, and behavior patterns imitatively learned within the cultural setting. All three theories of aggression and violence fit into the adaptation-coping explanation. Violence is an attempt to cope with stressful situations and to resolve intolerable conflicts. Violence may have short-run adjustive value, even when the long-run adaptive consequences may in fact be adverse. It is the sometimes conflicting natures of adjustment and adaptation that are confusing and insufficiently appreciated. In some instances violence emerges when other more constructive coping strategies have failed. In other instances violence is used to enhance survival. Our species apparently has overabsorbed violence into our cultures as a survival technique. Children and adolescents have learned well the accepted violent behaviors of their elders.

All three theories help us understand violent behavior and hence suggest potential ways of reducing violence. In the following sections we consider current examples of violence from the perspective of those factors in our society that foster violence and from the standpoint of how these examples reflect the changing nature of adaptation.

PHENOMENON OF PRESIDENTIAL ASSASSINATION

Assassination is not an isolated historical quirk, eluding comprehension or analysis. The event is usually overdetermined by multiple but equally important factors: personal qualities of the assassin, a fatalistic posture assumed by the victim, and such factors in the social environment as political stereotypes, murder sanctions, and the symbolic nature of high offices.

Although assassination can strike down anyone, we have restricted our examination to assassination of presidents in America (15) by studying the personal qualities of "successful" assassins and of others who almost succeeded. Of the eight assassination attempts on American presidents, four have been successful. The following facts emerge. (i) All the assassination attempts were made with guns, all but one with pistols. (ii) All the assassins were shorter and weighed less than average men of the period. (iii) All the assassins were young adult Caucasian males. (iv) All the assassination attempts but one were made by individuals who were seriously disturbed or even paranoid schizophrenics (16). The exception was the final attempt of two Puerto Rican nationalists to kill President Harry S Truman. The successful assassins, for the most part, were mentally unbalanced and had persecutory and grandiose delusions.

Assassination provides a method for instantly satisfying a need for personal importance. The delusional assassin very probably had a fantasy that once the act was committed, an outcry of favorable opinion and acclaim would vindicate what he had done. In most of the instances of attempted or successful assassination, escape plans were inadequate or nonexistent.

The life pattern of most of the assassins included extreme resentment toward others—a resentment aggravated by a long history of isolation and loneliness. Often the isolation stemmed from poor and inconsistent relations with parents and others early in life, which resulted in most of the assassins having resentment and mistrust of parental figures. Their resentment toward parental figures might have included the President (political symbol of parenthood) as the head of the federal government. In response to imagined unfair treatment from others and a distortion of his own inadequacies, the assassin turned his anger on the chief of state.

Typically the assassin had struggled for importance, success, and manliness, but had failed. At the time of the attempted presidential assassination, the assassin was on a downward life course. Haunted by resentment and failure and plagued with disordered thinking and distortions of reality, the assassin took action. Shooting the President was thus an attempt to resolve conflicts with which he apparently could not otherwise cope. . . .

Our discussion of another important determinant of assassination—the victim's fatalistic attitude—is not restricted to presidential assassinations. The fatalistic thinking and actions of several assassination victims are reflected in their strong disinclination toward taking precautionary measures despite recognizing the existence of violent impulses in others toward presidents and presidential candidates. Robert Kennedy stated a view that he shared with Abraham Lincoln, Martin Luther King, Jr., and John F. Kennedy: "There's no sense in worrying about those things. If they want you, they can get you" (*17*). This attitude often leads to dangerous negligence that is an exaggerated form of denying that one is actually afraid of physical harm. Lincoln has been described as "downright reckless" (*18*) about personal safety. Robert Kennedy was quoted as saying, "I'll tell you one thing: If I'm President, you won't find me riding around in any of those awful [bullet-proof] cars" (*17*). The fatalistic attitude illustrated by statements like this is encouraged by our tradition of expecting physical courage in our leaders. Men who repeatedly and publicly proclaim their vulnerability may be unwittingly encouraging assassination by offering an invitation to the delusional, grandiose, and isolated person who dreams of accomplishing at least one important and publicly recognized act in his life. "Mixing with the people" is firmly embedded in the American political tradition, but it is also an accomplice to assassination. One way to cope with this problem would be legislation to restrict the contact and exposure of a President with crowds when his presence has been announced in advance.

MASS MEDIA AND VIOLENCE

Television could be one of our most powerful tools for dealing with today's violence. It could provide education and encourage, if not induce, desired culture modification. Unfortunately, it does little of either today, perhaps because the harmful effects of televised violence have been glossed over. However, all the mass media do little to discourage and much to encourage violence in America. The Ugly American as a national stereotype is rapidly being displaced in the eyes of the world by the Violent American, his brother of late. This stereotype is fostered by the media but is sustained by the violent acts of some of our citizens. Armed with shotgun, ignorance, frustrations, or hunger, this Violent American can be seen today throughout our society. We are not all violent Americans, but mass media are giving us the violence we seem to want.

What effect do the mass media have (*19*)? All of us are probably affected by the media to some degree, but most research has focused on children, since an immature and developing mind is usually less capable of discrimination when responding to a given stimulus. One comprehensive review (*20*) described short-term effects that include the child's emotional reactions to what he views, what the child actually learns as a result of his exposure, may include vocabulary, factual information, belief systems, and such altered personality characteristics as increased aggressiveness. No one selects all the media materials available, nor does anyone absorb or retain the selected materials consistently or completely. Prior information, differing needs, and quality of life adjustment also help to filter the child's processing of the offered materials. Mass media effects also depend somewhat on the applicability of the learned material to the child's own life situation.

Similarly, as shown by another researcher (*21*), frustration, the anger evoked by it, the overall situation, the apparent severity and justification of the violence viewed in a film—all relate to whether or not children use these aggressive responses.

A large study in Great Britain (*22*) showed that certain portrayals of violence are more disturbing to children than others. Unusual motives, settings, and weapons are more disturbing than stereotyped violence. For example, knives or daggers are more upsetting than guns or fist fights. Similarly, seeing violence or disasters in newsreels bothered children more than dramatized violence.

Another study (*23*) found that the average American child from 3 through 16 years old spends more of his waking hours watching television than attending school. First-graders spend 40 percent and sixth-graders spend 80 percent of their viewing time watching "adult" programs, with Westerns and situation comedies being most popular. By the eighth grade, children favor crime programs.

Can we justifiably say that the media teach violence? Television teaches more than vocabulary and factual information to the impressionable young viewer, who learns by identification and social imitation. Learning theorists have shown that children readily mimic the aggressive behavior of adults and that the degree of imitation is comparable whether the behavior is live or televised. In another study (*24*) nursery school children watched a film of adults aggressively hitting an inflatable plastic figure, a Bobo doll. Later these and other children were first mildly frustrated and then led individually into a room in which they found the Bobo doll and other materials not shown in the film. Those who had seen the film imitated precisely the film's physical and verbal aggression and made more aggressive use of other toys, such as guns, that had not been in the film. Film-watchers showed twice as much aggressiveness as those who had not seen the film.

These children were all from a "normal" nursery school population, and all showed some effect. This finding seriously questions the claim that such violence is learned only by deviant individuals. The findings apply equally to real, fictional, and fantasy violence. The impact on children observing aggressive behavior has been further corroborated in experiments in which live models, cartoons, and play materials were used. The idea that watching television satisfactorily releases pent-up aggressions (the catharsis theory) loses credibility in the face of these data from social-learning experiments. Watching dramatized violence may actually lead to subsequent aggressive behavior.

A tendency toward repeating certain behaviors viewed in the media clearly exists. The mass media teach the alphabet of violence, but whether or not the actual performance of violent behaviors occurs depends on personality, subcultural values, and other factors. The research to date indicates that the learning of violence must be distinguished from the performance of it. One fear we have is that restraints and taboos against violent behavior may diminish as the result of observing prohibited behavior being condoned and rewarded on the screen. Violence depicts a way of life; it is disguised by a cloak of history or locale and becomes acceptable. We are never taught "in this School for Violence that violence in itself is something reprehensible" (25). . . .

Given the effectiveness of the mass media in achieving culture modification, we should determine whether the content of the media produces desirable or undesirable modification. How frequently is violent content offered in our media? According to a 1951 New Zealand study (26), 70 American films had roughly twice as much violence per film as did 30 films from other countries. A 1954 study of network television programs (27) found an actual doubling from one year to the next in the number of acts or threats of violence, with much of the increase occurring during children's viewing hours. These studies were all conducted before the documentary and news depiction of violence became common, and thus these studies dealt essentially with fictional violence. More recent studies reflect the same trends, however. A New York *Times* headline from July 1968, reads "85 Killings Shown in 85½ TV Hours on the 3 Networks" (28).

Thus the media's repetitive, staccato beat of violence and the evidence of its impact upon the most impressionable members of our society show that violence is valued, wanted, enjoyed. In teaching that violence is a good quick way to get things done, television and other media teach that violence is adaptive behavior.

Part of the tragedy is that the mass media could effectively promote adaptive behaviors like nonviolent protest and other alternatives to violence. The communications personnel and we consumers alike share the responsibility for seeing that our mass media develop their own constructive educational potential. At the very least, violence in the media must be reduced. The statement is hackneyed, the conclusion is not.

MENTAL ILLNESS, VIOLENCE, AND HOMICIDE

What is the relationship between mental illness and violence (29)? Generally the stereotype of the mentally ill person as a potentially dangerous criminal is not valid. The act of homicide often raises the question of psychosis, but only a relatively few psychotic individuals are potential murderers. The stereotype is kept alive, however, by the sensationalist news coverage of the few homicides committed by psychotics.

Mental illness does not usually predispose one to commit violent acts toward others. The patient with severe mental illness (psychosis) is frequently so preoccupied with himself and so disorganized that he is more likely to commit suicide than homicide. A main exception is the fairly well-organized paranoid patient with persecutory delusions concerning one or more particular individuals, intense hostility and mistrust for others, and a pervasive tendency to blame his troubles on the world. However, this type of mentally disordered person constitutes a small minority and does not greatly increase the low incidence of violent acts committed by those identified as mentally ill. In fact, several comparative studies indicate that patients discharged from mental hospitals have an arrest rate considerably lower than that of the general population. . . .

Since mental illness of itself is not predictive of violence or homicide, we must look for other predisposing conditions. Predicting specifically who will murder is difficult because over 90 percent of the murders committed are not premeditated and 80 percent involve an acquaintance or family member (30). One often demonstrated factor related to homicide is the excessive use of alcohol (31). Overindulgence in alcohol has been cited as one feature of the "pre-assaultive state" (31). Persons who are preassaultive usually show some combination of the following five factors: (i) difficulty enjoying leisure time often associated with the heavy use of alcohol; (ii) frequent clashes with close friends, spouse, and others; (iii) history of many fistfights and evidence of past violence (such as scars) reflecting difficulty with impulse control; (iv) fondness for guns and knives; and (v) being relatively young, usually under 45 years old. Comparing homicide rates for males and females universally indicates that a potential murderer is more often male than female. This difference reflects more frequent use of guns and knives ("male" weapons) for murdering as well as sex differences in expressing aggression.

Case histories of homicide reveal repeatedly that a person uses murder as a means of conflict resolution in an unbearable situation for which he can find no other solution. Predisposing factors for homicide include alcoholism, subcultural norms accepting violence as a means of settling conflict, a setting in which the individual experiences intolerable frustration or attack, helplessness resulting from the unavailability of or the inability to perceive alternative actions, intense emotions, and distortion of reality (perhaps even to the point where reality disappears because of personality disintegration). In the instance of blind rage, a person sometimes murders without realizing what he is doing.

The act of homicide may be viewed as attempted coping behavior. Homicide eliminates the immediate problem at a time when there seems to be no future or when the future seems unimportant, and the long-range consequences of the act are not considered. Put another way, homicide has adjustive rather than adaptive value.

FIREARMS CONTROL AND VIOLENCE

Violence by firearms has recently caused great concern (32, 33). The question of whether there is a gun problem is complicated by regional variations in both the actual incidence and the reporting of crime and multiple psychosocial variables, such as individual "choice" of homicide, population density, age, race, socioeconomic status, religion, and law-enforcement effectiveness.

Even so, the following statistics (30, 34) estimating the involvement of guns in various forms of violence in America indicate that a problem does exist. In 1967 firearms caused approximately 21,500 deaths—approximately 7,700 murders, 11,000 suicides, and 2,800 accidental deaths. In addition, there were also about 55,000 cases of aggravated assault by gun and 71,000 cases of armed robbery by gun. Between 1960 and 1967, firearms were used in 96 percent (that is, 394) of 411 murders of police officers. More than 100,000 nonfatal injuries were caused by firearms during 1966.

The number of guns owned by citizens is unknown, but estimates run from 50 to 200 million (30). In 1967 approximately 4,585,000 firearms were sold in the United States, of which 1,208,000 were imports (34). Lately, data from a 1963 World Health Organization survey of 16 developed countries (30) give America an overwhelming lead in death rates for both homicide and suicide by firearms.

These data speak for themselves. What they do not show are the steady increases in all categories for gun-related mortality cited during the past few years. Firearms sales increased by 132 percent between 1963 and 1967.

Responsibility for legal restrictions on guns has generally been left to the states. Consequently, regulations on the sale of guns vary greatly. The lack of uniform laws and the ability (until recently) to buy guns in one state and transport them to another state have made it difficult to compare accurately the gun laws of different states. Even the so-called strict gun laws may not possess sufficient strength to reduce gun killings significantly.

Until 1968 there were only two federal laws of note (35). The National Firearms Act of 1934 imposes a tax on the transfer of certain fully automatic weapons and sawed-off shotguns. The Federal Firearms Act of 1938 requires a license for interstate sale of firearms and prohibits interstate shipment of guns to convicted felons, fugitives, and certain other persons. Two bills passed in 1968 go somewhat further but do not include firearm registration (32). The Omnibus Crime Control and Safe Streets Act restricts interstate and foreign commerce in hand guns. The Gun Control Act also adds mail-order sale of rifles and shotguns to this restriction and prohibits over-the-counter sales to out-of-state residents, juveniles, convicted felons, drug users, mental defectives, and patients committed to mental hospitals.

Although the data do not provide an ironclad indictment against weak, inconsistent legislation, we believe that they make a convincing argument. What is more, more than two-thirds of the American people continue to favor stronger gun-control legislation (33). Even the frightening regularity of assassination has not resulted in strong legislation (that is, legislation requiring registration of guns and owners). How then can we account for the successful opposition to strong gun legislation?

Diverse groups comprise the one-third or less of Americans who do not favor stricter gun control laws. The most visible opposition group is the large (about 1 million members), well-organized National Rifle Association (NRA). With an immense operating budget (approximately $5.7 million in 1967), the NRA is an especially effective "gun lobby" (36). Another group, the Black Panthers, sees arms as necessary for survival. Eldridge Cleaver, Defense Minister of the Black Panthers, wrote, "We are going to keep our guns to protect ourselves from the pigs [police]" (37). Protection is also the issue in Dearborn, Michigan, where housewives are arming against the potential rioter and looter who might "invade" Dearborn from Detroit. Tragic escalation continues around the interplay of urban and suburban action and reaction.

COLLECTIVE AND SANCTIONED VIOLENCE

An additional dilemma is that killing is neither legally nor socially defined as an unequivocally criminal act. The existence of capital punishment and war gives qualified sanction to violence as a means of resolving conflict. Both the general public and their leaders always seem to be able to justify any violence perpetrated on their fellow man. Thus in practice the legitimacy of violence is arbitrary and demands more on the will of powerful men than on moral, ethical, or humane considerations. In a sense, all sanctioned violence is collective, since it has group social approval. Certainly the existence of sanctioned violence abrades the concept of law and order.

We desperately need research on the psychological processes that permit an individual or group to view some violence as good (and presumably adaptive) and other forms of violence as bad (and presumably maladaptive). Although the history of violence in man is polymorphous, there likely are psychological mechanisms common to all cultures and times. For instance, the psychology of sanctioned violence everywhere depends on attributing evil motives to the "outsiders." Then because "they" are violent (evil), "we" *have* to be violent, or (twisted even further) because "they" are violent, it is *good* for "us" to be violent.

Thus people who have seen sanctioned violence being committed in the name of law, order, justice, moral obligation, and duty come to use violence themselves as a "just" means of solving their own problems. The people are acting as their government's representatives have acted—if the cause is just, the grievance real, then unlimited power and force can be used.

Nowhere do we better find this thinking reflected than in the actions of rioters (38). Study of the 1967 Detroit uprising (39) showed that the rioters (young, better educated men who had experienced frustration of their rising expectations) viewed violence against the "system" as justified. Not surprisingly, their views of what justifies violence differed greatly from those of the law enforcers and of the middle-aged black citizens. To the rioters violence was a means of accomplishing goals seemingly not attainable by nonviolent means. Their belief in the power of violence is understandable. Civil disorders are serving in part as a catalyst for change and an instrument of achievement. Some uprising participants reported that violence provided a sense of manliness and strength. But do these supposed gains outweigh the damage of escalations of counterviolence and potential suppression? At least the hypothesis that violence purifies, enhances manliness, and strengthens identity is subject to empirical study.

The results of social-psychiatric field investigations like those in Detroit and at Brandeis University's Lemberg Center for the Study of Violence are useful steps toward understanding the psychological processes and conditions evoking collective violence. For instance, a Lemberg report (40) cited four socio-psychological antecedents to ghetto uprisings: (i) a severe conflict of values between dominant and minority groups; (ii) a "hostile belief system" held by the aggrieved group, based considerably on reality; (iii) a failure of communication between the aggrieved and dominant groups; and (iv) a failure in social control resulting from either overcontrol or undercontrol. In short, these studies show that psychiatrists and psychologists can and must help to resolve the crisis of violence through field studies, facilitating communication between opposing groups, and making recommendations for social change.

But what of war? Behavioral scientists have grasped at all sorts of explanations for this species' warring behavior. Perhaps even this attempt to explain war is a cause of war; our ability to justify any form of violence is part of man's magnificent cerebral endowment. Many causes of war have been suggested: contiguity, habituation, social learning, predation, psychological defenses (for example, rationalization, blaming, denial, counterphobic tendencies among others), the host of fears associated with the human condition, territoriality and power, intolerable frustration, biologically rooted aggressive instincts, and sadism (41–43). One wonders whether the mere distance and speed with which we kill are factors rendering meaningless the signals of submission that other animals use to halt violent encounters (42). Often we literally no longer have to touch the results of our violence. The impersonal factor shows up in another way. Since war is an activity between organized nation states rather than angry individuals, decisions producing war often are made in a calculated manner by those who do not participate directly in any personal acts of violence.

The evidence of history is that war proves everything and nothing. An adequate analysis of the Vietnam war and of the myriad of other wars dotting history is far too great a task for this discussion, despite the relevance of war to the current crisis of violence (43).

Although preventive measures are difficult to administer in the face of the contradicting sanctioned and unsanctioned violence, there are remedies to violence, and we have discussed some of them. More effort could be expended trying to understand the all-important relation between the excessive use of alcohol and homicide. Disseminating currently available information on how to identify a potential murderer will help. Despite Americans' conflicting feelings about guns, there is a gun-death problem today, and more effective and uniform gun legislation can keep guns out of the hands of those who are likely to act impulsively. The mass media can play an increasingly responsible and educational role, while reducing the amount of violence for violence's sake. Many positive potentials of the media have not yet been tapped. Citizen complaint agencies can be established, of which one possibility might be homicide prevention centers along the lines of the suicide prevention centers. Frustrated minority groups will become less frustrated when they are not blocked from responsible participation and self-determination. Peaceful resolution of conflict (44) such as nonviolent protest and negotiation, reducing the amount of sanctioned violence, encouraging a shared sense of humanity, and moving toward rehabilitation rather than retribution in dealing with crime—all these are promising directions. Violence must be studied scientifically so that human behavior can be sustained by knowledge.

CHANGING NATURE OF HUMAN ADAPTATION: SOME SPECULATIONS

Violence is unique to no particular region, nation, or time (43). Centuries ago man survived primarily as a nomadic hunter relying on violent aggression for both food and protection. Even when becoming agricultural and sedentary, men struggled against nature, and survival still required violent aggression, especially for maintaining territory when food was scarce.

Then in a moment of evolution man's energies suddenly produced the age of technology. Instead of adapting mainly by way of biological evolution, we are now increasingly subject to the effects and demands of cultural evolution. Instead of having to adapt to our environment, we now can adapt our environment to our needs. Despite this potential emancipation from biological evolution, we retain the adaptive mechanisms derived from a long history of mammalian and primate evolution, including our primitive forms of aggression, our violence, bellicosity, and inclination to fight in a time of emergency. Where these mechanisms once responded more to physical stress, they now must respond more to social, cultural, and psychological stress, and the response does not always produce adaptive results. Where violent aggressive behavior once served to maintain the human species in times of danger, it now threatens our continued existence.

In this new era, culture changes so rapidly that even time has assumed another dimension—the dimension of acceleration. Looking to the past becomes less relevant for discerning the future.

In the current rapidly expanding technological era, many once useful modes of adaptation are transformed into threats to survival. Territorial exclusivity is becoming obsolete in an economy of abundance. Vast weapons, communication, and transportation networks shrink the world to living-room size and expand our own backyard to encompass a "global village." Yet war and exclusivity continue. Our exploitation of natural resources becomes maladaptive. Unlimited reproduction, once adaptive for advancing the survival of the species, now produces the overcrowded conditions similar to those that lead to destructive and violent behavior in laboratory experiments with other species.

The rate at which we change our environment now apparently exceeds our capacity for adapting to the changes we make. Technological advances alter our physical and social environments, which in turn demand different adaptive strategies and a reshaping of culture. The accelerated civilization of technology is crowded, complex, ambiguous, uncertain. To cope with it, we must become capable of restructuring knowledge of our current situation and then applying new information adaptively. Several factors give us reason to hope that we can succeed.

1) Our social organization and intellectual abilities give us vast potential for coping. Knowledge and technology can be harnessed to serve goals determined by man. Automation makes possible the economics of abundance, but only our cultural values can make abundance a reality for all people. Medicine permits us to control life, but we have not yet seen fit to use this power to determine the limits of population. The technologies of communication and travel shrink the world, but man has not yet expanded the horizon of exclusion. We can learn to unite in goals that transcend exclusivity and direct cultural evolution in accordance with adaptive values and wisdom. The past need not be master of our future.

2) Violence can be understood and controlled. The crisis is one of violence, not of aggression, and it is violence that we must replace. Aggression in the service of adaptation can build and create rather than destroy. The several theories of aggression and current issues of violence suggest many complementary ways of controlling and redirecting aggression. We have suggested some in this article. Furthermore, our brief review of theory and issues points to many possibilities for multidimensional research—an approach that we believe is needed rather than "one note" studies or presentations.

3) Greater attention can be focused on both social change and adaptation processes. Cultural lag in the technological era produces not stability but a repetitious game of "catch up" characterized by one major social crisis after another and by behaviors that are too often only adjustive in that they bring relief of immediate problems while doing little to provide long-range solutions. Expanding our knowledge of the processes of social change and understanding resistance to change are of highest priority. Unforeseen change produces intolerable stress, anxiety, and increased resistance to rational change. These reactions inhibit solution-seeking behavior; evoke feelings of mistrust, loss, and helplessness; and lead to attacks on the apparent agents of change. We must develop the ability to foresee crises and actively meet them. We must dwell more on our strengths, assets, and potential as the really challenging frontier.

CONCLUSION

The current examples of violence and the factors encouraging it reflect our vacillation between the anachronistic culture of violence and the perplexing culture of constant change. We feel alienated and experience social disruption. Current demands for change are potentially dangerous because change activates a tendency to return to older, formerly effective, coping behaviors. Social disruption caused by change tends to increase violence as a means of coping at a time when violence is becoming a great danger to our survival.

America's current crises of violence make it difficult for us to cope with our changing world. Today's challenge, the crisis of violence, is really the crisis of man. This crisis is especially difficult because violence, a once useful but now increasingly maladaptive coping strategy, seems to be firmly rooted in human behavior patterns. We conquer the elements and yet end up facing our own image. Adaptation to a changing world rests on how effectively we can understand, channel, and redirect our aggressive energies. Then man can close his era of violence.

REFERENCES

1. Eiseley, L. *The immense journey.* New York: Random House, 1946.
2. Daniels, D. N., Gilula, M. F. and Ochberg, F. M. (Eds.). *Violence and the struggle for existence.* Boston: Little, Brown, in press.
3. Dr. T. Bittker, C. Boelkins, Dr. P. Bourne, Dr. D. N. Daniels (co-chairman); Dr. J. C. Gillin, Dr. M. F. Gilula, Dr. G. D. Gulevich, Dr. B. Hamburg, Dr. J. Heiser, Dr. F. Ilfeld, Dr. M. Jackman, Dr. P. H. Leiderman, Dr. F. T. Melges, Dr. R. Metzner, Dr. F. M. Ochberg (co-chairman); Dr. J. Rosenthal, Dr. W. T. Roth, Dr. A. Siegel, Dr. G. F. Solomon, Dr. R. Stillman, Dr. R. Taylor, Dr. J. Tinklenberg, Dr. Edison Trickett, and Dr. A. Weisz.
4. Boelkins, R. C. and Heiser, J. Biological aspects of aggression. In *Violence and the struggle for existence*, D. N. Daniels, M. F. Gilula, F. M. Ochberg (Eds.). Boston: Little, Brown, in press.

5. Carthy, J. D. and Ebling, F. J. (Eds.). *The natural history of aggression.* New York: Academic Press, 1964.
6. Dobzhansky, T. *Mankind evolving.* New Haven: Yale University Press, 1962.
7. Silber, E., Hamburg, D. A., Coelho, G. V., Murphey, E. B., Rosenberg, M. and Pearlin, L. I. Title unavailable. *Archives of General Psychiatry,* 1961, **5**, 354.
8. Fenichel, O. *The psychonanalytic theory of neurosis.* New York: Norton, 1945.
9. Lorenz, K. *On aggression.* New York: Harcourt Brace Jovanovich, 1966.
10. Storr, A. *Human Aggression.* New York: Atheneum, 1968.
11. Solomon, G. F. Case studies in violence. In *Violence and the struggle for existence,* D. N. Daniels, M. F. Gilula, F. M. Ochberg (Eds.). Boston: Little, Brown, in press.
12. Scott, J. P. *Aggression.* Chicago: University of Chicago Press, 1958.
13. Berkowitz, L. *Aggression: A social-psychological analysis.* New York: McGraw-Hill, 1962.
    Dollard, J., Doob, L. W., Miller, N. E., Mowrer, O. H. and Sears, R. R. *Frustration and aggression.* New Haven: Yale University Press, 1939.
14. Bandura, A. and Walters, R. H. *Social learning and personality development.* New York: Holt, Rinehart and Winston, 1963.
    Ilfeld, F. Environmental theories of aggression. In *Violence and the struggle for existence.* D. N. Daniels, M. F. Gilula, F. M. Ochberg (Eds.). Boston: Little, Brown, in press.
    Wolfgang, M. E. and Ferracuti, F. *The sub-culture of violence.* New York: Barnes and Noble, 1967.
15. Taylor, R. and Weisz, A. The phenomenon of assassination. In *Violence and the struggle for existence,* D. N. Daniels, M. F. Gilula, F. M. Ochberg (Eds.). Boston: Little, Brown, in press.
16. Freedman, L. Z. Assassination: Psychopathology and social pathology. *Postgraduate Medicine,* 1965, **37**, 650–658.
    Hastings, D. W. The psychiatry of presidential assassination. Part I: Jackson and Lincoln. *Journal Lancet,* 1965, **85**, 93.
17. *San Francisco Examiner.* "It's Russian roulette every day," said Bobby. June 6, 1968.
18. Cottrel, J. *Anatomy of an assassination.* London: Muller, 1966.
19. Siegel, A. E. Mass media and violence. In *Violence and the struggle for existence,* D. N. Daniels, M. F. Gilula, F. M. Ochberg (Eds.). Boston: Little, Brown, in press.
    Larsen, O. N. (Ed.). *Violence and the mass media.* New York: Harper & Row, 1968.
20. Maccoby, E. A. Effects of the mass media. In *Review of child development research,* L. W. Hoffman and M. L. Hoffman (Eds.). New York: Russell Sage Foundation, 1964.
21. Berkowitz, L. Impulse, aggression and the gun. *Psychology Today,* September, 1968, **2**, 18–23.
22. Himmelweit, H. T., Oppenheim, A. N. and Vince, P. *Television and the child.* New York: Oxford University Press, 1958.
23. Schramm, W., Lyle, J. and Parker, E. B. *Television in the lives of our children.* Stanford, California: Stanford University Press, 1961.

24. Bandura, A., Ross, D. and Ross, J. Imitation of film-mediated aggressive models. *Abnormal Social Psychology*, 1963, **66**, 3–11.
25. Wertham, F. *A sign for Cain*. New York: Macmillan, 1966.
26. Mirams, G. Drop that gun! *Quarterly of Film, Radio, Television*, 1951, **6**, 1–19.
27. Purdue Opinion Panel. *Four years of New York television*. Urbana, Illinois: National Association of Educational Broadcasters, 1954.
28. Associated Press Report of July 25, 1968.
29. Gulevich, G. D. and Bourne, P. Mental illness and violence. In *Violence and the struggle for existence*, D. N. Daniels, M. F. Gilula, F. M. Ochberg (Eds.). Boston: Little, Brown, in press.
30. Bakal, C. *No (sic) right to bear arms*. New York: Paperback Library, 1968.
31. deLeon, C. A. Threatened homicide—A medical emergency. *Journal of the National Medical Association*, 1961, **53**, 467.
32. Gillin, J. C. and Ochberg, F. M. Firearms control and violence. In *Violence and the struggle for existence*, D. N. Daniels, M. F. Gilula, F. M. Ochberg (Eds.). Boston: Little, Brown, in press.
33. Daniels, D. N., Trickett, E. J., Tinklenberg, J. R. and Jackman, J. M. The gun law controversy: Issues, arguments, and speculations concerning gun legislation. In *Violence and the struggle for existence*, D. N. Daniels, M. F. Gilula, F. M. Ochberg (Eds.). Boston: Little, Brown, in press.
34. Criminal Division, U. S. Department of Justice. *Firearms Facts*. June 16, 1968; based in large part on the Federal Bureau of Investigation, *Uniform Crime Reports*, Washington, D.C. U. S. Government Printing Office, 1968.
35. *Congressional Quarterly*. King's murder, riots spark demands for gun controls. April 12, 1968, 805–815.
36. Harris, R. Annals of legislation: If you love your guns. *The New Yorker*, April 20, 1968, **44**, 56–155.
37. Cleaver, E. A letter from jail. *Ramparts*, June 15, 1968, **6**, 17–21.
38. Bittker, T. E. The choice of collective violence in intergroup conflict. In *Violence and the struggle for existence*, D. N. Daniels, M. F. Gilula, F. M. Ochberg (Eds.). Boston: Little, Brown, in press.
39. Darrow, C. and Lowinger, P. The Detroit uprising: A psycho-social study. In *Science and Psychoanalysis, Dissent*, Vol. 13, J. H. Masserman (Ed.). New York: Grune and Stratton, 1968.
    Lowinger, P., Luby, E. D., Mendelsohn, R. and Darrow, C. Case study of the Detroit uprising: The troops and the leaders. Detroit: Department of Psychiatry, Wayne State University, School of Medicine, and the Lafayette Clinic, 1968.
40. Spiegel, J. Title unavailable. *Psychiatric Opinion*, 1968, **5**, 6.
41. Frank, J. D. *Sanity and survival: Psychological aspects of war and peace*. New York: Random House, 1967.
    Ziferstein, I. Psychological habituation to war: A sociopsychological case study. *American Journal of Orthopsychiatry*, 1967, **37**, 457.
42. Freeman, D. Human aggression in anthropological perspective. In *The natural history of aggression*, J. D. Carthy and F. J. Ebling (Eds.). New York: Academic Press, 1964.
43. Richardson, L. F. *Statistics of deadly quarrels*. Pittsburgh: Boxwood Press, 1960.

44. Ilfeld, F. and Metzner, R. Alternatives to violence: Strategies for coping with social conflict. In *Violence and the struggle for existence*, D. N. Daniels, M. F. Gilula, F. M. Ochberg (Eds.). Boston: Little, Brown, in press.

MALE DOMINANCE? YES, ALAS. A SEXIST PLOT? NO.

Lionel Tiger

The feminists' angry rebuke to us males could not be more correct and more justified. Women everywhere earn less money than men, possess less power over their communities than men, have more difficulty becoming eminent than men, and do so far less often; as a group they have lower status than men and less public prestige. Surely no one, myself included, would want to argue that such a situation is good or even tolerable: this must be the moral given or baseline from which all discussion of the feminist movement proceeds. However, if you want to change a system you have to understand it.

The feminist critique is rooted in the assumption that there are no important differences between the sexes (except reproductive) which are not culturally determined and that, in fact, any differences which do exist result mainly from a universal conspiracy among males to keep females different—and inferior.

"Groups who rule by birthright are fast disappearing," says Kate Millett in her "Sexual Politics," "yet there remains one ancient and universal scheme for the domination of one birth group by another—the scheme that prevails in the area of sex." She claims that new research "suggests that the possibilities of innate temperamental differences seem more remote than ever. . . . In doing so it gives fairly concrete positive evidence of the over-whelmingly *cultural* character of gender, i.e., personality structure in terms of sexual category."

Not only do men keep women subordinate, goes the argument, they also make an elaborate pretense of placing them on a pretty pedestal—by means of literature and social science designed to make women feel they are most feminine, most productive and most natural when they raise men's children, cook men's food, share men's beds, and believe in the ideology that what's good for men and boys is best for women and girls.

As well as being of general intellectual interest, the feminists' attack on males is also one of the strongest indictments of science and the scientific method that it is possible to make. On generous scientific grounds, it seems

From *New York Times Magazine*, October 25, 1970, p. 35. Reprinted by permission of International Famous Agency. Copyright 1970 by Lionel Tiger.

clear to me that the evidence which feminists such as Kate Millett and Ti-Grace Atkinson use to support their case is, on balance, irresponsible in its selection and so narrowly and unfairly interpreted that it will finally do damage to the prospects of women's actual liberation.

Briefly, there is considerable evidence that differences between males and females do not result simply from male conspiracy, that they are directly related to our evolution as an animal, that they occur in such a wide variety of situations and cultures that the feminist explanation is inadequate in itself to help us understand them, and that there are biological bases for sexual differences which have nothing to do with oppressing females but rather with ensuring the safety of communities and the healthy growth of children. Furthermore, these differences reach back not only to the early states of our history as a civilization, but further back to our formative time as a species; accordingly, sexual differences in physique, hormone secretions, energy and endurance, and possibly even in ways of relating to other people, may be linked to our genetic heritage in direct and influential ways. To say that these differences have existed for a long time and have some biological basis is not—as some people too hastily conclude —to say that human beings are condemned to live in ancient arrangements with no hope of real change. But without understanding what they are and how they came about in the first place, the women and men who want to change our sexual patterns will fail.

First, we have to look at the unpleasant facts. In all communities, the central political decisions are overwhelmingly taken by males and the "public forum" is dominated by males. In a few progressive countries women may be actively involved in legislatures—for example, in Finland and Norway—but by and large the pattern is that even where females have had the vote for many years and where there is open encouragement of female political activity, the number of women participating in managing governments is tiny. The rule is, the higher up the hierarchy you look, the less likely it is you'll find a woman official. The same pattern applies in labor unions, businesses, recreational groups and religious hierarchies. All over the world armies and other fighting groups are all-male. In a few places where women are trained to fight, it remains unusual for them to join men in the front lines (except where defense of home territory is involved, as is sometimes the case for the Vietnamese, for example, and for Israelis living in some border kibbutzim). The task of forming a raiding and fighting party and leaving the home bases to attack elsewhere is universally and unexceptionally male. So is controlling other persons by force, as in police work and similar enterprises.

Other things being equal, women's work is of lower status than men's, and when women begin to move in on an occupation, it loses standing in comparison with others. Though in this country individual women have considerable power to dispose of family income and wealth, typically their investment decisions are guided by males; the products they buy and the manner in which they are stimulated to do so are managed by men. Even proponents of the kibbutz system in Israel—still the most radical, long-term effort at constructing the ideal society which we can observe—concede that insofar as relations between men and women are concerned, the result of over two generations of extremely shrewd and wholehearted effort is far from acceptable to sexual egalitarians. And in this country, those who have set up communes to avoid the effects of private property, patriarchy, restrictive sexual and familial life, and technocracy have discovered that simply because there is more heavy physical labor on the commune, the distinction between men's work and women's work is far sharper than in the larger society from which they hope to escape.

The political misfortune in this is clear. However, the scientific question remains: why is this the case? I've already noted the feminist answer: patriarchy exists because it has existed for so long and so universally. Despite enormous variation in standard of living, religious belief, economies, ecologies, political history, ideology and kinship systems of different societies, the same pattern broadly prevails *because* males have always dominated females in an effective and widespread scheme. But coming from feminists, this is a curious explanation, because it implies that all men everywhere are sufficiently clever and persistent to subdue permanently all women everywhere. If this is so, the conclusion follows mercilessly that men *should* govern. And if women so universally accept this state of affairs, then perhaps they are actually incapable of political action. That is nonsense, and unflattering to women, and unduly optimistic about male political acumen.

In all this general discussion, one of the most useful laws of science has been overlooked, the so-called Law of Parsimony (or Occam's Razor[1]). This dictates that you cannot explain a behavioral phenomenon by a higher, more complex process if a lower or simpler one will do. To take a simple case: The other day in the paperback section of Brentano's in Greenwich Village, a beautiful women was looking at books. She wore no bra and her blouse was aggressively unbuttoned; all the supposedly cerebral men around couldn't take their horn-rimmed eyes off her. Now it is possible that the reason we stared was that we had been brainwashed by sexist books like Mailer's and Henry Miller's and our male chauvinist egos were aroused by the challenge of conquest. But the law of parsimony demands we consider that since sexual attraction is a basic signaling system which all animals have, this woman was signaling something which the men around her were dutifully responding to. Obviously, there were some higher processes involved, too, but the simple erotic one was probably primary in this case.

[1] Named after William of Occam, 14th-century English philosopher, because he frequently invoked the law of parsimony to explain phenomena. It is called his "razor" because the law, in effect, shaved away more complex, metaphysical explanations of nature provided by scholastic theologians.

If male dominance extends over the whole species—and has existed for so long—we seem constrained by the law of parsimony to look first into the biological information and theory at our disposal for an explanation. This includes comparative information about the other primates who exhibit many of the behavior patterns which feminists claim are unique impositions on human females by human males. It also requires us to see what effect our evolution in the past has on our behavior in the present, which feminists—along with many of the social scientists they criticize— by and large are unwilling to do.

Their reasoning derives from the Pavlovian biology of the nineteen-twenties and thirties, which taught that habit and conditioning could account for almost all men's behavior—and inherited characteristics for very little. Like the Lysenkoists in Russia and the positivists in this country, the feminists believe that changing the environments of the human animal will soon change the animal itself. For this, there is no evidence. Moreover, the argument ignores the theory that remains one of the strongest in science today—Darwin's explanation of the evolution of the species through natural selection and inheritance.

Modern biology in part represents an extremely important synthesis of sociology and genetics: we are able to understand the complicated social behavior of animals and can also work out how this behavior can be transmitted in the genetic codes. By now, many people are familiar with the work of the animal ethologists such as Konrad Lorenz, George Schaller and Jane Goodall. Through their experiments and field studies, and those of their colleagues, we have come to appreciate that higher animals other than man also live in relatively elaborate social systems, with traditions, much learning, and considerable variation among different groups of the same species. And yet there remains a central pattern of behavior which is common to a species and appears to be passed down genetically from generation to generation. Three decades ago, how this was transmitted would have been difficult to say. But now we know that the intricate DNA genetic code makes it possible for the individual to inherit not only simple physical characteristics, such as size, shape and chemical makeup, but also a whole set of propensities for particular social behavior which goes with a given physiology. And we can deduce from systematic observations of behavior that these propensities can be inhibited or released in the encounter with other members of the species, and modified over generations by the process of natural selection. This is most important, because it is a decisive advance from the notion of "instinct," which was defined as a relatively automatic matter of feeling hunger, blinking, and kicking softly at the doctor who hits one's knee with a small hammer.

Now we see that the question of what can be inherited is much more complex than we once thought, that all animals are "programed" not only to grow, come to sexual maturity, reproduce, become old and die, but also to interact with each other in rather predictable ways. Of course, there is considerable variation in how animals behave, just as there is in how they look, how quickly they run or swim, how much food they eat, and how large they grow. Just as with humans, there is considerable diversity but also a great amount of consistency and predictability.

We now want to know what the human biological inheritance is, or put another way, what is "in the wiring" of the average male and female, and how it got there. Almost certainly the most dismal difference between males and females is that men create large fighting groups, then with care, enthusiasm, and miserable effectiveness proceed to maim and kill each other. Feminists associate this grim pattern with *machismo*—the need for men to assert themselves in rough-and-tumble ways and to commit mayhem in the name of masculinity. Why men show *macho* and not women, the feminists do not wholly clarify, but the fact that women don't and men do is strikingly plain enough. Yet, among the possible reasons, there is a simple and clear biological factor the feminists overlook—the effect of the sex hormones on behavior.

In a report to a UNESCO conference on aggression I attended in Paris last May, David Hamburg of the department of psychiatry at Stanford described the role of testosterone in stimulating aggressive behavior. In experiments on primates, when both males and females are given extra testosterone, they show much more aggressive hyper-male activity. Humans have similar reactions under artificial manipulation of hormone levels. Among boys and girls before puberty, boys show more testosterone than girls. But at adolescence, the changes are startling: Testosterone in boys increases at least tenfold, and possibly as much as 30 times. On the other hand, girls' testosterone levels only double, from a lower base to begin with. These levels remain stable throughout the life cycle.

In one sense this seems unimportant, because the absolute amounts of these hormone substances are so tiny. And yet hormones are like poisons— a tiny amount can have a gross effect. Hence we see adolescent males— not only among humans but in some other primate species, too—flooded at puberty with a natural chemical which apparently stimulates marked aggressive behavior. When females are given extra amounts, their behavior— independent of socialization, advertising, the male conspiracy—becomes more male-like, more aggressive, more assertive. I choose the example of aggression to discuss "the wiring" and its effect on what we do because no one is likely to claim any longer that the male capacity for violent corporate aggression is a sign of superiority or courage in the world we live in.

Other differences, too, are not unusual in the world of little boys and girls. Parents and teachers are familiar with the marked difference in the rate of maturity between girls and boys: the girls generally outpace the boys for at least the first 14 years of life in school performance, physical control, ability to withstand disease and accident, emotional control, and capacity to engage in detailed work. The pattern persists into sexual maturity; the earlier social competence of women is widely recognized when women marry men some years older than they. Among humans the contrast in rates of maturation are nowhere as marked as in some of the primates—for example, those whose females may mature at 3½ years of age and males at 7. As John Tanner of London University has shown in his book, "Human Growth," girls at adolescence are about 18 months ahead of boys, just as they have been physically more mature than boys at all ages from birth. These differences are tangible, measurable and cross-cultural; they must reflect in some degree the genetic heritage which underlies such predictable regularities—though it must be emphasized that we are speaking of propensities that overlap and not absolute differences.

Now what could be the advantage to the human species of this extensive difference of male-female production of testosterone—given its implication for behavior? In a real if extremely simplified sense, evolution is conditioning over time. In other words, just as dogs can be rewarded for salivating at the sound of a bell, so members of a species do things which become rewarded gentically by the greater ability of the performers of the effective actions to survive and to reproduce. So what our information about sex hormones may mean is that there was an advantage to the evolving human species in selecting males with high testosterone levels and females with much lower levels. Our new information about human evolution from archeological research gives us a reason for this difference: hunting.

From all the available evidence, hunting was the critical human adaptation as long ago as 2 million, or 14, or even 20 million years ago. We have been farming for 13,000 years at most, and until about 5,000 years ago the majority of us were hunter-gatherers. We have been industrialized for barely 200 years. For 99 per cent of our history our survival depended on what bio-anthropologist William Laughlin of the University of Connecticut calls "the master pattern of the human species."

During this vast time span, the hunting-based behavioral adaptations which distinguish us from the other primates were selected in the same way we evolved our huge higher brains, our striding walk, our upright posture, and the apparatus for speech. And one of the most important of our evolutions underlies precisely the feminists' complaint: males hunted and females did not, and my suggestion is that, in addition to other indices such as size, running and throwing ability, and endurance, the differences between male and female hormone patterns reflect this reality.

It's worth reviewing this briefly. Among the other primates, an individual who is old enough gathers virtually all the food he or she will eat. Almost no primates eat meat, and there is no division of labor as far as getting food is concerned. Among humans, however, a division of work on the basis of sex is universal. A strong explanation for this is that our hunting past stimulated a behavioral specialization—males hunted, females gathered—which is clearly still very much part of us, though often in only symbolic and contorted forms. The ancient pattern seems to persist: men and women unite to reproduce young, but they separate to produce food and artifacts.

Highly volatile adolescent males are subjected to rigorous and frequently painful initiations and training in the active manly arts; females—more equable, less accident-prone, less gripped by symbolic fantasies of heroic triumph—rarely undergo initiations as violent and abusive as those males suffer. That is, it appears that females are much less truculent, much less in need of control, much less committed to extensive self-assertion. The possibility must be faced that this general characteristic of the species reflects the physiological one—that female bodies are less driven by those internal secretions which mark the rambunctious and often dangerous males.

If millions of years of evolution have a lot to do with the temperament of the individual male, it may also help explain the deep emotional ties that bind men together in groups. In a book that I published [1969], "Men in Groups," I suggested that there is a biological program that results in a "bonding" between males which is as important for politics as the program of male-female bonding is for reproduction. The results of this male bonding propensity could be seen easily and everywhere: in sports, rock groups (who ever said males weren't emotional?), the American Legion, the men's houses of Indians, the secret societies of both Yale seniors and Australian aborigines, and—most unhappily of all—the bizarre and fantasy-ridden male enterprises called armies.

So not only were there traditional and casual barriers to female participation in the powerful groups of human communities but more elusive and fundamental ones as well. It might take far more radical steps than we feared to approach the sexual equality we say we want.

I have said that males hunted and females gathered. This is not to imply that what females did was less valuable for survival. In his detailed studies of the Kalahari Bushmen, my colleague Richard Lee of Rutgers has shown that in this group, at least, the food women gather is 80 per cent of the diet. What the Kalahari males bring back from the hunt is useful, but not essential. How representative the Bushmen are of all hunters, and particularly of our ancestors, is another question, but Lee's general suggestion presumably applies in many hunting-gathering communities. Nonetheless, all societies make some distinction between men's work and women's work. As Cynthia Epstein of Queens College has pointed out in her excellent study, "Woman's Place" (the most sensitive and probing modern analysis of the sociology of female employment), these distinctions are not necessarily sensible or logical. Still and all, we are an animal as committed to sexual segregation for certain purposes—particularly those having to do with hunting, danger, war, and passionate corporate drama—as we are to sexual conjunction for others—in particular for conceiving and rearing children, and sharing food.

Once again, we get perspective of this matter from studying other primates. While among the other primates there is no sexual division of labor for food-getting, there is still considerable difference between what males and females do. In fact, from primatological work only now becoming available, an unexpected and fascinating body of information is emerging about encounters among primate females, their hierarchies, how they structure relationships over generations and how they learn their social roles. From the work of researchers at the Japanese Monkey Center, from Vernon Reynolds and his wife, Frankie, of Bristol University, from Jane Lancaster of Rutgers, Suzanne Ripley of the Smithsonian Institution and Phyllis Jay Dolhinow of the University of California, we are beginning to learn that there are indeed elaborate patterns of female bonding and that these are based to a large extent on kinship relationships rather than the political ones that frequently bind males. Furthermore, these kinship-like structures appear to be essential for comfortable and viable community life, and they provide security for the young in a web of affiliations which persist over their lifetimes. Hence, the core social bonds at the intimate level are mediated through the females, while at the public or political level, the central relationships remain very much a male monopoly. It is extremely unlikely for a female to assume political leadership of a group when a suitable adult male is available, even though the females may be far more experienced than a young leader-male, and though females seem perfectly capable of leading groups in interim periods when no suitable male is present.

One possible, if elusive, clue to the different social roles of male and female is suggested by research into the frequency of their smiles by Daniel G. Freedman of the Committee for the Study of Human Development at the University of Chicago. The underlying proposition is that smiling is an affiliative gesture of deference, a permissive, accommodating expression rather than a commanding or threatening one. Certainly among other primates, the smile is associated with fear, and humans too talk of the "nervous smile." Freedman and his associates found that among human infants two days old, females smiled spontaneously at a significantly higher rate than males. This was *eyes-closed smiling*—in the absence of a social relationship—and suggests the affinity for this particular motor pattern which girls have.

In another study—using the ingenious method of looking at photos of students in high school and college yearbooks since 1900—the same sexual difference was maintained. While everyone smiled less during periods of economic depression (they also had fewer babies), still the significant sexual difference persisted. And in his field studies of primates, Irven De Vore of Harvard University has found that females smile more often than males as a result of fear.

Intriguingly enough, some of the techniques of political organization which feminists are exploring suggest significant differences from conventional male procedures. For one thing, the principle of competitive, individual leadership is rejected in favor of an attempt at cooperative, group action. In their "consciousness-raising" sessions, the exchange and discussion of personal intimacies serves as a basis for eventual political activity; these groups gather in a circle, formalities are minimal and sisterhood is emphasized. In a sense, the feminist approach to politics is genuinely radical; if it works, it could well be an important contribution not only to the lives of women but to the political conduct of men and the body politic in general.

So far I have argued that the feminist critique takes for granted what important scientific evidence does not permit us to take for granted: that only explicit cultural control—in fact, conspiracy—lies behind the very great differences in certain male and female social behaviors. Feminists such as Kate Millett suggest that once upon a time there was a matriarchy that became corrupted by patriarchal force, which to this day oppresses women. However, the archeological facts available suggest that there is an unbroken line from the male-dominated primate systems I have described here through the hunting stage of our evolution—from which we have not changed genetically—to the most sophisticated and complicated, male-dominated technocratic societies.

Because they ignore biological factors (like many other reformers), the feminists run the risk of basing their legitimate demand for legal and economic equality on a vulnerable foundation. Their denial of significant physiological differences can also deter real occupational and educational success by women—a possibility that is suggested by a variety of studies of the menstrual cycle. The relationship of the cycle to social performance is by no means simple, nor is the evidence conclusive. But studies such as those done over a period of some 15 years by Katherina Dalton of University College, University of London, must be considered: One of her estimates is that roughly 40 per cent of women suffer from a variety of distressing symptoms during the final week or so of the menstrual cycle (other researchers see a higher figure). Dalton's investigation of admission to mental hospitals revealed that 46 per cent of the female admissions occurred during the seven or eight days preceding and during menstruation; at this time, too, 53 per cent of attempted suicides by females occurred.

In another of her studies, 45 per cent of industrial employes who reported sick did so during this period; 49 per cent of crimes committed by women prisoners happened at this time and so did 45 per cent of the punishments meted out to schoolgirls. Dalton also discovered that schoolgirls who were prefects and monitors doled out significantly greater numbers of punishments to others during the menstrual period, and she raises the question of whether or not this is also true of women magistrates, teachers and other figures in authority.

She presents evidence that students writing examinations during the premenstruum earn roughly 14 to 15 per cent poorer grades than they do at other times of the month. If what happens in England also happens here (there could well be cultural and psychological differences between the reactions of the two female populations), then an American girl writing her Graduate Record Examinations over a two-day period or a week-long set of finals during the premenstruum begins with a disadvantage which almost certainly condemns her to no higher than a second-class grade. A whole career in the educational system can be unfairly jeopardized because of this phenomenon. In another sphere, a study by the British Road Research Laboratory suggests that about 60 per cent of all traffic accidents of females occur during about 25 per cent of the days of the month—apparently before and during menstruation. Since women are generally safer drivers than men, certainly in the younger age groups, this may not be a considerable hazard to the public. But for individual women driving cars or writing examinations, these findings may be relevant—and important.

So the paradox is that when they deny there are meaningful differences between males and females because of such a predictable phenomenon as menstruation, feminists may help make it more difficult for women to compete openly and equally for scholarships, jobs, entry to graduate schools, and the variety of other prerequisites of wealth and status. This emphatically does not mean women shouldn't have responsible or competitive jobs; it may mean that in a community committed to genuine equal opportunity examinations and schedules of work—for example, the flying time of women pilots—could be adjusted to the realities of female experience and not, as now, wholly to the male-oriented work week and pattern. (Interestingly, Valentina Tereshkova-Nikolayeva, the first woman astronaut, affirms that women can be as capable astronauts as men, but that allowance should be made for the effect of the cycle on physiology.)

The human species is faced with two overwhelming problems—war and overpopulation. The first results from the social bonding of males, and is not our concern here. The second results from the sexual bonding of males and females. Men and women make love and have children not simply because the patriarchal conspiracy offers women no other major form of satisfaction, but because an old pattern rooted in the genetic codes and reflected in our life cycles—particularly in the flurries of adolescence—draw men and women to each other and to the infants their conjunction yields.

There is no conspiracy in becoming adolescent and sprouting breasts and becoming interested in boys in a new way. Madison Avenue did not invent the fact that female bodies and the movement and sound of women are stimulating to men. Anyone who has pushed a baby carriage down the street will know how many passers-by peek at the young infant and how quickly the presence of a baby will help strangers talk. Throughout the primates, females with newborn infants enjoy high status and babies are enormously attractive to all members of the community. Can it be that human females, who have more of a stake in maternity than males, are responding to the crisis of population and devaluation of this role in the stringent, probing, feminist way? In other words, is the rhetoric about sexual politics really political, or is it, ironically, another expression of sexual difference? More poignantly still, may it perhaps reflect also the currently drastic excess of females over males of marriageable age—because of the disruptions of the Second World War and the baby boom which followed—

and hence the probability that a huge number of mature women remain "sexually unemployed" insofar as they will probably be unable to arrange reproductive lives in the limited ways our sexual rigidities allow?

Child-rearing remains the most labor-intensive task left to members of mechanized societies, and it can't be speeded up. Day-care centers for children can obviously be a sensible feature of a civilized society. But it is another thing for Kate Millett to recommend that child care be entrusted to "trained persons of both sexes"—an idea which is not promising in view of the experiences of orphanages and foster homes. As John Bowlby has argued in his book on child-rearing and deprivation, "Attachment," children need inputs of behavior as much as they require food, and there is considerable evidence that those who do not have a mother or mother-figure on which to focus their affections and security in early childhood suffer irreparable difficulty later on.

Now, it is not clear that fathers cannot do as well. Millions of children are currently being raised by fathers without wives, and it is true that adult males obviously have, as Margaret Mead has suggested, a strong interest in infants. On the other hand, the long and intimate relationship a pregnant woman has with her gestating child must prime her to respond to the child differently from even the most doting father. Even if this has not been demonstrated conclusively, it remains a possibility, just as it is possible that breast-feeding mothers—still the majority at the present time —have, in comparison to fathers, some different if not more substantial commitment to their children because of the hormonal and other physiological processes involved. And if nothing else, the fact that the whole human species has overwhelmingly elected to have children raised at least in the first years by women suggests conformity to nature rather than to male conspiracy.

There is good psychological and primatological evidence that it is necessary for young children to separate themselves increasingly from their parents as they mature. But unless the day-care program of the women's liberationists takes carefully into account what mothers know too well—the routinely incessant and innocent demands of young children for both care and encounter—then too many women who have spent too many days with this understanding will reject the more appealing aspects of the movement. A rejection of the intimacies of family life such as they are, and an implication that females interested sexually in males as husbands and progenitors are somehow inferior and don't know their own minds, can also serve only to frighten off potential supporters.

The theorists who proclaim the withering away of the state of sexual differences may well be proved as wrong as those Marxists who assumed that the State would wither away once it had changed the social arrangements of the people. The problem the feminists face is not just to change a culture and an economy, but to change a primate who is very old genetically and who seems stubbornly committed to relatively little variation in basic sexual structures. This is not to say that some change cannot and will not be achieved, if for no other reason than that the population crush may affect this animal as it has some others—by drastically altering his behavior patterns (though we may as yet be far from the densities which will seriously inhibit breeding).

In an article on the relationship between women's rights and socialism (New Left Review, November-December, 1966), the English sociologist Juliet Mitchell called the feminist struggle "The Longest Revolution." If there is to be a revolution, it will be of infinitely greater duration than Mitchell anticipated. Our biological heritage is the product of millions of years of successful adaptation and it recurs in each generation with only tiny alterations. It is simply prudent that those concerned with changing sex roles understand the possible biological importance of what they want to do, and take careful measure of what these phenomena mean. If they do not, the primary victims of their misanalysis, unfortunately, will be—as usual—women and their daughters.

5 Crisis and Change

The articles in this section consist of a theoretical essay and a case history. The essay, *Toward a Modern Approach to Values*, by a noted psychotherapist and theorist, Dr. Carl R. Rogers, explores the origins and implications of individuals' values and what happens when we permit our values to be determined by people other than ourselves. Dr. Rogers' ideas are of fundamental importance in an age in which many people are seeking to reestablish contact with themselves and to learn to live self-directed, satisfying lives.

The case history, *The Case of Johnny*, by Dr. Sheldon Cotler, Dr. Ronald E. Smith, and Dr. John G. Martire, is a fairly detailed description of how a team of psychotherapists worked with a boy who was so extremely withdrawn that he was considered psychotic. Note that the team relied on a variety of techniques—behavior therapy as well as traditional talk-it-through methods. Note too that treatment of the child also required treatment of the parents' problems. Their problems, particularly the mother's, had created the conditions which led to the boy's problems. It was only when the parents were able to deal with their own difficulties that the pressures on the boy were relieved sufficiently to permit him to deal with his troubles.

TOWARD A MODERN APPROACH TO VALUES: THE VALUING PROCESS IN THE MATURE PERSON

Carl R. Rogers

There is a great deal of concern today with the problem of values. Youth, in almost every country, is deeply uncertain of its value orientation; the values associated with various religions have lost much of their influence; sophisticated individuals in every culture seem unsure and troubled as to the goals they hold in esteem. The reasons are not far to seek. The world culture, in all its aspects, seems increasingly scientific and relativistic, and the rigid, absolute views on values which come to us from the past appear anachronistic. Even more important, perhaps, is the fact that the modern individual is assailed from every angle by divergent and contradictory value claims. It is no longer possible, as it was in the not too distant historical past, to settle comfortably into the value system of one's forebears or one's community and live out one's life without ever examining the nature and the assumptions of that system.

In this situation it is not surprising that value orientations from the past appear to be in a state of disintegration or collapse. Men question whether there are, or can be, any universal values. It is often felt that we may have lost, in our modern world, all possibility of any general or cross-cultural basis for values. One natural result of this uncertainty and confusion is that there is an increasing concern about, interest in, and a searching for, a sound or meaningful value approach which can hold its own in today's world.

I share this general concern. As with other issues the general problem faced by the culture is painfully and specifically evident in the cultural microcosm which is called the therapeutic relationship, which is my sphere of experience.

As a consequence of this experience I should like to attempt a modest theoretical approach to this whole problem. I have observed changes in the approach to values as the individual grows from infancy to adulthood. I observe further changes when, if he is fortunate, he continues to grow toward true psychological maturity. Many of these observations grow out of my experience as therapist, where I have had the mind stretching opportunity of seeing the ways in which individuals move toward a richer life. From these observations I believe I see some directional threads emerging which might offer a new concept of the valuing process, more tenable in the modern world. I have made a beginning by presenting some of these ideas partially in previous writings (Rogers, 1951, 1959); I would like now to voice them more clearly and more fully.

From the *Journal of Abnormal and Social Psychology*, 1964, *63*, 160–167. Copyright 1964 by the American Psychological Association and reproduced by permission.

Some Definitions

Charles Morris (1956, pp. 9–12) has made some useful distinctions in regard to values. There are "operative values," which are the behaviors of organisms in which they show preference for one object or objective rather than another. . . .

There are also "conceived values," the preference of an individual for a symbolized object. "Honesty is the best policy" is such a conceived value.

There is also the term "objective value," to refer to what is objectively preferable, whether or not it is sensed or conceived of as desirable. I will be concerned primarily with operative or conceptualized [conceived] values.

Infant's Way of Valuing

Let me first speak about the infant. The living human being has, at the outset, a clear approach to values. We can infer from studying his behavior that he prefers those experiences which maintain, enhance, or actualize his organism, and rejects those which do not serve this end. Watch him for a bit:

> Hunger is negatively valued. His expression of this often comes through loud and clear.
>
> Food is positively valued. But when he is satisfied, food is negatively valued, and the same milk he responded to so eagerly is now spit out, or the breast which seemed so satisfying is now rejected as he turns his head away from the nipple with an amusing facial expression of disgust and revulsion.
>
> He values security, and the holding and caressing which seem to communicate security.
>
> He values new experience for its own sake, and we observe this in his obvious pleasure in discovering his toes, in his searching movements, in his endless curiosity.
>
> He shows a clear negative valuing of pain, bitter tastes, sudden loud sounds.

All of this is commonplace, but let us look at these facts in terms of what they tell us about the infant's approach to values. It is first of all a flexible, changing, valuing *process*, not a fixed system. He likes food and dislikes the same food. He values security and rest, and rejects it for new experience. What is going on seems best described as an organismic valuing process, in which each element, each moment of what he is experiencing is somehow weighed, and selected or rejected, depending on whether, at that moment, it tends to actualize the organism or not. This complicated weighing of experience is clearly an organismic, not a conscious or symbolic function. These are operative, not conceived values. But this process can nonetheless deal with complex value problems. I would remind you of the experiment in which young infants had spread in front of them a score or more of dishes of natural (that is, unflavored) foods. Over a period of time they clearly tended to value the foods which enhanced their own survival, growth, and development. If for a time a child gorged himself on starches, this would soon be balanced by a protein "binge." If at times he chose a diet deficient in some vitamin, he would later seek out foods rich in this very vitamin. The physiological wisdom of his body guided his behavioral movements, resulting in what we might think of as objectively sound value choices.

Another aspect of the infant's approach to values is that the source or locus of the evaluating process is clearly within himself. Unlike many of us, he *knows* what he likes and dislikes, and the origin of these value choices lies strictly within himself. He is the center of the valuing process, the evidence for his choices being supplied by his own senses. He is not at this point influenced by what his parents think he should prefer, or by what the church says, or by the opinion of the latest "expert" in the field, or by the persuasive talents of an advertising firm. It is from within his own experiencing that his organism is saying in nonverbal terms, "This is good for me." "That is bad for me." "I like this." "I strongly dislike that." He would laugh at our concern over values, if he could understand it.

Change in the Valuing Process

What happens to this efficient, soundly based valuing process? By what sequence of events do we exchange it for the more rigid, uncertain, inefficient approach to values which characterizes most of us as adults? Let me try to state briefly one of the major ways in which I think this happens.

The infant needs love, wants it, tends to behave in ways which will bring a repetition of this wanted experience. But this brings complications. He pulls baby sister's hair, and finds it satisfying to hear her wails and protests. He then hears that he is "a naughty, bad boy," and this may be reinforced by a slap on the hand. He is cut off from affection. As this experience is repeated, and many, many others like it, he gradually learns that what "feels good" is often "bad" in the eyes of significant others. Then the next step occurs, in which he comes to take the same attitude toward himself which these others have taken. Now, as he pulls his sister's hair, he solemnly intones, "Bad, bad boy." He is introjecting the value judgment of another, taking it in as his own. To that degree he loses touch with his own organismic valuing process. He has deserted the wisdom of his organism, giving up the locus of evaluation, and is trying to behave in terms of values set by another, in order to hold love.

Or take another example at an older level. A boy senses, though perhaps not consciously, that he is more loved and prized by his parents when he thinks of being a doctor than when he thinks of being an artist. Gradually he introjects the values attached to being a doctor. He comes to want, above all, to be a doctor. Then in college he is baffled by the fact that he repeatedly fails in chemistry, which is absolutely necessary to becoming a physician, in spite of the fact that the guidance counselor assures him he has the ability to pass the course. Only in counseling interviews does he begin to realize how completely he has lost touch with his organismic reactions, how out of touch he is with his own valuing process.

Perhaps these illustrations will indicate that in an attempt to gain or hold love, approval, esteem, the individual relinquishes the locus of evaluation which was his in infancy, and places it in others. He learns to have a basic *dis*trust for his own experiencing as a guide to his behavior. He learns from others a large number of conceived values, and adopts them as his own, even though they may be widely discrepant from what he is experiencing.

Some Introjected Patterns

It is in this fashion, I believe, that most of us accumulate the introjected value patterns by which we live. In the fantastically complex culture of today, the patterns we introject as desirable or undesirable come from a variety of sources and are often highly contradictory. Let me list a few of the introjections which are commonly held.

> Sexual desires and behaviors are mostly bad. The sources of this construct are many—parents, church, teachers.
> Disobedience is bad. Here parents and teachers combine with the military to emphasize this concept. To obey is good. To obey without question is even better.
> Making money is the highest good. The sources of this conceived value are too numerous to mention.
> Learning an accumulation of scholarly facts is highly desirable. Education is the source.
> Communism is utterly bad. Here the government is a major source.
> To love thy neighbor is the highest good. This concept comes from the church, perhaps from the parents.
> Cooperation and teamwork are preferable to acting alone. Here companions are an important source.
> Cheating is clever and desirable. The peer group again is the origin.
> Coca-Colas, chewing gum, electric refrigerators, and automobiles are all utterly desirable. From Jamaica to Japan, from Copenhagen to Kowloon, the "Coca-Cola culture" has come to be regarded as the acme of desirability.

This is a small and diversified sample of the myriads of conceived values which individuals often introject, and hold as their own, without ever having considered their inner organismic reactions to these patterns and objects.

Common Characteristics of Adult Valuing

I believe it will be clear from the foregoing that the usual adult—I feel I am speaking for most of us—has an approach to values which has these characteristics:

The majority of his values are introjected from other individuals or groups significant to him, but are regarded by him as his own.

The source or locus of evaluation on most matters lies outside of himself.

The criterion by which his values are set is the degree to which they will cause him to be loved, accepted, or esteemed.

These conceived preferences are either not related at all, or not clearly related, to his own process of experiencing.

Often there is a wide and unrecognized discrepancy between the evidence supplied by his own experience, and these conceived values.

Because these conceptions are not open to testing in experience, he must hold them in a rigid and unchanging fashion. The alternative would be a collapse of his values. Hence his values are "right."

Because they are untestable, there is no ready way of solving contradictions. If he has taken in from the community the conception that money is the *summum bonum* and from the church the conception that love of one's neighbor is the highest value, he has no way of discovering which has more value for *him*. Hence a common aspect of modern life is living with absolutely contradictory values. We calmly discuss the possibility of dropping a hydrogen bomb on Russia, but find tears in our eyes when we see headlines about the suffering of one small child.

Because he has relinquished the locus of evaluation to others, and has lost touch with his own valuing process, he feels profoundly insecure and easily threatened in his values. If some of these conceptions were destroyed, what would take their place? This threatening possibility makes him hold his value conceptions more rigidly or more confusedly, or both.

Fundamental Discrepancy

I believe that this picture of the individual, with values mostly introjected, held as fixed concepts, rarely examined or tested, is the picture of most of us. By taking over the conceptions of others as our own, we lose contact with the potential wisdom of our own functioning, and lose confidence in ourselves. Since these value constructs are often sharply at variance with what is going on in our own experiencing, we have in a very basic way divorced ourselves from ourselves, and this accounts for much of modern strain and insecurity. This fundamental discrepancy between the individual's concept and what he is actually experiencing, between the intellectual structure of his values and the valuing process going on unrecognized within—this is a part of the fundamental estrangement of modern man from himself.

Restoring Contact with Experience

Some individuals are fortunate in going beyond the picture I have just given, developing further in the direction of psychological maturity. We see this happen in psychotherapy where we endeavor to provide a climate favorable to the growth of the person. We also see it happen in life, whenever life provides a therapeutic climate for the individual. Let me concentrate on this further maturing of a value approach as I have seen it in therapy.

As the client senses and realizes that he is prized as a person[1] he can slowly begin to value the different aspects of himself. Most importantly, he can begin, with much difficulty at first, to sense and to feel what is going on within him, what he is feeling, what he is experiencing, how he is re-acting. He uses his experiencing as a direct referent to which he can turn in forming accurate conceptualizations and as a guide to his behavior. Gendlin (1961, 1962) has elaborated the way in which this occurs. As his experiencing becomes more and more open to him, as he is able to live more freely in the process of his feelings, then significant changes begin to occur in his approach to values. It begins to assume many of the character-istics it had in infancy.

Introjected Values in Relation to Experiencing

Perhaps I can indicate this by reviewing a few of the brief examples of introjected values which I have given, and suggesting what happens to them as the individual comes closer to what is going on within him.

> The individual in therapy looks back and realizes, "But I *enjoyed* pulling my sister's hair—and that doesn't make me a bad person."
>
> The student failing chemistry realizes, as he gets close to his own ex-periencing, "I don't like chemistry; I don't value being a doctor, even though my parents do; and I am not a failure for having these feelings."
>
> The adult recognizes that sexual desires and behavior may be richly satisfying and permanently enriching in their consequences, or shallow and temporary and less than satisfying. He goes by his own experiencing, which does not always coincide with social norms.
>
> He recognizes freely that this communist book or person expresses attitudes and goals which he shares as well as ideas and values which he does not share.
>
> He realizes that at times he experiences cooperation as meaningful and valuable to him, and that at other times he wishes to be alone and act alone.

Valuing in the Mature Person

The valuing process which seems to develop in this more mature person is in some ways very much like that in the infant, and in some ways quite different. It is fluid, flexible, based on this particular moment, and the degree to which this moment is experienced as enhancing and actualizing. Values are not held rigidly, but are continually changing. The painting which last year seemed meaningful now appears uninteresting, the way of

---

[1] The therapeutic relationship is not devoid of values. When it is most effective it is, I believe, marked by one primary value, namely, that this person (the client) has *worth*.

working with individuals which was formerly experienced as good now seems inadequate, the belief which then seemed true is now experienced as only partly true, or perhaps false.

Another characteristic of the way this person values experience is that it is highly differentiated, or as the semanticists would say, extensional. The examples in the preceding section indicate that what were previously rather solid monolithic introjected values now become differentiated, tied to a particular time and experience.

Another characteristic of the mature individual's approach is that the locus of evaluation is again established firmly within the person. It is his own experience which provides the value information or feedback. This does not mean that he is not open to all the evidence he can obtain from other sources. But it means that this is taken for what it is—outside evidence—and is not as significant as his own reactions. Thus he may be told by a friend that a new book is very disappointing. He reads two unfavorable reviews of the book. Thus his tentative hypothesis is that he will not value the book. Yet if he reads the book his valuing will be based upon the reactions it stirs in *him*, not on what he has been told by others.

There is also involved in this valuing process a letting oneself down into the immediacy of what one is experiencing, endeavoring to sense and to clarify all its complex meanings. I think of a client who, toward the close of therapy, when puzzled about an issue, would put his head in his hands and say, "Now what *is* it that I'm feeling? I want to get next to it. I want to learn what it is." Then he would wait, quietly and patiently, trying to listen to himself, until he could discern the exact flavor of the feelings he was experiencing. He, like others, was trying to get close to himself.

In getting close to what is going on within himself, the process is much more complex than it is in the infant. In the mature person it has much more scope and sweep. For there is involved in the present moment of experiencing the memory traces of all the relevant learnings from the past. This moment has not only its immediate sensory impact, but it has meaning growing out of similar experiences in the past (Gendlin, 1962). It has both the new and the old in it. So when I experience a painting or a person, my experiencing contains within it the learnings I have accumulated from past meetings with paintings or persons, as well as the new impact of this particular encounter. Likewise the moment of experiencing contains, for the mature adult, hypotheses about consequences. "It is not pleasant to express forthrightly my negative feelings to this person, but past experience indicates that in a continuing relationship it will be helpful in the long run." Past and future are both in this moment and enter into the valuing.

I find that in the person I am speaking of (and here again we see a similarity to the infant), the criterion of the valuing process is the degree to which the object of the experience actualizes the individual himself. Does it make him a richer, more complete, more fully developed person? This may sound as though it were a selfish or unsocial criterion, but it does not prove to be so, since deep and helpful relations with others are experienced as actualizing.

Like the infant, too, the psychologically mature adult trusts and uses the wisdom of his organism, with the difference that he is able to do so knowingly. He realizes that if he can trust all of himself, his feelings and his intuitions may be wiser than his mind, that as a total person he can be more sensitive and accurate than his thoughts alone. Hence he is not afraid to say, "I feel that this experience [or this thing, or this direction] is good. Later I will probably know *why* I feel it is good." He trusts the totality of himself, having moved toward becoming what Lancelot Whyte (1950) regards as "the unitary man."

It should be evident from what I have been saying that this valuing process in the mature individual is not an easy or simple thing. The process is complex, the choices often very perplexing and difficult, and there is no guarantee that the choice which is made will in fact prove to be self-actualizing. But because whatever evidence exists is available to the individual, and because he is open to his experiencing, errors are correctable. If this chosen course of action is not self-enchancing this will be sensed and he can make an adjustment or revision. He thrives on a maximum feedback interchange, and thus, like the gyroscopic compass on a ship, can continually correct his course toward his true goal of self-fulfillment.

Some Propositions Regarding the Valuing Process

Let me sharpen the meaning of what I have been saying by stating two propositions which contain the essential elements of this viewpoint. While it may not be possible to devise empirical tests of each proposition in its entirety, yet each is to some degree capable of being tested through the methods of psychological science. I would also state that though the following propositions are stated firmly in order to give them clarity, I am actually advancing them as decidedly tentative hypotheses.

Hypothesis I. There is an organismic base for an organized valuing process within the human individual.

It is hypothesized that this base is something the human being shares with the rest of the animate world. It is part of the functioning life process of any healthy organism. It is the capacity for receiving feedback information which enables the organism continually to adjust its behavior and reactions so as to achieve the maximum possible self-enhancement.

Hypothesis II. This valuing process in the human being is effective in achieving self-enhancement to the degree that the individual is open to the experiencing which is going on within himself.

I have tried to give two examples of individuals who are close to their own experiencing: the tiny infant who has not yet learned to deny in his awareness the processes going on within; and the psychologically mature person who has relearned the advantages of this open state.

There is a corollary to this second proposition which might be put in the following terms. One way of assisting the individual to move toward openness to experience is through a relationship in which he is prized as a separate person, in which the experiencing going on within him is empathically understood and valued, and in which he is given the freedom to experience his own feelings and those of others without being threatened in doing so.

This corollary obviously grows out of therapeutic experience. It is a brief statement of the essential qualities in the therapeutic relationship. There are already some empirical studies, of which the one by Barrett-Lennard (1962) is a good example, which give support to such a statement.

Propositions Regarding the Outcomes of the Valuing Process

I come now to the nub of any theory of values or valuing. What are its consequences? I should like to move into this new ground by stating bluntly two propositions as to the qualities of behavior which emerge from this valuing process. I shall then give some of the evidence from my experience as a therapist in support of these propositions.

Hypothesis III. In persons who are moving toward greater openness to their experiencing, there is an organismic commonality of value directions.

Hypothesis IV. These common value directions are of such kinds as to enhance the development of the individual himself, of others in his community, and to make for the survival and evolution of his species.

It has been a striking fact of my experience that in therapy, where individuals are valued, where there is greater freedom to feel and to be, certain value directions seem to emerge. These are not chaotic directions but instead exhibit a surprising commonality. This commonality is not dependent on the personality of the therapist, for I have seen these trends emerge in the clients of therapists sharply different in personality. This commonality does not seem to be due to the influences of any one culture, for I have found evidence of these directions in cultures as divergent as those of the United States, Holland, France, and Japan. I like to think that this commonality of value directions is due to the fact that we all belong to the same species—that just as a human infant tends, individually, to select a diet similar to that selected by other human infants, so a client in therapy tends, individually, to choose value directions similar to those chosen by other clients. As a species there may be certain elements of experience which tend to make for inner development and which would be chosen by all individuals if they were genuinely free to choose.

Let me indicate a few of these value directions as I see them in my clients as they move in the direction of personal growth and maturity.

They tend to move away from façades. Pretense, defensiveness, putting up a front, tend to be negatively valued.

They tend to move away from "oughts." The compelling feeling of "I ought to do or be thus and so" is negatively valued. The client moves away from being what he "ought to be," no matter who has set that imperative.

They tend to move away from meeting the expectations of others. Pleasing others, as a goal in itself, is negatively valued.

Being real is positively valued. The client tends to move toward being himself, being his real feelings, being what he is. This seems to be a very deep preference.

Self-direction is positively valued. The client discovers an increasing pride and confidence in making his own choices, guiding his own life.

One's self, one's own feelings come to be positively valued. From a point where he looks upon himself with contempt and despair, the client comes to value himself and his reactions as being of worth.

Being a process is positively valued. From desiring some fixed goal, clients come to prefer the excitement of being a process of potentialities being born.

Sensitivity to others and acceptance of others is positively valued. The client comes to appreciate others for what they are, just as he has come to appreciate himself for what he is.

Deep relationships are positively valued. To achieve a close, intimate, real, fully communicative relationship with another person seems to meet a deep need in every individual, and is very highly valued.

Perhaps more than all else, the client comes to value an openness to all of his inner and outer experience. To be open to and sensitive to his own *inner* reactions and feelings, the reactions and feelings of others, and the realities of the objective world—this is a direction which he clearly prefers. This openness becomes the client's most valued resource.

These then are some of the preferred directions which I have observed in individuals moving toward personal maturity. Though I am sure that the list I have given is inadequate and perhaps to some degree inaccurate, it holds for me exciting possibilities. Let me try to explain why.

I find it significant that when individuals are prized as persons, the values they select do not run the full gamut of possibilities. I do not find, in such a climate of freedom, that one person comes to value fraud and murder and thievery, while another values a life of self-sacrifice, and another values only money. Instead there seems to be a deep and underlying thread of commonality. I believe that when the human being is inwardly free to choose whatever he deeply values, he tends to value those objects, experiences, and goals which make for his own survival, growth, and development, and for the survival and development of others. I hypothesize that it is *characteristic* of the human organism to prefer such actualizing and socialized goals when he is exposed to a growth promoting climate.

A corollary of what I have been saying is that in *any* culture, given a climate of respect and freedom in which he is valued as a person, the mature individual would tend to choose and prefer these same value directions.

This is a significant hypothesis which could be tested. It means that though the individual of whom I am speaking would not have a consistent or even a stable system of conceived values, the valuing process within him would lead to emerging value directions which would be constant across cultures and across time.

Another implication I see is that individuals who exhibit the fluid valuing process I have tried to describe, whose value directions are generally those I have listed, would be highly effective in the ongoing process of human evolution. If the human species is to survive at all on this globe, the human being must become more readily adaptive to new problems and situations, must be able to select that which is valuable for development and survival out of new and complex situations, must be accurate in his appreciation of reality if he is to make such selections. The psychologically mature person as I have described him has, I believe, the qualities which would cause him to value those experiences which would make for the survival and enhancement of the human race. He would be a worthy participant and guide in the process of human evolution.

Finally, it appears that we have returned to the issue of universality of values, but by a different route. Instead of universal values "out there," or a universal value system imposed by some group—philosophers, rulers, priests, or psychologists—we have the possibility of universal human value directions *emerging* from the experiencing of the human organism. Evidence from therapy indicates that both personal and social values emerge as natural, and experienced, when the individual is close to his own organismic valuing process. The suggestion is that though modern man no longer trusts religion or science or philosophy nor any system of beliefs to *give* him values, he may find an organismic valuing base within himself which, if he can learn again to be in touch with it, will prove to be an organized, adaptive, and social approach to the perplexing value issues which face all of us.

REFERENCES

Barrett-Lennard, G. T. Dimensions of therapist response as causal factors in therapeutic change. *Psychol. Monogr.*, 1962, **76**, (43, Whole No. 562).

Gendlin, E. T. Experiencing: A variable in the process of therapeutic change. *Amer. J. Psychother.*, 1961, **15**, 233–245.

Gendlin, E. T. *Experiencing and the creation of meaning.* Glencoe, Ill.: Free Press, 1962.

Morris, C. W. *Varieties of human value.* Chicago: University of Chicago Press, 1956.

Rogers, C. R. *Client-centered therapy.* Boston: Houghton Mifflin, 1951.

Rogers, C. R. A theory of therapy, personality and interpersonal relationships. In S. Koch (Ed.), *Psychology: A study of a science.* Vol. 3. *Formulations of the person and the social context.* New York: McGraw-Hill, 1959. Pp. 185–256.

Whyte, L. L. *The next development in man.* New York: Mentor Books, 1950.

THE CASE OF JOHNNY: A FAMILY-ORIENTED APPROACH TO THE TREATMENT OF A PSYCHOTIC CHILD

Sheldon Cotler, Ronald E. Smith, and John G. Martire

It has been observed that seriously disturbed children frequently have seriously disturbed parents. Johnny, diagnosed as a psychotic child, came from maladjusted, immature, but non-psychotic parents. There was a remarkable similarity between Johnny's experiences and problems and those of his mother during the corresponding periods of her early life. The parallels indicate the extreme influence which the mother had upon this boy's personality development. These similarities plus specific trauma around 18 months of age are seen as precipitating the boy's pathological behavior. As might have been predicted, the therapeutic progress made by the mother was correlated with the psychological maturation of her son.

The boy was referred to our clinic because of a series of severe symptoms: a loss of meaningful speech at 18 months of age after having made normal language progress until that time; the institution of neologistic speech (i.e., containing 'made-up' words); hysterical and terrorized reactions to noises, radio, and television; and constant nervousness. He had little impulse control and was at various times excessively aggressive, demanding, petulant, non-responsive, withdrawn, and passive. He was not responding to the world as others saw it; and consequently, the therapists viewed much of his behavior as psychotic in nature.

The original diagnosis of psychosis, perhaps schizophrenia, was tentative since the examining physician had suggested the possibility of central nervous system damage. Nevertheless, treatment was begun on the assumption of an interpersonal origin for his disturbances; the therapeutic approach was eclectic and person-oriented in nature. For the boy, we saw the initial problem in treatment as helping him to again become realistically responsive to other people and to his physical environment. Primarily for mother and secondarily for father, our goal was to change their perceptions and attitudes, so that their actions toward the child would change. Specifically, Mother needed to replace her inconsistent extremes of overindulgence and screaming rejection with a more balanced approach of loving firmness. Both parents had to develop a positive relationship with their child for any psychotherapeutic intervention to be effective.

Family History

Mother and Father were married when she was only 17 and he 18 and had not yet finished high school. The marriage was precipitated by pregnancy

This article was especially written for this book of readings. The first two authors dedicate the article to the memory of the late Dr. John G. Martire, a sensitive and gifted clinician whose supervision was responsible for the success of this case.

with the patient, although the young people reportedly had planned a future marriage.

Mrs. T. was bright, attractive, vivacious, and originally a very unrealistic, immature, and self-centered young woman. In sharp contrast to his wife, Mr. T. was not talkative and tended to keep his feelings to himself. Father's primary goal was to achieve a comfortable, worry-free life and he resented anyone who disrupted the equilibrium. He denied family responsibilities and characteristically withdrew from any source of conflict. Clearly, the parents were not psychologically ready for their child and Johnny was perceived as interfering with their youthful social activities.

Mother saw herself accurately as self-indulgent, excitable, nervous, impulsive and "spoiled rotten." She got her way as a child by sulking, pouting, and temper tantrums, and she continued to use these manipulative techniques as an adult. For herself and others she stated: "I can't stand anyone not having his way." Apparently, she systematically avoided frustration and facing the painful realities of living. She could not stand violence, aggression, tragedy, and death; she wanted to continue her make-believe happy world of childhood. Strikingly, she too had had unintelligible speech until the age of four; only her family could understand her. She called herself a "problem child" as a youngster and noted that she used to run away from home.

Johnny's parents, especially his mother, treated him in an extremely inconsistent manner. On the one hand, mother was indulgent—giving in to his every whim, even to the point of learning to understand his idiosyncratic language. Her own level of confidence and security was such that she could not provide the loving firmness which the child needed. When she could no longer tolerate his insatiable demands, she would scream at the child, completely rejecting and terrorizing him. Another possible indication of mother's immature judgment and hostility is reflected in her selection of babysitters during the period of Johnny's most intense trauma. These girls were apparently irresponsible and left the boy alone at night to cry out in loneliness and terror. Interestingly enough, one babysitter went to a home for unwed mothers, while another went to a reform school.

Our thesis was that the child was traumatized by the violence of rejection by his parents and the neglect of babysitters. Concurrently, he was taught the non-adaptive and frequently pathological behaviors of his mother, and to a lesser extent, of his father. The boy's withdrawal, loss of language, and the substitution of pathological language and action can be seen both as adaptation to the threats of his environment and as attempts to compensate and survive in this setting. Clearly, Johnny was the psychological and behavioral child of his parents and of the complex interactions among the family members. Multiple factors account, then, for his psychopathology and for the severity of his symptoms.

Focus on the Child

When first seen, Johnny presented a picture of complete physical health—he had a suntan, was well proportioned, and there was no evidence of frailty. The findings of pediatric and hearing examinations were negative. There was no evidence of neurological or physical impairment and his development was reportedly normal. Each professional person who saw the child independently reported the same striking things about his behavior: Johnny was exceptionally distractable, and seemingly disinterested in the people and activities around him. There was basically no interaction with his social environment except to satisfy his immediate needs. The child showed no responsivity or emotionality toward people; he also strongly avoided physical contact and frequently became aggressive when adults tried to touch or hold him. He reportedly did, however, turn to other children for attention, although he did not engage in any constructive or cooperative play with them.

Johnny was first seen for psychotherapeutic play sessions when he was 30 months old. At this time Johnny's social withdrawal was not complete—he accepted gifts of food and made some attempts at verbal communication. His mother discontinued treatment after six sessions because she could not tolerate the clinic's demands for her own personal involvement in the therapy. The family returned to the clinic when Johnny was 46 months old because the boy's psychological status was progressively deteriorating. There was essentially no social approach behavior and Johnny was exceptionally hyperactive and irritable. He was frightened of anything which made noise (e.g., radio or T.V.) and unexpected noises would throw him into a panic, which included loud crying and trembling of the body. He had no apparent fear of injury and frequently would hurt himself since he was enthralled with climbing. Among his idiosyncratic behaviors were his obsessions with lights and with water and plumbing. He carried around a large collection of light bulbs and he frequently washed himself, with or without his clothes on.

PHASES OF TREATMENT

A striking and essential feature of this case was the concommitant and parallel progress made by parents and child in the course of our family-oriented therapeutic program. Therefore, this program has been divided into five phases in order to more easily demonstrate these parallels. In addition, the phases illustrate how the utilization of various therapeutic procedures were determined by the ability of the child and the parents to profit from them. While this paper provides some information about how a severely disturbed child may be treated, the primary purpose is to demonstrate the parallels between the treatment and changes of this child and his mother.

Phase I—Relationship: Beginning Stages

A primary goal in the beginning of therapy was to create a satisfactory therapeutic relationship with the child and his parents. For the child the initial relationship phase of treatment was predicated upon three basic suppositions: One, that he suffered severe social trauma and tended to be very frightened by interpersonal relationships; two, that he was fighting very hard, albeit unsuccessfully, to predict and respond appropriately to environmental stimuli; and three, that the parental pattern of punitiveness and rejection coupled with overindulgence greatly contributed to his maladaptive behavior.

The mother was unsophisticated about human relationships and quite unaware of the influence which she and her husband had on the personality development and behavior of their son. Her own immature personality was characterized by an inability to face the unpleasant realities of adult living and a resultant distortion of reality to conform to her Pollyannaish concept of how things should be. She could discipline her over-demanding child only when his attention-getting behavior became too much for her to tolerate. At these times mother's permissiveness became transformed into a violent temper tantrum in which mother screamed, spanked, and rejected her child. She often made threats to the boy without carrying them out and, as a result, the child was incapable of predicting her behavior and structuring a most important part of his world. In addition, her own immature tantrum behavior hardly provided Johnny with an acceptable model for dealing with frustration in a constructive manner, and it is not surprising that he came to react with an explosive lack of control similar to hers.

The early therapeutic intervention consisted of providing the child and his mother with rather firm guidelines for behavior, accompanied by thorough and repetitive explanations of proper conduct. The atmosphere was permissive to the extent that Johnny was permitted to explore the plumbing and the lighting systems to satisfy his curiosity and gain some control of his surroundings. On the other hand, he was required to respect the property in the playroom and was not permitted to assault the therapist. The therapist labored to gradually constrict the patient's confused world so that Johnny could at least learn to appropriately deal with a few elements of the environment. During this early period of treatment the boy was primarily characterized as functioning very primitively, roughly at about the 15 to 18 month level.

Treatment for mother during this phase was coordinated with that of Johnny and followed essentially the same pattern. Mother was expected to help fulfill Johnny's need for firmer structure in his life, but this could be accomplished only after Mrs. T. was able to introduce structure and control in her own life. She was urged to stop acquiescing to her son's unreasonable demands and was helped to deal with the aggression and tantrums which resulted from disciplining and frustrating her son. A goal during this phase was to help Mrs. T. develop a loving firmness in her relationship with Johnny which would become mutually reinforcing. Likewise, the mother needed to become convinced that she could change in terms of assuming more adult feelings and responsibilities. She was helped to recognize that she needed a degree of self-discipline to correspond to the discipline she now sought to impose upon Johnny. In frank discussion sessions, Mr. and Mrs. T. were helped to plan and regulate their activities and to establish pre-determined standards and expectancies for their son's behavior. The evolving confidences of the trusting therapeutic relationship provided the conditions enabling Mrs. T. to experiment with new forms of behavior both as a mother and an adult. The changes in Mrs. T. were tentative, but as Johnny became more responsive, she became more highly motivated to attempt further change. At this time Mr. T. maintained a neutral position regarding treatment—he made few independent contributions, but did acquiese to some of the therapist's suggestions.

Phase II—Building—Greater Reality Orientation

Whereas therapeutic activities during the first phase were geared to providing primitive structure to the child, the goal at this second phase was to help the child begin to divert his raw and diffuse emotional experiences into appropriate and expressive physical play. Prior to the tenth play session, the youngster's dog was killed. The therapist was aware of this event and provided the materials and encouragement for communicating his concerns in a socially meaningful way. The boy reenacted the entire scene with dolls, a truck, and a toy dog, with tremendous hostility directed toward the truck driver. He repeatedly crashed the truck into the wall, throwing the driver out of the truck and, presumably, to his death. In instances such as this, the therapist repeatedly reinforced all attempts at appropriate verbal and motoric communication by empathizing with his feelings and showing the boy that this was the kind of behavior other people could understand.

Further evidence of Johnny's increasing ability to cope with his world occurred after fourteen interviews and eight months of treatment. The child developed compulsive features similar to those that existed when he was two years old. Johnny became very determined about maintaining complete order in the playroom and became upset with any foreign substance on his person. This is in contrast to two months earlier when he systematically covered his body with tempera paints. Further, limited compulsive behaviors (such as arranging toys in a certain way at the end of the hour) were introduced to this child as a means of continuing to provide structure for his world.

The second phase of treatment with Mrs. T. and sometimes with Mr. T. promoted the beginnings of a growing, personalized involvement of the parents with their child and with each other. A truly family-oriented therapeutic program evolved only after the parents came to realize that Johnny's maladjustment stemmed from early trauma and neglect resulting from their inability to accept and assume mature parental roles. The parents, like Johnny, needed to learn to cope with the demands of reality and their therapist sought to provide the information so that this could be accomplished. The emphasis was on promoting the occurrance of new behaviors which were likely to satisfy the needs of other family members and thus be rewarded.

It was the considered intention of the therapists to demonstrate to the parents and child the importance of achieving mastery over their lives. The parents tended to perceive what occurred in their lives as contingent upon forces outside of themselves, and they were encouraged to see themselves as being able to exert influence over what happened to them. It was our thesis that the rewards occurring from predictability in their lives would yield a continuing and growing tendency to create and maintain explicit structure in their family relationships.

Mr. T.'s characteristic response to life was one of passivity and withdrawal, leaving most of the responsibility for family affairs and social activities to his extroverted wife. Only when confronted with Johnny's excessive petulance did Mr. T. become emotional, and then he very hostilely spanked and screamed at the child. After the father came to acknowledge the idea that he could influence him and his family's destiny, he began to take a firmer stand as a father and husband. Father's demonstration of loving firmness and concern resulted in his finally becoming a male figure with whom Johnny could identify. After father broke all of his son's light bulbs and insisted that Johnny no longer sleep with his mother, the parents immediately noted a more attentive and responsive boy.

Mrs. T. made continued efforts to grow beyond the immature features of her personality during this period. She was helped to come to terms with her own rights of self determination and to lessen her dependency ties with her parents. As she achieved this, she also began to allow her son greater responsibility as well as more structure for his own behavior. Mrs. T. matured enough to more readily accept her husband as he was and to develop compromises in their relationship. She was encouraged to more openly and directly communicate with her husband and, in doing so, added a new positive dimension to their already sexually-satisfying marriage. The parents stood together in their attempts to encourage Johnny's growth by providing for more organization, structure and emotional involvement within the family, and they were pleased that Johnny began to respond more realistically to them and to others.

Phase III—Social Maturation

After a year of therapeutic contact, including only 17 treatment sessions, the child was beginning to directly express positive feelings toward the therapist. J. began to climb onto the therapist's lap, and refused to leave the playroom when the hour ended. He even initiated some attempts at verbal communication, and these were reinforced even though the speech was not comprehensible.

As the therapist became a source of comfort and reward for the child, he was able to directly attack inappropriate behavior and provide meaningful alternatives for the child. The process was, in fact, a behavior shaping procedure and the child was pushed, prodded, and cajoled into establishing more appropriate contact with his environment. There were times when the therapist became an insistent taskmaster so that the child only received what he wanted if he stayed within the prescribed boundaries of playroom procedure. Appropriate verbal expression was encouraged by responding less and less to Johnny's idiosyncratic language and gestures, by frequently asking him to pronounce words more clearly, and by responding immediately and positively whenever he complied. Language would improve, it was assumed, as it served Johnny's needs.

The youngster became able to act out family conflicts with dolls and a playhouse and began to show considerable aggression toward the mother figure. The boy was becoming more expressive and aggressive, but in a modulated and meaningful fashion. As this occurred, his activity level and frustration tolerance became more normal and there was no evidence of tantrum behavior in the therapy situation after about one year of treatment. The child still tended to respond rather openly to anxiety generated by the psychotherapeutic interaction and this provided cues which enabled the therapist to regulate the pace and extent of his interpretations and demands. The therapist no longer responded to atypical behavior by quickly empathizing and providing external control, as in the earlier phases of treatment. He began to ignore the idiosyncracies and to positively reinforce all attempts at symbolic representation, constructive activity, and appropriate expression of aggression and discontent. It was crucial that the child learn to express his fears, especially his hostility, without any concern about retribution or rejection. But whenever he lapsed into his old, regressed manner of expression, he was provided with little or no attention.

During this third phase of treatment, Mrs. T. continued to explore her own problems, relationships, and immaturities. It became possible to encourage her to test her interactions with reality, a parallel of what was simultaneously occurring, on a more primitive level, in Johnny's treatment. She was able to institute new means of coping with her internal hedonistic demands and respond more adequately to external frustration. As she became forced to acknowledge and accept the unpleasant aspects of life, she found that she could interact with the world without becoming harmed or hurting others (e.g., her husband and son) in the process of fulfilling her needs. The same conditions were established for Father and through direct teaching and his own behavioral experimentation, he gained confidence that he could cope with adversity by using means other than passive withdrawal or explosive hostility.

At this point in the on-going therapeutic process, both therapists began leaves of absence from the clinic and although Mrs. T. and Johnny were reassigned they did not resume sustained psychotherapeutic contacts. After a period of nine months, Mrs. T.'s therapist (JGM) returned to the clinic and therapeutic contacts were resumed, with a new therapist (RES) seeing Johnny. During this interim period, the parents were unable to maintain their recently acquired adaptive behavior patterns and lapsed into their previous customary modes of responding to Johnny and to each other. Not surprisingly, Johnny began to regress to his former level of adjustment as his environment not only failed to encourage and support the more adaptive behavior patterns which he had acquired, but also began once again to provide him with models for nonadaptive behaviors. The parents reverted to a pattern of overindulgence (occasionally interspersed with periods of rejection) which, in essence, was their way of submitting to and contributing to the tyranny of their disturbed child. The regression, for both child and parents, demonstrated how tenuous the previous changes in this family had been and indicated that internal resources had not yet evolved to maintain more adequate levels of functioning.

Phase IV—Concern for Others

The dominant theme during this phase of treatment was Johnny's increasing tendency to emerge from his egotistically constructed world into the world of other people.

When therapy was reinstituted, the child, then five years, nine months of age, appeared at least two years retarded in his overall personality development. After Johnny and his parents had been treated for three sessions, the child began to demonstrate a degree of social responsivity that surpassed his previous level of adjustment. As a partial explanation, the child's return to the clinic represented a very positive development for him. The renewed order and general predictability in his life yielded immediate compensations. The family had seen that therapy produced certain payoffs. After the therapists began to enforce their old demands, the family once again achieved a more settled state.

A first and significant indication that Johnny was beginning to venture into the world of others occurred while the therapist was reading him a story. He became engrossed in the plot and began to empathize with characters in the story. When the therapist read that "the donkey was very, very sad," he pounded the desk and cried out. When it was related that "the donkey was very happy," he clapped his hands and giggled. In addition, the child began to engage in truly cooperative activity with the therapist— he copied geometric figures and participated in puppet play.

An early example of Johnny's emerging ability to empathetically appreciate and respond to the feelings of others occurred at home, where Johnny often asked his mother or father to lie on his bed with him until he was asleep at night. On one occasion, he heard a favorite television program of his mother's beginning and told her to go and watch it. This concern for others was merely one aspect of the larger pattern of responding to people not merely as objects to satisfy his desires, but as people. The boy's progress significantly encouraged and supported his parents' attempts to look beyond themselves when evaluating the effects of their behavior.

As Johnny became truly responsive in a two-person interaction, the therapist was able to more effectively bring social reinforcement to bear on a number of problems, such as his speech. The boy began to enjoy recording his speech on a tape recorder and listening to it. The importance of the therapist's lavish praise of Johnny's attempts to speak clearly seemed to outweigh the advantages of his idiosyncratic language, and Johnny's speech became progressively more normal.

As Johnny increased his attention toward the external world he took more of the initiative in structuring this world and determining his role and place in it. With increasing security the child's normal tendencies toward inquisitiveness and exploration began to free themselves from his constricted and defensively insulated personality. There was now a driving curiosity in the boy to seek answers to questions which had already been answered for the normal child his age. In addition to providing him with useful information his questions may be seen as having had two other functions: first, they allowed him to demonstrate his capacity to exert some control over significant others. That is, when he repeatedly asked questions, adults almost invariably responded to him and in a predictable fashion. Secondly, Johnny often asked questions to which he knew the answers and welcomed the request that he answer his own question. This suggested that it was important to Johnny that he demonstrate to others the degree of knowledge and mastery that he had achieved. The implication was that what other people, primarily his parents, thought of him had become a matter of concern. He was now in a home where the parents permitted him some degree of influence and control and were interested in his opinions and his judgment. It should be noted that at this time we regarded the foregoing phases of therapy as, in part, laying the foundation for psychotherapeutic effort directed at broader aspects of his maladjustment.

As Johnny's interpersonal relationships became stable and solidified, a deluge of material centering around sex, eliminative processes, and aggression began to emerge. As the child developed more trust, he was able to safely express normal concerns. Since many of these manifested themselves at a relatively late age, the information proved to be particularly interesting and revealing because of the verbal labels Johnny was able to attach to these experiences.

While engaged in doll play during this second year of treatment, Johnny began to lift up the dresses of the female dolls and tried to tear the clothing off one of them. He was also reported to have several times looked under the dresses of female classmates in school. In addition, the child expressed eliminative concerns, which were possibly related to his sexual concerns. His mother reported that, for awhile, he refused to go to the bathroom with the other children at school. His explanation was: "I don't want them to see me, and I don't look at them." The therapeutic efforts were routine, geared mainly toward establishing conditions both by words and specific play materials that would promote expression of concern. The therapist focused on the idea that Johnny was like other boys and that sexual curiosity and elimination were acceptable and natural processes. The parents became the real key to treatment during this phase. Their increasing maturity made them capable of understanding their son's fears and his feelings. Mother, in particular, was helped through role-playing and discussion to learn how to deal directly with her son's emerging concerns. During the course of treatment she, like Johnny, had become sensitized not only to her own needs and feelings, but to those of others, specifically her husband and her son. She was no longer the immature, hedonistic adolescent; she was a responsible adult. Within a month, Johnny asked his parents to show him how to urinate "like the other boys do." He related that the other boys had been poking fun at him because he pulled his trousers down rather than unzipping his pants. This response to the social sanctions of his peer group was but another of the many behavioral referents which indicated an increasing commerce with his social environment.

Aggression which occurred in the absence of an identifiable cause was conceived of as an irrational response to past hurt and deprivation. During one therapy session Johnny suddenly and without apparent reason, hurled a large metal airplane at the therapist. This was looked upon as a positive development, since it indicated that Johnny now felt secure within the therapeutic relationship. On this occasion the therapist stated, "Sometimes boys feel very angry without knowing why. We're here to find out where these feelings come from." A more dramatic example of these aggressive impulses was told by Johnny's mother, who related that for no apparent reason, he had come to intensely dislike a female classmate in school. Johnny would say only that he "hates her" and that "she smells bad." His first outward aggression toward the little girl took the form of throwing rocks at her. He later asked his mother if he could take his pocket knife to school. After the refusal, she found him holding his knife and staring at a picture of the little girl. When she asked him what he was doing, he answered: "Might cut Sally."

The new nature of his interpersonal relationships and his direct confrontation with several areas of concern began paying additional dividends as Johnny began to re-experience some of his past trauma. For a period of several months, he became very upset whenever his mother tried to leave him alone, even if only to go into the back yard. He seemed to fear that he would again be deserted by his parents, as he was earlier in life. Spontaneous verbalizations indicated that he remembered the babysitter who was outside the house while he screamed. He remembered when he "pooped on the icebox" and recalled his Granny's death. Mrs. T. was encouraged to help Johnny bring out this kind of open talk about events, and discuss them with him. It was felt that the warm and understanding nature of the developing relationship between Johnny and his parents, particularly his mother, would allow him to re-experience his past concerns in an atmosphere stripped of the negative emotional remnants of the past, and would make possible a series of corrective emotional experiences. The child accurately recalled events even though they had occurred two to three years earlier, a time at which the child was not communicating with normal language. Whether or not such re-experiencing is a sufficient or even necessary condition for positive change in a child of this type, it appears to have occurred here in a rather classical sense.

This fourth phase of treatment was marked by extensive and enduring changes in Johnny, in his parents, especially mother, and in their family relationships. It was increasingly apparent that Johnny's mother had become the focal point of his world, his most "significant other." Mrs. T. continued to mature and spoke enthusiastically of her own expanding and developing relationships outside the home. She wanted and was offered guidance on how to handle problems as they arose. For example, she was told that it was perfectly all right for Johnny to talk back and express himself, although in similar fashion, parents have the responsibility to determine what children do and do not do. She developed her capacity to accept selfishness in herself and others, to overcome her fears of rejection, to seek attention in a mature fashion, and to have some determination over her own life.

During this eight month period, each person became more positively involved with the other. Father was taking his boy fishing and obviously was becoming proud of him. Mother became freer and more spontaneous and was determined to assume her proper role, and take the responsibility for helping her son to direct his activities. The boy was turning out toward children his own age and developing relationships with them. He turned to teasing others, listening to them, and playing with the neighborhood children; he even stole for a brief period of time. It seemed that a new equilibrium had become established—each member of the family was encouraged and supported in his progress by changes in the other two.

Phase V—Autonomous Development

The phase, which comprised the final three months of therapeutic contact with the family, witnessed an amazing rate of psychological growth in the child and in his parents. In essence, Johnny came to be very much like other boys his age. The key to these positive changes is seen to be the increasing evolvement of a more mature and normalized relationship with his mother and father. As the parents gained confidence in their role and began to see their child mature, the family became identified as a source of pleasure and pride.

By this time, Johnny was able to draw upon extra-therapeutic relationships since he found that it was safe to relate to and trust others. The therapist focused on the child's expanding world by helping him to acquire and use the appropriate verbal labels for feelings, objects, and events. Essentially, a socializing process was rapidly taking place so that normal aggressive or fearful feelings were dealt with cognitively as well as behaviorally.

As the child's feelings were dealt with in a reassuring and understanding manner, Johnny became willing and able to use the therapeutic setting as a forum in which he could engage in mature problem-solving behavior. One incident appears to have been particularly revealing in this regard. One day, in response to the therapist's suggestion that "it's important for a boy to have a place where he can come and talk about things he wonders about or thinks of, but never talks about," he abruptly stated: "Teacher shouldn't have a stick." Exploration revealed that Johnny was very concerned about the fact that his teacher was employing corporal punishment in school. He had seen several children taken from the classroom into the corridor where they were struck with a ruler. The therapist immediately supported this concern and sought to explain the role of punishment in maintaining discipline, emphasizing the difference between appropriate and inappropriate measures. Then Johnny played the role of a child who had been overtly aggressive in school (since the children in school had been punished for this) and the therapist played the role of a teacher who used warmth and reasoning rather than physical punishment. This was done to illustrate that authority and punishment could be of a benign nature. It was in these instances that the therapist stressed the importance of communication so that other people would understand and help Johnny deal with his concerns.

This incident seemed to have had a good deal of impact on Johnny, for Mrs. T. later reported that he broached the subject of the teacher's behavior to her and had told her that he feared that if he were struck by the teacher he would die. Mrs. T. dealt with this irrational remnant of Johnny's past fears in a sympathetically reassuring and understanding manner, and this appears to have been a milestone in their relationship. Johnny now began to confide in her to a greater extent, and her own increased maturity enabled her to deal with his concerns in an effective manner. Indeed, in a very real sense, Mrs. T. became Johnny's most important "therapist" at this point. Johnny's expressiveness was surely promoted and reinforced by his mother's demonstration that she could comprehend her son's concerns. Father, too, was interested in participating in his son's affairs, but mainly in sports and recreation. While Father did not appear ready or able to deal with his son in a verbal problem-centered way, he was providing a suitable model and companion for Johnny.

As Johnny grew psychologically, he was, in turn, increasingly able to make use of his family relationships with their growth-inducing potential. In addition, because of the appropriateness of his behaviors, he was well-accepted by his peers in school and began to develop meaningful relationships with them. As time passed, these family and peer relationships gradually came to replace the therapeutic relationship in importance. The child's growth, however, was impressively clear during the therapeutic hour; his play became quite constructive and his formerly repetitive questions were gradually replaced by queries which reflected a more mature approach to understanding his world. The relationship between child and therapist moved toward the status of a friendship as the child, largely through interacting with peers, learned the rudiments of social intercourse.

During the final two months of therapy, one could detect little difference between Johnny's behavior and that of the average six year old, a dramatic and gratifying change indeed when one considers his status of several years before. He did not become a model child but seemingly a more responsive, socially oriented and happy child. His old fears were eliminated; he was able to tolerate frustrations and comply to parental requests. He turned to parents and teachers for help and counted on them for support. Johnny no longer feared going to school alone and his demands for constant attention decreased. He became an active participant in class, learned well, and played cooperatively with the other youngsters. He was fortunate to have had a perceptive, understanding, and helpful first grade teacher. The quality of Johnny's speech improved markedly and his use of language became more and more appropriate and meaningful to others, although the remaining impediment was considered to be of sufficient severity to require speech therapy.

Since Johnny appeared to have developed sufficient resources to profit maximally from his new home and peer group environments, the possibility of terminating therapeutic contacts could now be considered. Both Johnny and his mother shared the conviction that they were able to continue their course of growth in the absence of therapeutic intervention. When the subject of termination was introduced and Johnny was asked how he felt about it, he replied, "I used to need to come here, but now I don't anymore."

DISCUSSION AND SUMMARY

The case of Johnny focuses on issues that are frequently involved in treating a seriously disturbed child and his parents. The child's first years of life were spent in a rejecting, traumatizing home environment. The parents were immature and were not prepared for or interested in caring for a dependent. There was a similarity between the behavior of the child and his mother, both in terms of their initial non-adaptive behavior and their subsequent and concurrent adaptive changes. Most importantly the treatment program involved a closely coordinated effort directed at both child and parents. The therapists adopted specific goals at various stages of treatment and simultaneously applied similar techniques with parents and child to achieve these goals.

A number of historical factors which appear to have contributed heavily to Johnny's severe disturbance can be enumerated. He was a child conceived out of wedlock and born to parents who responded with hostility and rejection to his interference with their adolescent activities. Johnny understandably developed a basic sense of mistrust which was repeatedly reinforced not only by his parents' behaviors, but also by the irresponsible and unconcerned people assigned to care for him, e.g., his babysitters. In addition, the child suffered from a lack of adequate learning experiences. There was little positive reinforcement for his appropriate behavior since his parents attended primarily to the unacceptable aspects of his behavior. Secondly, and perhaps more importantly, the parents themselves did not possess sufficient maturity to provide him with acceptable models for socially mature behavior. This threatening and hurtful atmosphere finally resulted in Johnny's withdrawal into a regressed and psychotic world.

The therapeutic approach was family-oriented and eclectic and was adapted to the child's and the parents' needs at the several stages of treatment. No effort was made to utilize any single theortical framework; principles were derived from relationship, psychoanalytic and learning orientations. Methods were designed to fulfill the therapeutic requirements at a given time. As one reads through the various phases of treatment, it is to be noted that as the child and the parents improved, the therapeutic procedures were gradually altered to take advantage of their new-found strengths.

Progress in the treatment of this child and his parents was dependent upon certain sequential phenomena. When adequate therapeutic relationships were established, both parents and child saw the therapists as being able to help them impose order and structure on their worlds. Father became more assertive and confident in family affairs, mother took charge in a constructive and non-impulsive manner, and Johnny found himself being more influential in a more predictable environment. The emphasis was on teaching all three people to construct and deal with a more orderly world. The decrease of personal threat and the increased self control set the stage for rewarding interpersonal relationships, with the family members becoming a prime source of comfort and gratification for each other. With the emergence of an integrated family unit, whose members had acquired the capacity to provide for individual and group needs, psychotherapy was no longer necessary.

6 Special Topics

Part One   Language

Suppose that one evening you and your spouse are quietly watching yet another rerun of *The Forsyte Saga* when a small Evil Demon suddenly materializes atop your TV set. With the self-confident insolence so common to Evil Demons, he announces that you are soon to become parents and that your child will be born either blind or deaf, but that you get to choose which affliction the child will have. Which would you choose?

Most people, after being asked this question, unhesitatingly state that they would prefer for the child to be born deaf rather than blind. The thought of consigning someone to a life of darkness is too dreadful for most of us to even consider—not being able to hear seems minor when compared to never having seen the color of a flower, the magnificence of a sunset, or the face of a lover. But most of us overlook one very important point when comparing blindness and deafness; a person who is deaf from the time of birth (congenitally deaf) is cut off from the most fundamental instrument of human interaction, spoken language.

Now you may argue that sign language and speechreading (lip-reading) are common skills of the deaf and therefore the problem can't be all that serious. However, congenitally deaf children frequently receive no training in these skills until they are four, five, or even six years old—two to three years beyond the optimal period for language acquisition. As a result, few ever acquire adequate language skills—they have consistently smaller vocabularies and they read, write, and speak considerably less well than normal-hearing children and adults of comparable ages. The most immediate effect of these language deficiencies is to hamper educational progress (few go far in school), and the long-range effect is to relegate the deaf to marginal employment at menial jobs.

An obvious step toward preventing this dreadful waste of human beings would be to introduce the deaf to sign language during the crucial language acquisition stage when they are very young. This could be done by teaching the members of deaf children's families to use sign language while they orally talk to each other, thus providing a language-rich environment that is comparable to the environment experienced by normal-hearing youngsters. The problem with this is that many professional teachers of the deaf are of the opinion that success in teaching language via signing (called the *manual method*) reduces deaf children's motivation to learn to speechread and to speak. As a result, most schools for the deaf prohibit their pupils from using sign language (even outside of classes), and most parents of deaf children are advised not to use it at home. Because parents want their deaf children to become as "normal" as possible, that is, to be able to speechread and to speak reasonably intelligibly, they follow the professionals' prescription. The professionally preferred method is to have the children learn to speechread by being around people when they talk and by undergoing special preschool training (called the *oral method*).

There is much current controversy over the manual versus oral methods of teaching the deaf and our first two readings examine this controversy. The first of the two, Dr. Kathryn Meadow's *Early Manual Communication in Relation to the Deaf Child's Intellectual, Social, and Communicative Functioning*, presents evidence about the supposed ill effects of early use of sign language and the second, Drs. McCay Vernon and Soon Koh's *Effects of Oral Preschool Compared to Early Manual Communication on Education and Communication in Deaf Children*, examines the supposedly beneficial effects of preschools that stress the oral method of training.

The last reading also deals with a controversy about language skills and how to teach them. It arises from the fact that a large number of Americans do not speak the Standard English that is used in the public schools. Instead, they speak one or another dialects of English which, while useful in communicating with family and friends, are not easily understood by the population as a whole. The most common of these dialects are spoken by many Black Americans. Dialects evolve over hundreds of years and the people who use them are not speaking English incorrectly—rather, they are speaking another language. Unfortunately, the problem (and controversy) arises when we try to decide how schools should deal with children who speak a dialect of English but for whom Standard English is a foreign language. Some people argue that the teachers should teach using the dialect. Other people argue that the children should learn Standard English in order to improve their communications with the broader population and to provide them access to a greater variety of jobs, and so forth. This is no small problem, and it is explored in Dr. Joan Baratz's *Should Black Children Learn White Dialect?*

EARLY MANUAL COMMUNICATION IN RELATION TO THE DEAF CHILD'S INTELLECTUAL, SOCIAL, AND COMMUNICATIVE FUNCTIONING

Kathryn P. Meadow

The basic impoverishment of deafness is not lack of hearing, but lack of language. To illustrate this, we have only to compare the four-year-old hearing child, with a working vocabulary of between two and three thousand words, to a child of the same age, profoundly deaf since infancy, who may have only a few words at his command. Even more important than vocabulary level, however, is the child's ability to use his language for expressing ideas, needs, and feelings. By the age of four, the hearing child in all cultures has already grasped the rules of grammar and syntax which enable him to combine words in meaningful ways.

There are those who feel that existing research points to the inability of the individual ever to recapture those phases of linguistic development which are by-passed (McNeill, 1965; Sigel, 1964). Data on the linguistic achievement of deaf adolescents and adults tend to confirm this notion. It is estimated that the average deaf adult reads at about the fifth grade level, or even below (Furth, 1966, p. 205). An investigation of language comprehension of deaf students in 73 schools in Canada and the United States showed that only 12 per cent of the sixteen-year-olds scored above the fifth grade level on the Metropolitan Achievement Tests Elementary Battery (Wrightstone, *et al.*, 1962, pp. 13–14).

It has been suggested that the experiential deficiency resulting from communicative inadequacy influences the personality characteristics which have been noted among the deaf. One of the most consistent findings is that deaf persons are less "mature" than hearing individuals with whom they are compared. Levine, on the basis of a Rorschach study of normal deaf adolescent girls, described the complex which she summarized as "emotional immaturity" in terms of egocentricity, easy irritability, impulsiveness, and suggestibility (1956, p. 143). Neyhus characterized the deaf adults whom he studied (also using the Rorschach) as "restricted in breadth of

Reprinted from *American Annals of the Deaf*, 1968, *113*, 29–41. By permission of The American Annals of the Deaf and the author.

This investigation was supported in part by a fellowship from the Vocational Rehabilitation Administration. Preliminary work was done while the author was a participant in an NIMH Training Program in Personality and Social Structure. Of the many persons who were helpful during the course of research, a particular debt of gratitude is due Dr. John A. Clausen, University of California (Berkeley); Dr. Hilde Schlesinger, Langley-Porter Neuropsychiatric Institute; Dr. Hugo Schunhoff and Mr. Myron Leenhouts, California School for the Deaf (Berkeley).

experience, rigid and confused in thought processes, and characterized by an inability to integrate experiences meaningfully." He found that the "distorted perception" noted in younger persons was apparent in adulthood as well. However, this characteristic was diminished at the older age levels, "suggesting a delayed period of maturation in the deaf" (Neyhus, 1964, p. 325). Altshuler describes deaf persons as lacking in empathy, egocentric and dependent, handling tensions with "considerable impulsivity" and without much thoughtful introspection (1964, pp. 63–64).

On the one hand, deaf persons have been found to be noticeably deficient in their educational and intellectual functioning, compared to hearing persons, in spite of apparently normal capacities. On the other hand, findings have been presented which indicate many deaf persons to be less mature and more dependent than comparable groups of hearing persons. Since not all deaf persons exhibit these responses, we may assume that there is nothing inherent in early profound deafness which makes these deficiencies inevitable. Rather, we must look to environmental factors for explanations of developmental differences.

Because of the occasional genetic transmission of deafness, there are families in which both parents and children are deaf. "Nearly ten per cent of all children born to deaf subjects" in the survey of the deaf population in New York State, are also deaf. (Rainer, et al,. 1963, p. 27). The socialization experiences of these deaf children can be expected to differ markedly from those of deaf children with hearing parents. First, the emotional reaction of deaf parents to the birth of a deaf child is predicted to be less traumatic. Parental acceptance of and adjustment to the deaf child should be comparatively easier and more rapid. Secondly, most deaf children with deaf parents have a means of communication from earliest childhood, since most deaf adults utilize the manual language of signs as a matter of course.[1] These two basic differences in the family environments of deaf children with deaf parents and those with hearing parents provide the basis for a research design approximating a "natural experiment" for testing some hypotheses about the bases of differences in levels of social and intellectual functioning in deaf persons.

One reason for the presence of manual communication in deaf families and the absence of manual communication in hearing families with deaf children is related to a bitter controversy regarding the use of the language of signs with young deaf children. Most hearing parents are warned against the use of manual communication by the professionals with whom they

[1] In the New York State study, almost half of the 493 deaf respondents stated that they used "mainly signs" for communicating, while another 18 per cent report the "equal use of speech and signs." This compares to 29 per cent who use "mainly speech" (Rainer, et al., 1963, computed from Table 6, p. 119). Of seventy-one deaf parents of deaf children responding to the Stuckless and Birch survey, only five stated that they did *not* use the language of signs with their deaf child. Sixty-four per cent stated that they had used the language of signs with the child when he was a baby (Stuckless and Birch, 1966, p. 458).

come in contact. The reason for this proscription is the belief that if deaf children are not forced to rely exclusively on oral methods of communication, they will not be motivated to learn speech and speechreading: "the evidence is . . . impressive that speech seldom develops if signs come first" (DiCarlo, 1964, p. 115). Some social scientists, however, are not convinced that this statement is true. Furth, for instance, says that the insistence that the early use of signs is detrimental to the acquisition of speech *because* they are easier for the deaf to learn relies on "a mysterious doctrine of least effort." "Carried to its logical conclusion, this would mean that infants who are allowed to crawl would forever lack the motivation to learn to walk" (Furth, 1966). Kohl (1966) and Altshuler and Sarbin (1963) also believe that insistence on the exclusive use of oral communication with young deaf children has been carried to extremes. A comparison of the communicative functioning of deaf children who were exposed to manual communication early in life, and those who had no exposure to it in the early years should provide parents and educators with additional evidence in this sensitive area.

The above discussion was designed to provide background for the rationale behind the selection of three crucial dependent variables examined in the research to be reported here: (1) the intellectual or academic functioning; (2) the social functioning; and (3) the communicative functioning of the deaf child. The major independent variable was defined as the parents' status, since this factor was believed to affect (1) the socialization climate and (2) the existence of a system of early family communication. . . .

Research Hypotheses for the Present Study — On the basis of the theoretical considerations and results from previous research the following hypotheses were formulated prior to the initiation of research procedures:

> Hypothesis 1 — Deaf children of deaf parents, compared to deaf children of hearing parents, are more likely to show a higher level of intellectual functioning.
> Hypothesis 2 — Deaf children of deaf parents, compared to deaf children of hearing parents, are more likely to show a higher level of social functioning, especially apparent in situations requiring "maturity" and "independence."
> Hypothesis 3 — Deaf children of deaf parents, compared to deaf children of hearing parents, are more likely to demonstrate a higher level of communicative competence, including competence in written and spoken, expressive and receptive language.

Research Population and Setting — All the children included in this study were enrolled at the California School for the Deaf in Berkeley between January and September, 1966. This is one of two residential schools for the deaf operated by the State. Minimum age for admission is five-and-one-half. Pupils either graduate or must leave the school by the age of twenty-one. School population is approximately 500. In January, 1966, sixty children (twelve per cent) were enrolled who had both a deaf father and deaf mother. One was eliminated because parents did not wish to participate. Thus, 59 deaf children with deaf parents formed the base of the study population. Each of these children was matched individually with a child whose father and mother both are hearing. Matching was done on the basis of sex, age, IQ test score, degree of residual hearing, and family size. Some attempt was made to equate family socio-economic status, using the father's occupation as a measure. . . .

Research Instruments and Procedures — A rating scale was devised which included items dealing with intellectual, social, and communicative functioning (Meadow, K., 1967, pp. 336–340). Each student was rated *independently* by three separate raters. Of these, the first was the classroom teacher, and the second a dormitory counselor. Children in the fifth grade or above, who participate in the vocational training program, were rated by their vocational arts teacher. For the younger children, the third rating was completed by a different counselor. The three ratings were summed, scores ranked from highest to lowest and trichotomized for most of the analyses (referred to as "high," "medium," and "low" scores). . . .

In addition to teacher-counselor ratings for intellectual functioning, Stanford Achievement Test scores, administered by the School in May, 1966, were utilized for evaluating students in this area. The Craig Lipreading Inventory (Craig, 1964) was administered to evaluate this area of communicative functioning.[2, 3]

Research Findings

Intellectual Functioning — There were thirty-two pairs of children for whom Stanford Achievement Test scores were available for both members. (These tests are administered only to children who are beyond the second grade in school). The scores are expressed in terms of standardized "grade level" achievement, for "reading," "arithmetic," and "grade average." Table 1 shows the results of a pair-by-pair comparison, evaluated by means of a t test of differences. This table shows that differences in grade level achievement, reading, and arithmetic, *favoring children with deaf parents* in each instance, were significant at the one per cent level of confidence or beyond. The average discrepancy in scores was greater than one year for grade level and arithmetic, and greater than two years for reading.

Social Functioning — The areas of social and personal "adjustment" or behavior were evaluated by means of the Index of Teacher-Counselor

[2] The following persons gave a great deal of assistance in the development of the research instruments: Mr. Jacob Arcanin, Mr. Bernard Bragg, Mr. Ralph Jordan, Mr. Erwin Marshall, Mr. Hubert Summers.

[3] I am grateful to Mr. Hartley Koch for administering this test, and to Dr. William Craig, who loaned the films and test forms which he developed.

Table 1

Matched-Pair Comparisons of Stanford Achievement Test Scores:
1966 Grade Average, Reading, and Arithmetic

	Mean difference	(N) (pairs)	t
Grade average	+1.28 years	(31)*	2.84**
Reading	+2.10 years	(31)*	2.56**
Arithmetic	+1.25 years	(32)	3.67**

*one tied observation dropped from the analysis.
**p ≤ .01

Ratings. The pair-by-pair analysis of these items is shown in Table 2. Ratings for the nine items describing social functioning all favor the children with deaf parents, most beyond the one percent level of confidence.

In addition to the support which these findings give to the initial research hypothesis, they are of interest because of their relationship to previous comparisons of deaf and hearing subjects. As was stated earlier, a number of investigators have found deaf subjects to be "immature" compared to

Table 2

Index Ratings of Social Adjustment Variables for Matched
Pairs of Children with Deaf or Hearing Parents

Rating Scale Item	No. of Pairs	No. where Children with Deaf Parents Rated Higher	Wilcoxon T value	z
Mature	56	39 (70%)	430.0	2.99**
Responsible	55	38 (69%)	432.5	2.83**
Independent	53	40 (75%)	281.0	3.85**
Enjoys new experiences	55	36 (65%)	501.0	2.25*
Friendly, Sociable	55	42 (76%)	405.0	3.06**
Popular with classmates	55	40 (73%)	434.0	2.82**
Popular with adults	52	34 (65%)	427.5	2.38**
Responds to situations with appropriate emotion	55	34 (62%)	535.5	1.97*
Shows appropriate sex-role behavior	54	33 (61%)	509.5	2.01*

**p ≤ .01   *p ≤ .05

hearing subjects (Rainer, 1963; Neyhus, 1964; Levine, 1956). Several researchers have evaluated the "social maturity" of deaf children, using the Vineland Social Maturity Scale, designed to measure the "degree of independence or self-sufficiency." Streng and Kirk (1938), Avery (1938), Myklebust and Burchard (1945) and Myklebust (1960) all found that deaf children received lower scores on this Scale than did hearing children. Myklebust (1960, p. 215), reported that the discrepancy between the two groups increased with age. It has been suggested that the immaturity which seemingly characterizes deaf children and adults may result from the high proportion who attend residential schools, where the development of independence and responsibility may be attenuated (Barker, 1953).

The results of the present study suggest that there is nothing inherent in the condition of deafness itself—that is, in the lack of auditory contact with the environment—which produces characteristics of immaturity which so many have noted. Since all subjects in the present study are students in a residential school for the deaf, and there are significant differences among them, the fact of residential living by itself would not seem to lead necessarily to immaturity. Rather, we should look to other conditions in the deaf child's environment to discover those which produce differences *within* the deaf population which may be as great as those between the deaf and hearing groups. (Of course, the hypothesized differences upon which the present study was designed relate to the presence or absence of early communication, and the quality of family relationships.)

Another similarly suggestive area is that represented by the item, "appropriate sex-role behavior," shown in Table 3 to be significantly more frequently rated higher among the children with deaf parents. Here, differences are attributable almost entirely to higher ratings given to *boys* with deaf parents (Meadow, K., 1967, p. 193). The New York group found indications of a higher incidence of sexual maladjustment among their clinic patients than would be expected (Rainer, *et al.*, 1963, p. 148, 245).

The significance of differences found in these critical areas of "socal adjustment" (maturity, sociability, sex-role behavior), is underscored by the *absence* of significant findings for a number of traits for which there is no evidence of deaf-hearing difference. These areas included traits summarized as "happy, calm, generous, obedient, kind, neat, mannerly, emphatic" (Meadow, K., 1967, p. 191). . . .

Communicative Functioning — If the deaf child is to communicate effectively with the hearing world, he must acquire facility in speech, speechreading, and writing. If he is to communicate effectively within the deaf community, he must acquire both receptive and expressive facility in fingerspelling and the language of signs. In addition, he should feel comfortable about his own communicative skills, and be willing to use these skills to communicate with strangers, both deaf and hearing. All these items were included in the rating scale which teachers and counselors completed for this study. Table 3 shows the results of the matched-pair comparisons of children with deaf and with hearing parents on these items.

The critical communicative areas, for most parents and educators of deaf children, are represented by *speechreading* and *speech*. Table 3 shows that the differences between children with deaf and hearing parents on these two variables are not significant. Twenty-two of 46 available score-comparisons favor children with deaf parents in ratings of speechreading ability; 21 of 51 comparisons favor children with deaf parents in ratings of speech aptitude and performance. The analysis of the additional six items dealing with communicative skills shows that children with deaf parents are given higher ratings in a significant proportion of the comparisons.

The results of the Craig Lipreading Inventory were essentially the same as those of the teacher-counselor ratings: no significant differences appeared in the scores of children with deaf parents and those with hearing parents. Of thirty-five pairs for whom a "Word Score" was available, differences favored children with deaf parents in eighteen instances. Of twenty-eight pairs for whom a "Sentence Score" was available, differences were in the

Table 3

Matched-Pair Comparisons of Index Ratings for Communicative Functioning, Children with Deaf or Hearing Parents

Rating Scale Item	No. of Pairs	No. where Child w/Deaf Parents Rated Higher	Wilcoxon T value	z
Speechreading ability	46	22 (48%)	623.0	.10
Speech aptitude and performance	51	21 (41%)	758.0	.89
Facility in written language	49	35 (71%)	263.5	3.47**
Ability to fingerspell	54	50 (93%)	18.5	6.23**
Ability to read others' fingerspelling	52	49 (94%)	25.0	6.09**
Ability to use the language of signs	55	46 (87%)	117.0	5.47**
No apparent frustration from inability to communicate	56	39 (70%)	319.0	3.89**
Willingness to attempt communication with strangers	45	30 (67%)	335.5	2.06*

**p ≤ .01   *p ≤ .05

predicted direction in eighteen instances (not statistically significant).

Because of the great interest in the relationship between proficiency in oral and in manual communicative skills, scores on the Lipreading Inventory were compared to Index Ratings for other aspects of communicative functioning. A significant positive relationship emerged between speech-reading score and ratings for speech, expressive fingerspelling, and language of signs usage. (Relationships with written language facility and receptive fingerspelling were in the same direction but were not statistically significant at the five per cent level of confidence). These findings fail to provide support for the notion that the knowledge and use of manual communication prevent the acquisition of speechreading skills. This contention is the heart of the oralist argument which forbids the use of manual communication with young deaf children. The findings of the present research agree substantially with those reported by Montgomery, who studied 59 prelinguistically deaf Scottish students and concluded that: "There are no negative correlations between any of the measures of oral skills and the manual communication rating: indeed there are no negative correlations at all. Positive significant correlations are recorded between the manual communication rating and the Donaldson Lipreading Test." (Montgomery, 1966, p. 562). Like the present author, Montgomery concludes that, "There . . . appears to be no statistical support for the currently popular opinion that manual communication is detrimental to or incompatible with the development of speech and lipreading" (*ibid.*).

Another variable which may well contribute to the deaf student's communicative functioning is the extent of the early oral training which he receives. From interviews with 34 deaf and 34 hearing families, it appears that the parents' hearing status is related to preschool training. About 40 per cent of the children with deaf parents had attended preschool classes for deaf children, compared to 80 per cent of those with hearing parents. Both children with deaf parents and those with hearing parents are more likely to score above the median on the lipreading inventory if they received some early oral training. (Approximately two-thirds of the groups with some early training scored above the median, compared to about one-third without early training. Because of the small numerical base, however, these differences were not statistically significant.)

Summary and Conclusions

The findings confirm the initial research hypotheses regarding the superior intellectual and social functioning of deaf children with deaf parents, compared to deaf children with hearing parents. Data from Stanford Achievement Tests (reading, arithmetic, and overall grade level), as well as teacher-counselor ratings for intellectual functioning, disclosed significant differences between the sets of matched pairs in the predicted direction. In the area of social functioning, differences favoring children with deaf parents were particularly impressive in areas of behavior which have often been cited as "characteristic" of deaf individuals. These include traits such as "maturity," "responsibility," "independence," "sociability," and "appropriate sex-role behavior."

The results of ratings and speechreading test, measuring communicative functioning, were less clear-cut. No differences were found between children with deaf parents and those with hearing parents on the ratings for speechreading and speech. Children with deaf parents received significantly higher ratings for facility with written language, receptive and expressive fingerspelling, and use of the language of signs. On the other hand, various measures of manual communication were positively related to facility in speechreading, as measured by the Craig Inventory. Early oral training seems to be related to later communicative functioning, and is less likely to have been experienced by children with deaf parents.

None of the evidence from the research reported above would seem to justify the strong injunctions placed by professional educators on the use of manual communication by parents of young deaf children. Children in this study who had been exposed to early manual communication performed at a higher level by almost every measure employed. This conclusion is not meant to discourage early oral training for deaf children. On the contrary, some evidence was reported to the effect that children who are most likely to be judged as having good communicative skills are those who were exposed to both oral and manual training at an early age.

BIBLIOGRAPHY

Atshuler, K. Z., "Personality Traits and Depressive Symptoms in the Deaf," Wortis, J. (ed.), *Recent Advances in Biological Psychiatry*, Vol. VI, N. Y.: Plenum Press, 1964.

———— ————, and M. Bruce Sarlin, "Deafness and Schizophrenia: A Family Study," in John Rainer, *et al.* (eds.) *Family and Mental Health Problems in a Deaf Population*, N. Y.: Dept. of Medical Genetics, New York State Psychiatric Institute, 1963, pp. 204–213.

Avery, Charlotte D., "The Social Competence of Pre-School Acoustically Handicapped Children," *Journal of Exceptional Children*, 15 (1948), 71–73.

Barker, Roger G., in collaboration with Wright, Beatrice A., Myerson, Lee, and Gonick, Mollie R., *Adjustment to Physical Handicap and Illness: A Survey of the Social Psychology of Physique and Disability*, N. Y.: Social Science Research Council Bulletin 55 (rev.), 1953.

Craig, William N., "Effects of Preschool Training on the Development of Reading and Lipreading Skills of Deaf Children," *American Annals of the Deaf*, 109 (1964), 280–296.

DiCarlo, Louis M., *The Deaf*, Englewood Cliffs, N. J.: Prentice-Hall, 1964.

Furth, Hans G., *Thinking Without Language, Psychological Implications of Deafness*, N. Y.: The Free Press, 1966.

Kohl, Herbert R., *Language and Education of the Deaf*, N. Y.: Center for Urban Education, 1966.

Levine, Edna S., *Youth in a Soundless World, A Search for Personality*, Washington Square, N. Y.: New York University Press, 1956.

McNeill, David, "The Capacity for Language Acquisition," in *Research on Be-*

havioral Aspects of Deafness, Proceedings of a National Research Conference on Behavioral Aspects of Deafness, New Orleans, May, 1965, Vocational Rehabilitation Administration.

Meadow, Kathryn Pendleton, *The Effect of Early Manual Communication and Family Climate on the Deaf Child's Development*, Unpublished Ph.D. Dissertation, University of California, Berkeley, 1967.

Montgomery, G. W., "The Relationship of Oral Skills to Manual Communication in Profoundly Deaf Students," *American Annals of the Deaf*, 111 (1966), 557–565.

Myklebust, H., and Burchard, E. M. L., "A Study of the Effects of Congenital and Adventitious Deafness on Intelligence, Personality, and Social Maturity of School Children," *Journal of Educational Psychology*, 34 (1945), 321.

Myklebust, H., *The Psychology of Deafness, Sensory Deprivation, Learning, and Adjustment*, N. Y.: Grune and Stratton, 1960.

Neyhus, Arthur I., "The Social and Emotional Adjustment of Deaf Adults," *The Volta Review*, 66 (1964), 319–325.

Rainer, John D., Altshuler, Kenneth Z., Kallmann, Franz J. (eds.), *Family and Mental Health Problems in A Deaf Population*, N. Y.: Department of Medical Genetics, N. Y. State Psychiatric Institute, Columbia University, 1963.

Sigel, Irving E., "The Attainment of Concepts," in Hoffman, M., and Hoffman, L. W. (eds.), *Review of Child Development Research*, Vol. 1, N. Y.: Russell Sage Foundation, 1964.

Streng, Alice and Kirk, S. A., "The Social Competence of Deaf and Hard-of-Hearing Children in A Public Day School," *American Annals of the Deaf*, 83 (1938), 244–254.

Stuckless, E. Ross, and Birch, Jack W., "The Influence of Early Manual Communication on the Linguistic Development of Deaf Children," *American Annals of the Deaf*, 111 (1966), 452–460, 499–504.

Wrightstone, J. W., Aronow, Miriam S., and Moskowitz, Sue, "Developing Reading Test Norms for Deaf Children," *Test Service Bulletin, No. 98*, New York: Harcourt Brace Jovanovich, 1962.

EFFECTS OF ORAL PRESCHOOL COMPARED TO EARLY MANUAL COMMUNICATION ON EDUCATION AND COMMUNICATION IN DEAF CHILDREN

McCay Vernon and Soon D. Koh

The value of early childhood education is a subject of major controversy in psychology, education, and government. Once seen as a near panacea for many of the ills of our school system, Head Start and other preschool

From *American Annals of the Deaf*, 1971, *116*, 569–574. By permission of The American Annals of the Deaf and the authors.

programs have produced results which have raised fundamental doubts about their lasting educational values. Defenders and critics of early childhood education have presented their respective and conflicting views in prestigious journals with no general accepted conclusions (Circelli, Evans, and Schiller, 1970; Smith and Bissell, 1970).

In deafness there has occurred a parallel series of events. Many educators have expressed the hope and belief that oral preschools would be the educational breakthrough needed to enable deaf children to master communication skills and academic subject matter. Two rather comprehensive studies of the actual results of oral preschool education have been conducted (Craig, 1964; Phillips, 1963). These investigations included over 200 deaf children from the leading oral preschools in the East such as Lexington and the American School. Results showed that while there were initial differences favoring deaf children with oral preschool training, by the age nine both groups were at the same level in academic, speech, and communication skills. Interestingly, Craig and Phillips were both carrying out their separate research work at about the same time and in many of the same schools. Thus, their studies were to some extent replications of one another. Such independently conducted investigations yielding almost identical findings deserve considerable weight in an objective evaluation of oral preschool education.

PROBLEM

Although the landmark work of Craig and Phillips was done in the early sixties, there have been no other objective comparative research studies since. The present investigation, an attempt to fill this void, will compare the academic and communicative achievement of three groups: 1) deaf children who have had three years of oral preschool education; 2) deaf children of deaf parents ("manual" children); and 3) deaf children who had no preschool education but who had hearing parents. Only by objectively evaluating various preschool programs will we know whether they are making progress toward remediating the handicap of deafness or simply helping us tread water and waste resources.

METHOD

The John Tracy Clinic is the pioneer in early education for deaf children. Its program remains one of the most highly regarded in the world. Deaf children there are provided intensive day long oral instruction and the best of modern amplification. Parents are taught to work with their children in oral communication and academic learning and are given psychological counseling and therapy.

The present study is a follow-up of every graduate of the Tracy Clinic Oral Preschool (not the correspondence course) from 1944 through 1968 who attended the California School for the Deaf, Riverside. These orally educated children are matched with deaf children of deaf parents and deaf children of hearing parents who had no pre-school training. Hearing loss in the speech range (500-2000 Hz) for all cases was 60 db or greater (ASA 1951).

RESULTS

Academic Achievement

Using rigorous matching criteria on the variables of IQ (no difference greater than 5 points), age (within 6 months), and sex, it was possible to match 23 graduates from the Tracy Clinic with 23 deaf children of deaf parents who had had no preschool education and with 23 deaf children who had had no preschool education and who had hearing parents. This last group was matched with the Tracy sample on the additional variable of etiology of deafness.

In effect, this matching results in a comparison between children given oral preschool education under the optimal conditions of the Tracy Clinic, children who had early manual communication but no oral preschool, and children with no oral preschool or manual communication who lived in an oral home environment.

The data on the academic achievement of the three groups [showed that] the deaf children of deaf parents (manual group) were superior to the other two groups by at least one full grade on all four subtests [i.e., paragraph meaning, word meaning, reading average, general average] of the Stanford [Linguistic Achievement Test]. The Tracy Clinic children and those children who had no preschool and hearing parents showed virtually identical grade point averages on the same four subtests.

These results indicate that the manual communication provided the deaf children of deaf parents resulted in better linguistic skills than did the three-year Tracy oral preschool program. The negligible lasting academic effects of the Tracy program on linguistic and general academic achievement are further demonstrated by achievement of deaf children who had no preschool and hearing parents. Their scholastic achievement is equal to that of Tracy Clinic graduates.

In the next data analysis we dropped the deaf children of hearing parents in order to increase the number of available subjects and make additional comparisons between deaf children of deaf parents (the manual group) and deaf graduates of the Tracy Clinic (pre-school oral group). By matching all available Tracy graduates and available deaf children of deaf parents on the variables of age (within 5 months), IQ (within 10 points), and sex, it was possible to obtain 56 pairs. In this matching, ten of the deaf children of deaf parents had had some speech therapy or preschool, but in no case was it nearly as extensive as that provided by the Tracy Clinic.

Once again, the group with early manual communication shows a superiority of approximately one full grade in all areas over the Tracy oral preschoolers. On all four Stanford Subtests the differences are statistically significant.

Another criterion of academic achievement is the circumstance under which a student leaves school, that is, graduation, dismissal for academic deficiency, etc. An analysis of this was made for all subjects 16 years of age or older from the matched samples of subjects previously reported. These data show that 90% of the children with early manual communication were in the top three categories indicative of academic success (passed college exams, academic graduates, and vocational diploma). Only 65% of the Tracy oral preschool children achieved this level. It is also noted that 68% of those with early manual communication passed college entrance examinations, whereas 47% of the Tracy group and only 34% of the [third] group did.

Communication

A critical education-communication variable for a deaf child is his ability to write. However, there are no standardized measures of this. Hence, this variable and those of speech intelligibility and speech reading were assessed by going to the school records of all students who had left the California school and using the ratings there which had been obtained independently of the present research. These were on a three point scale of one point for Good, two for Fair, and three for Poor. Teachers' ratings of students still in school were also used when available. In all cases the raters compared the child against other deaf children of his age, thus making it possible to drop the matching variable of age and leaving only sex and IQ as the matching variables.

Significant between-group differences exist in written language competence. Those with early manual communication were superior to the other two groups. On the variables of speech intelligibility and speech reading, there were no significant differences among the three groups. Thus, the evidence indicates that the extensive early oral training of the Tracy program resulted in no better speech than did the relative absence of early oral training in the children of deaf parents.

CONCLUSIONS

It is clear from these data that early exposure to manual communication results in linguistic competence and educational achievement superior to that of extensive oral preschool education. In fact, this research and that of Craig (1964) and Phillips (1963) indicate that by the age of nine, deaf children who have had no preschool at all achieve academically at the same level as children who have had three years of oral preschool. The gains achieved through early manual communication do not "wash out," whereas those of preschool oral training do.

There have been previous studies which have shown that early manual communication resulted in better academic achievement (Denton, 1965; Hestor, 1963; Meadow, 1966; Montgomery, 1966; Quigley, 1968; Quigley and Frisina, 1961; Stevenson, 1964; Stuckless and Birch, 1966; Vernon and Koh, 1970). This is the first time early manual communication has been compared directly with a three year intensive oral preschool program involving both education of the child and the parent. The superiority of the early manual group even when they had no oral preschool at all is as conclusive as research findings can be because the experimental condition (early manual communication) was tested under the most difficult of conditions and compared to one of the best of oral preschools.

Several other considerations need to be set forth in interpreting these data. First, the deaf parents as a group had extremely low educational levels. Based on national norms, 30% could be expected to be functionally illiterate, 60% grade level 5.3 or below, and only 5% at 10th grade or above (Boatner, 1965; McClure, 1966). Their linguistic competence could be expected to be even lower (Moores, 1967). By contrast, the Tracy parents represent an above average group educationally and socio-economically.

Second, the Tracy children had the best of early amplification and oral home and school environment. The children of deaf parents did not have an "oral" environment. Their parents could not hear and correct their speech nor provide them examples of normal speech.

Third, the parents of the Tracy children had group counseling and in some cases private psychotherapy to help them understand their deaf child and their own problems. The deaf parents had none of this but instead had the profound psychological, sociological, and educational deprivation of deafness. Related to this is the unproven idea that deaf parents accept deaf children more readily than hearing parents. The Tracy parents were specifically helped by professionals to accept their child. The deaf parents were not. The findings on speech intelligibility deserve special mention in view of the emphasis most professionals place on the importance of an early oral environment. The Tracy children had the epitome of an oral environment and the children of deaf parents had the most non-oral situation possible. Yet there were no significant differences in speech intelligibility, a finding noted in many other studies (Moores, 1970). This suggests two things. First, early oral training even under optimal conditions yields no better results than the absence of oral training and an oral environment. Corollary to this, it may be that speech instruction with deaf children pays its biggest yield when begun at regular school age.

Another point relates to the selectivity of the sample. The children from Tracy who came to Riverside had a mean IQ of 114. They represented 56 of the 123 graduates of the Tracy Clinic. An IQ of 114 places a person in approximately the upper 20% of the population, indicating Tracy has a very select population in terms of intelligence. Data from other leading private oral facilities such as Central Institute and Clarke School indicate that those accepted are, on the average, also in the upper 20% (Blish, 1967; Fiedler, 1969; Elliott, 1967). Those who graduate or are referred to regular public schools average close to 120 in IQ and thus are in the upper 10% of the population. These data, the present study, and previous research on results of adherence to just oral approaches as contrasted to the values of total oral-manual or primarily manual communication are a mandate for early total communication for all deaf children.

Reasonable men can disagree over individual research findings and their policy implications. However, as study after study gives evidence indicating the limitations to just oralism as destructive to deaf children, there should be some point at which responsible professionals act accordingly and in the interest of these children.

REFERENCES

Blish, S. C. A survey of the results of the educational and guidance program of the Clarke School for the Deaf. *Proceedings of the International Conference on Oral Education of the Deaf.* 1, 329–344, 1967.

Boatner, E. B. The need of a realistic approach to the education of the deaf. Paper given to the joint convention of California Association of Parents of Deaf and Hard of Hearing Children, California Association of Teachers of the Deaf and Hard of Hearing and the California Association of the Deaf, November 6, 1965.

Circelli, V. G., Evans, J. W. & Schiller, J.: A reply to the report analysis. *Harvard Educational Rev.*, 1970, **40**, 105–129.

Craig, W. N. Effects of preschool training on the development of reading and lipreading skills of deaf children. *Amer. Ann. Deaf*, **109**, 280–296, 1964.

Denton, D. M. A study in the educational achievement of deaf children. Proceedings of the 42nd meeting of the Convention of American Instructors of the Deaf, Flint, Michigan, 428–438, 1965.

Elliot, L. I. Descriptive analysis of audiometric and psychometric scores of students at a school for the deaf. *J. Sp. and Hearing Res.*, **10**, 21–40, 1967.

Fiedler, Miriam F. Developmental studies of deaf children. ASHA monograph **13**, 11, 1969.

Hestor, M. S. Manual communication in Doctor, P. V. (Ed.), *Rep. of Proceedings of Inter. Cong. on Ed. of Deaf and of 41st Meeting of Conv. Amer. Inst. Deaf*, Gallaudet College, Washington, D. C. 211–221, 1963.

McClure, W. J. Current Problems and Trends in the education of the deaf. *Deaf American*, 1966, **18**, 8–14.

Meadow, Kathryn P. Early manual communication in relation to the deaf child's intellectual, social, and communicative functioning. *Amer. Ann. Deaf*, **113**, 29–41, 1968.

Montgomery, G. W. Relationship of oral skills to manual communication in profoundly deaf students. *Amer. Ann. Deaf*, **111**, 557–565, 1966.

Moores, D. F. Projected trends in language development for the deaf. Deaf American, 1967, **20,** 5–7.

Moores, D. F. An investigation of the psycholinguistic functioning of deaf adolescents. *Exceptional Children,* 1970, **36,** 645–652.

Phillips, W. D. Influence of preschool training on achievement in language arts, arithmetic concepts, and socialization of young deaf children. Unpublished doctoral dissertation. Teachers College, Columbia, 1963.

Quigley, S. P. The influence of fingerspelling on the development of language, communication, and educational achievement in deaf children. Mimeographed report, 1968. Department of Special Education, University of Illinois, Champaign.

Quigley, S. P. & Frisna, D. *Institutionalization and Psychoeducational Development in Deaf Children.* Council for Exceptional Children Research Monograph, Series A, No. 3, 1961.

Smith, M. S. Bissell, Joan S. Report analysis: The impact of Headstart. *Harvard Educational Rev.,* **40,** 51–104, 1970.

Stevenson, E. A. A study of the Educational Achievement of Deaf Children of Deaf Parents. Published by the California School for the Deaf, Berkeley, 1964.

Stuckless, E. R. & Birch, J. W. The influence of early manual communication on the linguistic development of deaf children. American Annals of the Deaf, 1966, **111,** 452–462.

Vernon, M. & Koh, S. D. Effects of early manual communication on achievement of deaf children. *American Annals of the Deaf,* 1970, **115,** 527–536.

SHOULD BLACK CHILDREN LEARN WHITE DIALECT?

Joan C. Baratz

Should black children learn white dialect? No. Should black children be taught standard English? Yes.

Standardization is a socio-linguistic fact of life. Societies are socially stratified—be the organization by clan, tribe, or nation-state. We might wish for complex, socially stratified societies where the spectrum of standard language included under the heading of *standard* all the different grammars and usages of speakers of the many varieties of that language. Sad to say, human behavior doesn't operate like that. To date, wherever research has been done—in Europe, Asia, and Africa—one variety of a language invariably becomes the standard. Grammar books are written in it;

From *Journal of the American Speech and Hearing Association,* 1970, *12,* 415–417. By permission of the *Journal of the American Speech and Hearing Association* and author.

its orthography is established. It is studied by the populace in school. Language standardization is a universal aspect of language variation in a national context, particularly when literacy is involved. There is standard English, standard German, standard (literary) Arabic, standard Yoruba, and standard Hausa. Standardization is not a political invention of racist whites.

WHAT IS STANDARD ENGLISH?

Opponents of teaching standard English to black children do not understand language standardization. They falsely assume that the standardization of English in America is a white plot to exploit the Negro, rob him of his heritage, and deny his language.

Those who argue against teaching standard English dialect to black children confuse learning standard English with "talking like a honky." By standard English I mean that dialect which uses a set of grammatical patterns in oral production that are similar to those used in the written form of the language. A black child might be taught standard English from a frame of reference widespread in the black community of "talkin' proper." Talking proper refers to language usage that generally conforms to the rules of standard English grammar, but may or may not be ethnically marked in its phonology. For example, a black individual talking "proper" might say "He asked for something to write with" or "He aks fo' somethin' to wri' wif."

Within the black community, "talking proper" is contrasted with "talkin' country" or "talkin' bad," which refers to nonstandard varieties of black English (Mitchell, 1969). Although black speakers may use adjective reversal, e.g., 'He a bad (usually drawn out vowel) cat," to mean on occasion the positive "He's a great guy," "talkin' bad" is not used in this way. In the black community "talkin' bad" means speaking a Negro nonstandard dialect. By Negro nonstandard dialect (sometimes referred to as black English) I mean the use of a set of distinctive grammar patterns that are not in conformity with the written forms of English (excluding such art forms as the use of Negro nonstandard dialect or other dialects in poetry and in dialogues) and which are used by a large portion of the black community.[1] Talking bad is important for in-group solidarity and, indeed, talking proper in an all black social group may be seen as "putting on airs." Nonetheless, the community has a concept of standard English that is carried in the notion "talking proper."

[1] Although there are many features in black nonstandard English that are also present in other nonstandard dialects and in standard English, there are also many features that are not shared. The thing that makes black nonstandard English a distinct dialect is the sum total of its features, whether shared with other dialects or not.

THE OPPOSITION

Those who oppose teaching standard English often claim that the parents don't want it. But most black parents insist that they want their children to learn to read and write and talk proper. Indeed, the problem is not so much that parents don't want their children to learn standard English; on the contrary, they are often so anxious to have their children learn "proper English" that they do not want Negro nonstandard dialect in the classroom —even if it is the best way to achieve competence in speaking, reading, and writing standard English.

Another frequent argument of those who object to teaching standard English to black children who speak only Negro nonstandard is that "the black man always is the one who has to change." Again, I submit that this admits to the erroneous notion that to learn another dialect or linguistic system means to change one's original system. I insist that teachers who wish to teach standard English to Negro nonstandard speakers learn their students' dialect. In the process the teacher sees that acquiring an additional linguistic system does not change the initial dialect system. The notion that learning an additional system means eradication and replacement of the existing system is completely false; just as one does not change or forget one's native language by learning a foreign language, he does not necessarily forget his first dialect when he learns a second.

Another argument presented by opponents of teaching standard English contends that Negro nonstandard dialect and standard English are mutually intelligible, therefore a nonstandard speaker need not learn standard English. I would submit that claim to empirical test. Mitchell's "unhesitating opinion" (1969) that the two systems are mutually intelligible is based on the scanty data of Labov (1968), Baratz (1969a), and on her own data on sentence repetition. Such tests are hardly measures of mutual intelligibility except in the loosest sense. At present we do not know the extent of presumed mutual intelligibility, especially at the primary school level where reading and writing skills are introduced in standard English. Indeed, the failure of children in such programs to acquire reading and writing skills in standard English may in part be a testament to the lack of mutual intelligibility of the two systems for the young Negro nonstandard speaking child.

The final frequent argument against teaching standard English crassly dismisses the truism that economic ability is dependent upon acquisition of standard English skills. Thus, opponents of teaching standard English argue lack of economic mobility in the black community is the result of white oppression (failure to hire blacks)—not the result of blacks' ignorance of standard English. In addition, they argue, knowledge of standard English does not automatically grant black mobility within the white power structure. Knowledge of standard English is not a guarantee of job mobility, and discrimination has played a large role in the economic disadvantage of blacks; nevertheless, access to white collar and professional jobs is dependent upon knowledge of standard English both within and outside the black community.

EDUCATIONAL REALITY

The arguments against teaching standard English to black Negro nonstandard speakers cannot stand up to linguistic and social reality. The issue is not political; it is educational. Essentially our discussion asks: What is to be the language arts program in public education for black children who are monodialectical speakers of Negro nonstandard English? Whatever the political situation—separation or integration—we are ultimately faced with the question of language learning. Separatism in this country, if effected tomorrow, would do little to solve the language problems of black Negro nonstandard speaking children. What language would a black America use to sign a treaty with white America, and to conduct its other national and international affairs? Standard English? Negro nonstandard? Swahili? Whatever its language, this state would still confront the educational problems of teaching its citizens to read, write, and speak its national tongue. If the new nation chose standard English, as would be likely, the problems would remain unchanged. If Negro nonstandard were chosen, it would have the additional problems of producing an orthography for that language and developing grammar books and printing texts for reading, science, social studies, physics, etc., in Negro nonstandard. (In other words, it would have to "standardize" Negro nonstandard English.) It would also have to teach Negro nonstandard to all black speakers of standard English. Or if Swahili were chosen, the educators in the new state would be faced with the problem of teaching the entire nation to read, write, and speak Swahili. Whatever the politics, a language teaching problem remains—as can be seen by the language situation in newly independent African states.

We do not, however, at present have a separate state, and it is very unlikely that we ever will. What then are the language factors involved in educating black children in white America?

It is, I believe, the desire of black parents that their children learn standard English. A minority voice in the white liberal establishment and the middle class "militants" who already speak standard English argues against teaching standard English. But, the black parent wants "in" to the existing system and, therefore, wants his child to be educated to function in that system.

One can learn a second dialect without destroying one's culture and identity (e.g., witness experiences with Swiss-German dialect and standard German). Economic mobility is partially dependent on such knowledge. Yet, there is an even more important reason why children should be taught oral standard English: competence in reading and writing standard English (which everybody agrees is important) is highly dependent on oral language skills.

LINGUISTIC INTERFERENCE

One cannot overemphasize the relationship between the oral and the written language system. Although there are stylistic differences in standard speech as compared with the more formal written system, the grammar in both the written and oral forms of standard English is essentially the same. The black child who speaks Negro nonstandard English still must learn to read and write standard English. If he is not taught oral standard English, his difficulties with the written system are compounded by linguistic inter- ference. His knowledge of Negro nonstandard will interfere with his written performance in standard English.

Linguistic interference—knowledge of one linguistic system interfering with performance in another linguistic system—is well documented. The development of the contrastive grammar technique in second language teaching is aimed precisely at eliminating the linguistic interference of the primary language system during the acquisition of a second system.

The educational literature on written skills of Negro children clearly illustrates the interference of black nonstandard English on performance in standard English. Contrary to the educational interpretation of that litera- ture, their "mistakes" are not random errors but occure precisely at those points where standard English and Negro nonstandard English diverge. Thus, teachers make lists saying that their students overuse *be*, or overuse *do* (*be* takes *do* in the interrogative "He be working"—"Do he be work- ing!"), use double negatives, fail to mark the plural, fail to use auxiliary verbs, fail to mark the possessive, use double subjects, and fail to mark the past (Loban, 1963).

Interference from black English on standard English is most evident in oral language performance, the predominant area of the language arts curriculum in which speech specialists have worked. An experiment with third and fifth grade inner city black children demonstrated that knowledge of one system (standard or black English) will invariably interfere with regenerating sentences in another system (black English or standard Eng- lish). The children in this study were asked to render sentences in both standard and black English. The city children were predominantly black English speakers whereas the suburban children were all monodialectal standard English speakers. When asked to repeat the standard English utterance, "I asked Tom if he wanted to go to the picture at the Howard," 97% of the black children responded with "I aks Tom did he wanna go to the picture at the Howard." In response to "Does Deborah like to play with the girl that sits next to her in school?" 60% of the black children responded "Do Deborah like to play with the girl what sit next to her in school?" On the other hand, when white suburban children were asked to regenerate the black English sentence "I aks Tom do he wanna go to the picture that be playin' at the Howard," 78% said "I asked Tom if he wanted to go to the picture that was playing at the Howard." When asked to repeat "Do Deborah like to play wif the girl what sit next to her at school," 68% of the white suburbanites responded with "Does Deborah like to play with the girl that sits next to her at school?" (Baratz, 1969b).

Linguistic interference becomes a major problem to the black child when he learns to read. Without knowledge of standard English, the black child, when confronted with the printed page, is actually given two jobs instead of one. He must not only decode the little black marks on the page but he must also translate them into black English as well. Only then can he make sense out of the material. But how can he translate if he hasn't been taught standard English? The enormous reading failure of low income black children (the overwhelming majority of whom speak Negro nonstandard English) is a testament to their quandary and their need to learn standard English. One can deal with the black child's lack of knowledge of standard English by teaching him first to read in his dialect and then, with the aid of transition texts that teach him the difference between his dialect and standard English, shift to standard English texts. We are doing just that at the Education Study Center. But, in the process of teaching him to read standard English, we are also teaching him to speak standard English.

Standard English is the *lingua franca* of the mainstream in America. If the black child is to participate and compete in that mainstream he must be able to read, write, and speak standard English. If he wishes to opt out of the mainstream and not use these skills, that's his choice; he can make it. If, however, he does not learn these skills, he can not "choose" to opt out. He is automatically excluded. We educators must provide the child with the tools of proficiency in reading, writing, and speaking standard English so that then he can choose to use or not use these tools.

REFERENCES

Baratz, J. A bi-dialectal task for determining language proficiency in economically disadvantaged Negro children. *Child Development*, **40**, 889–901 (1969). (a)

Baratz, J. Teaching reading in an urban Negro school. In J. Baratz and R. Shuy. *Teaching Black Children To Read*, Center for Applied Linguistics, Washington, D.C. (1969). (b)

Labov, W. A study of the nonstandard English of Negro and Puerto Rican Speakers in New York City. Coop. Res. Proj. #3288, Vol. I, U.S. Office of Education (1968).

Loban, W. The language of elementary school children. *NCTE Res. Rep. 1*, Champaign, Ill.: NCTE (1963).

Mitchell, C. Language behavior in a black urban community. Doctoral dissertation, Univ. California, Berkeley (1969).

Part Two   Beliefs, Values, and Decisions

People's values are fundamental to how they interpret the events that occur around and within them and how they decide to react to these events. The first of the two articles in this section, *Long-Range Experimental Modification of Values, Attitudes, and Behavior,* by Dr. Milton Rokeach, explores the consequences of inconsistencies in people's values and how discovery of these inconsistencies can influence subsequent decision-making behavior. Note particularly that the behavior in question in this study is not merely what people say; people often say one thing and do another. Rather, opportunities are provided for the people to act in accordance with their stated values and Dr. Rokeach checks to see if they actually do so or not.

The second of the two articles, *When You Face a Difficult Decision,* by Isabel Rockower, outlines a level-headed, orderly approach to intuitive decision making. It clearly illustrates that everyday decisions need not be the chaotic, hit-or-miss affairs that most of us settle for—the investment of a little thought and careful consideration could reduce the hazards of decision making and help us be less hesitant about making decisions. (The theoretical essay by Dr. Carl Rogers in Section 5 is closely related to the above two articles, and it may be a good idea to look over Rogers' essay before reading these two articles.)

LONG-RANGE EXPERIMENTAL MODIFICATION OF VALUES, ATTITUDES, AND BEHAVIOR

Milton Rokeach

Since the summer of 1966, a major portion of the research effort at Michigan State University has been devoted to a systematic investigation of the effects of experimentally induced feelings of self-dissatisfaction on long-range changes in values, attitudes, and behavior. The theoretical approach used differs from other approaches in experimental social psychology in three major respects:

1. Contemporary social psychologists generally agree that a necessary prerequisite to cognitive or attitude change is the presence of a state of imbalance or inconsistency. Two major experimental methods generally employed to create such a psychological state are (*a*) to induce a person to engage in behavior that is incompatible with his attitudes and values and (*b*) to expose him to information about the attitudes or values of significant others that are incompatible with his own attitudes and values. In contrast to these two well-known methods, we have employed a third method, namely, to expose a person to information designed to make him consciously aware of states of inconsistency that exist chronically within his own value-attitude system below the level of his conscious awareness.

2. While the main theoretical focus of contemporary social psychology is on the concept of attitude and on theories of attitude change, the present focus is on the concept of value and on a theory of value change. This shift from attitudes to values is made on the assumption that values are more fundamental components within a person's makeup than attitudes and, moreover, that values are determinants of attitudes as well as of behavior. Such a shift in focus becomes scientifically possible only if clear conceptual and operational distinctions can be made between the attitude and value concepts. Relevant discussions concerning this distinction are presented elsewhere (Rokeach, 1968a, 1968b, 1968c, 1968–69, 1971) and need not be repeated here except to say that an attitude represents an organization of interrelated beliefs that are all focused on a specific object or situation, while a value refers to a desirable *end state of existence* (terminal value) or a desirable *mode of behavior* (instrumental value). Terminal and instrumental values are generalized standards of the means and ends of human existence that transcend attitudes toward specific objects and situations. Thus defined, a person is conceived to have many

From the *American Psychologist*, 1971, *26*, 453–459. Copyright 1971 by the American Psychological Association, and reproduced by permission.

The research reported herein was supported by a grant from the National Science Foundation. Support of this research is gratefully acknowledged.

This paper was presented as part of a symposium, Human Behavior and Its Control, at the annual meeting of the American Association for the Advancement of Science, Chicago, Illinois, December 30, 1970.

thousands of attitudes but only several dozens of values. These relatively few values are conceived to determine many or all of man's attitudes as well as his behavior.

3. A third way in which our theoretical approach differs from those of other workers in the field of attitude change is in the conception and measurement of psychological states of dissonance (imbalance, inconsistency, incongruity). To speak of dissonance meaningfully is to identify at least two elements X and Y that are in some "dissonant relation" to one another. In Festinger's theory (and in other balance formulations), X and Y are typically identified as two cognitions (beliefs, attitudes, values, or cognitions about behavior), and X and Y will necessarily vary from one situation to another. In the present formulation, X and Y are not two cognitions that vary from one situation to another, but are invariant across all situations: X = self; Y = one's perceived performance or behavior in whatever the situation. X and Y are dissonant with one another if the person's behavior in any given situation leads him to become dissatisfied with himself; X and Y are consonant if his behavior in a given situation leads him to remain satisfied with himself. Such states of dissonance or self-dissatisfaction can be routinely measured in any experiment by simply asking the subject to report the extent to which he is satisfied or dissatisfied with whatever he may have said or done in a given situation. Such a measure is not a generalized measure of self-esteem or the self-concept; it is a situation-specific measure.

To date, a number of experiments have been carried out and are now under way in which situation-specific states of self-dissatisfaction have been induced concerning one's values, attitudes, and behavior, and in which the long-range effects of such induced states have been objectively ascertained. The general procedure employed in all these experiments is basically the same, as follows:

The experimental subjects (college students at Michigan State University, 97% of whom are white) are first asked to rank 18 terminal values (see Table 1) in order of importance, and also to state their position in writing toward civil rights demonstrations. They are then shown Table 1 and Table 2 which are reproduced here. Table 1, the subjects are informed, shows the average rankings of the 18 terminal values that had been previously obtained from Michigan State University students. The experimenter draws specific attention to the data concerning two target values—equality and freedom. More precisely, their attention is drawn to the finding that previously tested college students had ranked freedom first and equality eleventh on the average. To arouse feelings of self-dissatisfaction, the experimenter then interprets these findings to mean that "Michigan State University students, in general, are much more interested in their own freedom than they are in the freedom for other people." The experimental subjects are then invited to compare their own rankings of the same 18 values with the results shown in Table 1.

Table 1

Rank Order of Importance to 298 Michigan State University Students

Rank	Value
13	A comfortable life
12	An exciting life
6	A sense of accomplishment
10	A world at peace
17	A world of beauty
11	Equality
9	Family security
1	Freedom
2	Happiness
8	Inner harmony
5	Mature love
16	National security
18	Pleasure
14	Salvation
15	Social recognition
4	Self-respect
7	True friendship
3	Wisdom

Then, to increase the level of self-dissatisfaction to an even greater degree, subjects are asked to state the extent of their sympathy with the aims of civil rights demonstrators as follows: (*a*) "Yes, and I have personally participated in a civil rights demonstration"; (*b*) "Yes, but I have not participated in a civil rights demonstration"; (*c*) "No." Immediately afterward, they are shown Table 2 which displays a highly significant positive relationship between attitude toward civil rights demonstrations and value for equality.

The experimenter then interprets the results shown in Table 2 as follows:

> This raises the question as to whether those who are *against* civil rights are really saying that they care a great deal about *their own* freedom but are indifferent to other people's freedom. Those who are *for* civil rights are perhaps really saying they not only want freedom for themselves, but for other people too.

Once again the subjects are invited to compare their own rankings of equality and freedom and their own position on the civil rights issue with the results shown in Table 2.

By this self-confrontation procedure, many of the experimental subjects become aware for perhaps the first time in their lives of certain inconsistencies existing within their own value-attitude systems. For example, some subjects discover to their dismay that they had placed a high value on

Table 2

Average Rankings of Freedom and Equality by
Michigan State University Students for and
against Civil Rights

Value	Yes, and have participated	Yes, but have not participated	No, not sympathetic to civil rights
Freedom	6	1	2
Equality	5	11	17
Difference	+1	−10	−15

freedom but a low value on equality; others discover that they had expressed a pro-civil-rights attitude, yet had ranked equality relatively low in their value hierarchy, etc.

At the end of the experimental treatment, measurements of self-dissatisfaction are obtained by having the subjects rate, on an 11-point scale, how satisfied or dissatisfied they are in general with what they had found out about their values and attitudes (general satisfaction-dissatisfaction). They also indicate whether they are satisfied or dissatisfied with their ranking of each of the 18 values considered separately (specific satisfaction-dissatisfaction).

The control group merely fill out the value and attitude scales and are then dismissed. They are not shown Tables 1 and 2 and thus have no opportunity to think about or to discover that they might hold incompatible values, or an attitude that is incompatible with one or more of their values, or that they had engaged in behavior that is incompatible with their values or attitudes.

Experimental and control subjects are typically tested in groups of 20–25 at a time. The experimental session lasts for about 30–40 minutes and the control session for about 20 minutes.

Experiment 1

A preliminary report of Experiment 1 has already been published (Rokeach, 1968a, 1968c), and a fuller report, along with the results obtained from all the work we have done to date, will be presented in a monograph now in preparation. The major findings of Experiment 1 were (a) that induced states of self-dissatisfaction concerning one's values and attitudes led to highly significant changes in values and attitudes that were evident three-five months after the experimental treatment. Moreover, (b) measures of self-satisfaction-dissatisfaction, obtained at the end of the experimental session, predicted the value changes that were to be observed three weeks and three–five months afterward.

We were extremely reluctant, however, to accept these experimental findings as evidence of real, genuine long-range changes in values and attitudes because it seems unlikely, given the present state of theory and fact in social psychology, that any single and brief experimental session could have resulted in such long-range changes. More convincing evidence that such changes are indeed real changes would require additional data concerning behavioral effects as well as effects on values and attitudes (measured by paper-and-pencil tests), following the experimental treatment. Experiments 2 and 3 were therefore carried out in order to determine the long-range effects of experimental procedures designed to induce feelings of self-dissatisfaction on real-life behavior as well as on values and attitudes.

Experiments 2 and 3

These two experiments are basically identical to Experiment 1 except for the fact that unobtrusive measures of behavioral effects were obtained as well as measures of value and attitude change. Moreover, posttest measures were extended to include a much longer time interval following the experimental treatment. Dependent measures (values, attitudes, and behavior) were obtained 3 weeks, 3–5 months, 15–17 months, and 21 months after the experimental treatment.

The subjects of Experiments 2 and 3 were entering freshmen (fall 1967) of two newly founded small residential colleges at Michigan State University: James Madison College, for students interested in the social sciences (Experiment 2); Lyman Briggs College, for students interested in the natural sciences (Experiment 3). Experiments 2 and 3 were identical in all respects except for the fact that they were carried out with these two different types of college freshmen. As already described, the experimental treatment was designed to induce feelings of self-dissatisfaction by making the subjects consciously aware that they held certain incompatible values or that they held an attitude that is incompatible with certain of their values. And, as already stated, the only difference in the treatment of the experimental and control subjects was that the experimental subjects were exposed to Tables 1 and 2, and to brief interpretations of these tables, while control subjects were not so exposed.

Pretest measures of values and attitudes showed no significant differences between experimental and control groups. More specifically, experimental and control subjects were not significantly different from one another in their pretest rankings of equality or freedom or position on civil rights for blacks. Posttest measures were obtained not only for values and attitudes, but also for various unobtrusive kinds of behavior. The best unobtrusive measure, obtained 3–5 months after and also 15–17 months after the experimental treatment, involved a direct solicitation by first-class letter from the National Association for the Advancement of Colored People (on NAACP letterhead and envelope) addressed to each subject individually. The letter invited the subject to join the NAACP. To join, the subject had to (*a*) fill out an application blank, (*b*) enclose $1, and (*c*) drop the pre-stamped return envelope into a United States mailbox.

The results pertaining to value and attitude change for the three posttest periods are shown in Table 3.

Table 3 shows that significant increases in value for equality and freedom were found for the experimental subjects on all three posttests. Fifteen to 17 months after the experimental session, for example, the experimental group had increased its ranking of equality an average of 2.68 units (on an 18-point ranking scale), while the control group had increased its ranking of equality only .32 units. Similarly, 15–17 months after the experimental session, the experimental group had increased its ranking of freedom an average of 1.59 units, while the control group had increased its ranking of freedom only .22 units. These findings, therefore, suggest long-range value change as a result of the experimental treatment.

Consider next the findings concerning attitude change (equal rights for Negroes). The findings at Posttest 1—three weeks after the experimental session—showed a "sleeper" effect: no change in the experimental group at Posttest 1, and in fact, a slight "backlash effect." But significant increases in pro-civil-rights attitude were found for the experimental group at Post-tests 2 and 3, suggesting long-range attitude change as well as value change. Table 3 also shows another important finding—that attitude change took place among experimental subjects following changes in values.

In contrast to all these findings for the experimental group, no significant value or attitude changes were observed in control subjects for any of the three posttest measures. After 15–17 months in college, the subjects in the control groups had essentially the same values for equality and freedom and the same attitude toward civil rights they had started with.

Consider next the results . . . that pertain to the first NAACP solicitation initiated three–five months after the experimental treatment. Forty subjects responded to this solicitation by joining the NAACP, and an additional 13 subjects responded by writing a sympathetic, pro-civil-rights letter asking for more literature or information about the NAACP as a civil rights or-ganization. Thus, a total of 53 persons out of 366 responded to the NAACP solicitation. Of these 53, 39 were experimental subjects, and only 14 were control subjects. This difference between experimental and control groups is statistically significant at the .002 level of confidence.

. . . An identical NAACP solicitation was initiated a full year after the first solicitation—15–17 months after the experimental treatment. All ex-perimental and control subjects still in school were once again invited to join the NAACP or, if they had previously joined, to renew their member-ship by paying their $1 annual dues. This second solicitation resulted in 6 new NAACP members—5 experimental and 1 control. It moreover yielded 11 additional letters, all favorable in tone, requesting more information about the NAACP, 7 coming from experimental subjects and 4 from control subjects. Six subjects renewed their membership, 3 renewals coming from

Table 3

Mean Increases in Value for Equality and Freedom and in Pro-Civil-Rights
Attitude for Experimental and Control Groups

Value	Posttest 1 (3 weeks later)		Posttest 2 (3–5 months later)		Posttest 3 (15–17 months later)	
	Experimental	Control	Experimental	Control	Experimental	Control
Equality	1.91***	.68	2.80***	.71	2.68***	.32
Freedom	1.48***	.20	1.16**	.21	1.59***	.22
Equal rights for Negroes	−.46	−.69	2.09**	.20	2.79***	.86

Note.—Madison and Briggs data combined.
* $p < .05$.
** $p < .01$.
*** $p < .001$.

experimental subjects and 3 from control subjects. Finally 2 subjects who had joined the previous year wrote indignant letters complaining that they had not heard from the NAACP all year. Both of these letters came from experimental subjects. All told, a total of 17 experimental subjects responded to this second NAACP solicitation as against 8 control subjects. While these findings fall somewhat short of statistical significance, they are highly consistent with those obtained from the first solicitation.

When the results of the NAACP solicitations from both years are combined, . . . a total of 69 persons out of 366—about 20%—had responded to the NAACP solicitations. Fifty-one of these were experimental subjects, and only 18 were control subjects.[1] This represents a response rate of about 1 out of 10 for the control subjects compared with 1 out of 4 for the experimental subjects. These findings are significant beyond the .001 level. When considered along with the findings previously presented, they suggest long-range behavioral effects as well as long-range value and attitude changes as a result of the experimental treatment.

It should be emphasized that the results . . . are for Experiments 2 and 3 combined. As already stated, Experiments 2 and 3 were experiments carried out with two very different samples of college students—one consisting of students interested in the social sciences, the other consisting of students interested in the natural sciences. Separate statistical analyses carried out for these two samples also show significant posttest differences between experimental and control groups in values, attitudes, and behavior.

The nonobtrusive NAACP solicitation was, of course, experimentally invented, with the full knowledge and cooperation of the local NAACP chapter. For the James Madison study (Experiment 2), the long-range behavioral effects of the experimental treatment were also tested by taking advantage of a totally unanticipated *natural* behavioral event. Students in the newly formed James Madison College were required to register for courses in one of the following five "core" areas: (*a*) ethnic and religious intergroup relations; (*b*) international relations; (*c*) justice, morality, and constitutional democracy; (*d*) socioeconomic regulatory and welfare policy problems; (*e*) urban community policy problems. The Madison students first heard of these five core areas about five months after the experimental treatment, at which time they were requested to select one of these to major in. Table 4 shows the number of experimental and control subjects who were officially registered in the ethnic core program in the fall of 1969—21 months after the experimental treatment.

These results, statistically significant beyond the .01 level of confidence, again suggest long-range behavioral effects as a result of the experimental treatment. The experimental treatment had the effect of doubling student enrollments in the ethnic core program, when compared with enrollments

---

[1] One subject wrote letters requesting more information in response to both NAACP solicitations.

Table 4

Number of James Madison Students Selecting the Ethnic Core Program: Experiment 2

Group	Ethnic core program	Other core programs	Total
Experimental	28	39	67
Control	14	50	64
Total	42	89	131

by control subjects. And it should be noted that these effects were observed four–six months after the second NAACP solicitation.

I turn, finally to present some data that throw light on the basic psychological processes that underlie the long-range changes reported here for the experimental groups, namely, data on the effects of self-dissatisfaction on subsequent change. Table 5 shows the amount of absolute change in rankings of equality and freedom for experimental subjects who had reported at the end of the experiment that they were "satisfied" and "dissatisfied" with their rankings of equality and freedom. While both groups changed their rankings of equality and freedom substantially over the long course of the experiment, it is obvious that those who reported they were "dissatisfied" changed their average rankings of equality and freedom significantly more than did those who reported they were "satisfied." In other words, reports of specific satisfaction or dissatisfaction obtained from

Table 5

Effects of Reported Satisfaction or Dissatisfaction with Equality and Freedom Rankings at End of Experiment on Absolute Change in Equality and Freedom Rankings Observed: 3 Weeks, 3–5 Months, and 15–17 Months Later

Value	Satisfied		Dissatisfied		
	N	M change	N	M change	p
Equality					
3 weeks later	116	2.56	36	5.22	.0001
3–5 months later	83	3.58	25	5.96	.0017
15–17 months later	85	3.12	30	5.77	.0002
Freedom					
3 weeks later	116	2.22	36	4.86	.0001
3–5 months later	82	2.54	26	4.54	.0006
15–17 months later	85	2.72	30	5.20	.0004

experimental subjects at the end of the experiment predicted the changes in value rankings that were to be observed 3 weeks after the experiment, 3–5 months afterward, and 15–17 months afterward. Indeed, we found that those subjects who had reported they were "dissatisfied" with their ranking of any 1 of the 18 values shown in Table 1 typically showed more subsequent change on that value than those who reported they were "satisfied" with their ranking of that value. Moreover, measures of *general* self-dissatisfaction also predicted subsequent value change, but not as well as measures of *specific* self-dissatisfaction. . . .

REFERENCES

Rokeach, M. *Beliefs, attitudes, and values.* San Francisco: Jossey-Bass, 1968. (a)

Rokeach, M. The nature of attitudes. In, *International Encyclopedia of the Social Sciences.* New York: Macmillan, 1968. (b)

Rokeach, M. A theory of organization and change within value-attitude systems. *Journal of Social Issues,* 1968, **24,** 13–33. (c)

Rokeach, M. The role of values in public opinion research. *Public Opinion Quarterly,* 1968–69, **32,** 547–559.

Rokeach, M. The measurement of values and value systems. In G. Abcarian & J. W. Soule (Eds.), *Social psychology and political behavior.* Columbus, Ohio: Charles E. Merrill, 1971.

WHEN YOU FACE A DIFFICULT DECISION

Isabel Rockower

Decision: Claire Fields is in a flap. She's trying to decide whether to move the family to a new, compact apartment in a good neighborhood or stay in their big, old place in a run-down area. The lease is nearly up and she has to give a month's notice. Yet every time she's on the brink of making up her mind to do it, she remembers the advantages she'll have to give up and she starts to back away.

Decision: It's not that Sue Gannet *wants* to play the heavy parent. She doesn't like asking her sixteen-year-old daughter to leave parties and dances before the other girls do, but she also disapproves of late hours for high schoolers. What's a mother to do? In the Gannet household, she argues— long, fruitless wrangles that have been going on ever since the girl started to date—all because Sue can't decide what an appropriate curfew should be.

Decision: Fran Simmons was all set to redecorate the living room. The family can afford it at last, and her husband has given the go-ahead. So where is Fran? At dead stop. Terrified of the responsibility for spending all that money, Fran is so afraid she'll make a mistake she doesn't know what she wants. Every swatch of carpeting and wallpaper represents an impossible choice, and Fran has lapsed into complete paralysis.

Every adult has to face decisions like these—large ones and small ones —every day of his life. People who can't deal with them and make up their minds waste enormous amounts of time and emotional energy. For them, the act of deciding becomes more important than the question to be decided. And that's debilitating. It can also snowball into even bigger problems, for an unresolved decision causes people to become so tense, irritable and unsure of themselves that their ability to make even simple, routine decisions breaks down.

Some people don't even realize just how indecisive they are. They don't *appear* to have any trouble with decisions. They just never make any. Rationalizing that things have a way of working themselves out, they let circumstances—not their own choices—control their lives. Take, for example, the man who delays a decision on a new job until the offer is no longer open, then shrugs off the loss as a sort of omen. "It's probably better for me to stay where I am anyway," he tells his friends.

At the other extreme are people who avoid choosing from an assortment of options by camouflaging their indecisiveness with fast, snap decisions— usually unwise. The girl who on an impulse pays more than she can afford for a new winter coat because "it's exactly what I was looking for," is merely refusing to deal with all the pros and cons of making a compromise on another model—one in the right price bracket.

Indecision is so universal that social scientists have made studies to find out why some people have trouble making up their minds and how some of the torture can be eliminated from decision-making. These studies reveal several psychological reasons for indecision. One of the most common is perfectionism. No decision is perfect. A woman like Claire Fields, who stews around trying to find *everything* she wants in an apartment, will probably never be satisfied with any decision she makes. A more flexible woman settles for the solution that most nearly suits her needs. She realizes that something has to give, that every alternative has some positive features that have to be sacrificed.

A fuzzy sense of values is another obstacle to decision-making. Sue Gannet can't take a firm position on her daughter's curfew because she's not sure of her own convictions. She gets them all mixed up with her daughter's feelings. Instead of sticking to her guns, she wishes her daughter would come home voluntarily at a decent hour. That way Sue would get what she wants without playing the heavy parent. Faced with a choice of options that involve personal values and standards, a person has to know who she is and what she stands for. Otherwise, she'll never be able to decide which values are most important.

A third handicap is fear—the fear of taking a risk and the fear of making a mistake. For Fran Simmons, every decision regarding her living room decorations is haunted by fear of criticism from husband, in-laws and friends. She lacks faith in her own taste. Let's face it: risk is inherent in any decision. To make a decision, a person has to take a risk. People who believe in themselves are not terrified of either failure or the unknown. They don't feel compelled to make an absolutely perfect decision every time.

Fran's dilemma is one of the most common that women face. We all feel more confident making decisions in areas that we're knowledgeable about than in those that are unfamiliar. That's why people often have trouble with some decisions but not others. It has been found that women, in general, are more likely to fall apart over decorating decisions than any other kind. The cost involved is one big worry. Also, the average woman hasn't had as much experience buying carpeting and couches as she has with clothing and housewares. She doesn't feel as qualified to judge durability, styling and quality. In a subtler sense, her home is a projection of herself. If she's not altogether sure of her self-image, she's bound to be thrown by a choice between, for instance, a dramatic, modern couch and an elegant, traditional model.

Notwithstanding all the tired jokes on the subject, indecision is just as common among men as it is among women. Behaviorists find that men— including chief executives of important companies—are equally susceptible. Proof lies in the number of complex systems, games and theories that management consultants devise to help businessmen handle the flow of decisions that cross their desks. Stripped to their essentials all of these systems use the same basic approach: identifying the problem, gathering the facts, considering the alternatives and then making the move.

You can follow the same procedure in making your decisions. Begin by setting a time limit for yourself to make sure you don't stall around. Stalling is just a good way to put off a decision.

Next, analyze and define the problem. Many people get off the track right at the start by confusing the issues. For example, if you're trying to decide whether your elderly mother should live with you or stay in her own house, better make sure these are the right alternatives. If what she really needs is professional nursing care, neither place will do.

After you've clarified the issues, start digging up all the pertinent information you can find on the subject. The element of risk decreases in direct proportion to the amount of solid information you have to go on. Before businessmen make an important decision, they'll assign fact-finding committees or hire special consultants to research a problem. You can enlist the aid of a school advisory service, interior decorator, family service counselor or travel agent if you have to.

Now jot down all the alternative courses of action open to you—with their advantages and disadvantages. And cross them out in order of their *unimportance*. If you still can't make up your mind, sleep on the matter overnight. Fresh perspective in the morning should bring the basic issues into focus. Finally, take the plunge. Make your decision and forget about it.

This formula *seems* simple enough. Why, then, do so many people end up making their choice in a mood of confusion and desperation? The answer is that they fall into booby traps along the way. According to management psychologist Peter Gilbert, some people overdo the fact-gathering, making it almost an end in itself. They wind up with so much extraneous information they can't tell what's important and what isn't. Some are so cautious or analytical, they try to foresee all possible eventualities and get too tangled up in alternatives to know what they really want. Others want everything and can't settle for less.

Every option has its advantages and its disadvantages. The basic conflict (and the real agony) sets in when you start to weigh your gains and losses. In a series of experiments to find out how people make up their minds, one psychologist found that his subjects began to procrastinate the minute they had to face the fact that they couldn't have everything. As soon as they tentatively chose one course of action, the option they were about to reject suddenly seemed twice as attractive. As a result, they wore themselves out with their shuttling back and forth. To imagine how they felt, picture yourself choosing between a much-needed coat of paint for the house or a much-wanted trip to Florida. Just as you're ready to opt for the paint, the prospect of warm sun and white sands suddenly seems so irresistible, and the mess of painting so unpleasant, you start examining the issues all over again.

This kind of a bind is common to three basic decision situations. The first is a choice between two equally attractive alternatives. A young girl who has to choose between two desirable boyfriends naturally doesn't want to give up either one. The second is a choice between two equally unpleasant courses. A woman trying to decide whether to undergo corrective surgery or live with her ailment finds the closer she gets to either of these unhappy choices, the more impossible each seems. The third and subtlest decision situation is one with a perfect balance of positive and negative factors. A wife who has the choice of a two-week vacation with her husband and the rest of the summer in town, or all summer in a country cottage that her husband can get to only on weekends, would have to be very clear about her own values to know how to choose.

Some people, to avoid all these emotional and mental gymnastics, cop out by making snap decisions without considering the alternatives. Although they appear to other people (and to themselves) as decisive men and women, they are actually resorting to "what might be called decision avoidance," explains psychologist Ladd Wheeler of New York University.

But snap decisions should not be confused with intuitive decisions. In making an intuitive decision, you consider all the available facts, but instead of deciding solely on rational grounds you let your feelings influence the way you interpret the facts. To some extent your feelings enter every decision. Even a matter-of-fact choice between steak and roast beef is influenced by what tastes best to you.

When it comes to decisions that involve people, ethics or the unknown future, you have to rely almost solely on your instincts. Take the woman who's deciding to go back to school so she can get a teaching job when her children are older. She can't be sure what their needs, her husband's attitude, the job market or her own physical capacity will be in three or four years. There are so many unknown quantities, she has to listen to her intuition. The difficulty, says psychologist Charles Hawkins, is that many people are not tuned in to themselves. They block off their feelings so that their real wants don't come through loud and clear. The acid test is how satisfied you are with a decision you've made. If you feel uneasy, chances are you either ignored your feelings or had no confidence in them. When that happens, experts advise, stop trying to be rational. Scrap the decision and do what you *feel* is right.

When it comes to joint decisions, one person's feelings aren't the only consideration, of course. It's what two or more people can agree on that matters. In one sense, joint decisions are easier because someone else shares the responsibility. In another, they are trickier because two people's individual values, priorities and personalities have to mesh. Dr. Orville Brim, President of the Russell Sage Foundation, found in a study of the decision-making behavior of a hundred married couples that the actual working mechanism of a joint decision was not so much a compromise as one person subordinating his desires to the other. In lower social-economic families, the husbands had the last word. In middle-class families, the final responsibility shifted back and forth between husbands and wives without any regard to traditional sexual roles. Recognizing that unanimity was required of them, these couples worked out a democratic arrangement whereby either partner would defer to the one who had the most experience or the strongest interest in the matter.

Since joint decisions require a certain amount of give-and-take, they are infinitely easier when husbands and wives are truly concerned about each other. A husband who knows his wife will be seriously upset if he accepts a promotion that means moving to another state may decide that the transfer would be too hard on her and turn down the job. On the other hand, if his wife knows how career-minded he is, she may swallow her objections and defer to his needs, realizing that she will benefit indirectly from his feelings of achievement.

This is the ideal way to reach a marital decision. At the other end are three destructive approaches that inevitably lead to trouble, says Sanford Sherman, associate executive director of Jewish Family Service. First, is the coerced decision: A husband removes himself from the problem abdicating all responsibility. He creates a vacuum, forcing his wife to make the decision by herself. Then he comes to life and accuses her of robbing him of his manhood.

Another fatal way to handle joint decisions is the unilateral approach.

Either the husband or the wife is incapable of making a shared, cooperative decision, so he or she simply decides alone. The knowledge that his opinion is neither sought nor respected hurts the partner who has to stand aside and receive the edict.

Finally, there is the omissive decision: neither partner ever gets around to making a decision. They live from day to day without any direction and without providing any guidance for their children.

Parents have to see to it that their children also learn to cope with decisions. Here's how to do it: When a child comes to you with *small* decisions, pass the buck right back to him. A youngster can learn only if he is allowed to confront problems, lay out options and accept the consequences on his own. Unfortunately, many parents stymie their children's development. Dr. Brim finds that overprotective or dominating parents usually don't give their children the freedom to experiment on their own. They make it impossible for them to acquire any decision-making know-how. Dr. Hawkins has found in his practice that parents who are inhibited themselves unwittingly train their children to repress emotion so that, eventually, they lose touch with their intuitive feelings. Psychiatrist Marthe Gassmann notices that mothers and fathers frequently damage a young child's will by confusing him. Some bewilder him with their inconsistencies. They can't make up their own minds or they can't agree on what they expect of the child. Others confuse their children by giving them too many choices before they're mature enough to handle them.

The most effective way to train children is by example. Indecision is highly contagious. A mother who backtracks, vacillates and postpones decisions communicates her uncertainty to her child. If, as a parent, you have trouble with decisions, you should make a point of cultivating decisiveness. Psychologists and psychiatrists insist it can be done. Let's review the guidelines.

• Use a clock. If you're a snap-decisionmaker, train yourself to "take ten" while you pause and consider consequences. If you tend to be a procrastinator, set a time limit and stick to it. Decisions can be neither left to chance nor postponed. If the alternatives are that evenly balanced, for heaven's sake flip a coin! But decide.

• Learn to define problems before you start looking for answers. Make sure you're not comparing apples and oranges.

• Lay out a decision; weigh the facts, and evaluate the options—but not interminably.

• If the facts are insufficient, trust your instincts.

• Learn to distinguish between important and unimportant decisions, and don't spend the same amount of time on both.

• Don't try to anticipate every eventuality—it's impossible.

• Don't try to have your cake and eat it too; every decision involves some compromise.

• Keep your cool. You need to be calm to exercise good judgment.
• Don't solicit too many people's opinions—it's confusing and an imposition to boot.
• Once a decision is made, forget it. Postmortems only undermine your confidence to handle future problems.

These guidelines can really expedite the mechanical or external phases of decision-making. They lead right up to the actual moment of decision. Then you're on your own. When the facts are in and counted, the final phase is a very private one that takes place deep within oneself. As the late President John F. Kennedy described it in his foreword to Theodore C. Sorensen's book, *Decision-making in the White House*, "The essence of ultimate decision remains impenetrable to the observer—often, indeed, to the decider himself." In the final hour, you have to draw on your own inner resources—your judgment, your values and your courage. That means you first have to know yourself, and then believe in yourself.

Part Three   Love, Marriage, and Sex

Fall in love, get married, settle down, raise a family—most of us regard this as the natural pattern of events. In fact, this pattern is so broadly accepted that anyone who does not follow it may be subjected to strong social pressure to conform, for example, the woman who is still unmarried at age 30, the couple that lives together without getting married, the married couple that elects to have no children. But, when you stop and think about it, the rationale for the traditional marriage-family pattern is becoming increasingly difficult to defend. For example, why should people commit themselves to lifelong marriage contracts when divorce rate makes it clear that such a contract is likely to be broken? Or, what is going to happen to the traditional marriage pattern as a result of the trend toward smaller families that will require that a shorter period in one's life be devoted to childrearing? Or, what will happen to marriage as more and more women become employed and, therefore, less dependent upon men for economic security? In short, it may well be time to consider alternatives to the traditional pattern, alternatives that might achieve the same positive ends as marriage but which may be better suited to current and future social conditions.

The first two of the three readings that follow examine marriage and some alternatives to marriage. In the first, *Marriage as a Wretched Institution*, Dr. Mervyn Cadwallader looks at the stresses that modern life places on marriage and at the inadequacy of the womens' magazines' prescription that everything will turn out OK if you work at a marriage hard enough.

The second article, *Marriage Versus the Counter Culture*, by Dr. Gail Putney Fullerton, is a case study of one alternative to the traditional pattern, the rural commune. Inclusion of this article does not mean that communal living is the best alternative. As you will see, communal life, like the traditional pattern it replaces, is not always very pleasant—the problem of retaining one's individuality while living with one or more other persons is difficult in any arrangment, traditional or otherwise.

The third reading is different from the first two in that it does not focus on marriage *per se*. However, it is similar to the others in that it is an argument for diversity; it demonstrates that what is desirable for some people may not be desirable for others. *What is Normal Sex Behavior?*, by Dr. Albert Ellis, examines a variety of definitions of "normal" (finding each inadequate) and describes how people's sexual norms and tastes reflect the constraints imposed by the culture in which they happen to live.

MARRIAGE AS A WRETCHED INSTITUTION

Mervyn Cadwallader

Our society expects us all to get married. With only rare exceptions we all do just that. Getting married is a rather complicated business. It involves mastering certain complex hustling and courtship games, the rituals and the ceremonies that celebrate the act of marriage, and finally the difficult requirements of domestic life with a husband or wife. It is an enormously elaborate round of activity, much more so than finding a job, and yet while many resolutely remain unemployed, few remain unmarried.

Now all this would not be particularly remarkable if there were no question about the advantages, the joys, and the rewards of married life, but most Americans, even young Americans, know or have heard that marriage is a hazardous affair. Of course, for all the increase in divorce, there are still young marriages that work, unions made by young man and women intelligent or fortunate enough to find the kind of mates they want, who know that they want children and how to love them when they come, or who find the artful blend between giving and receiving. It is not these marriages that concern us here, and that is not the trend in America today. We are concerned with the increasing number of others who, with mixed intentions and varied illusions, grope or fling themselves into marital disaster. They talk solemnly and sincerely about working to make their marriage succeed, but they are very aware of the countless marriages they have seen fail. But young people in particular do not seem to be able to relate the awesome divorce statistics to the probability of failure of their own marriage. And they rush into it, in increasing numbers, without any clear idea of the reality that underlies the myth.

Parents, teachers, and concerned adults all counsel against premature marriage. But they rarely speak the truth about marriage as it really is in modern middle-class America. The truth as I see it is that contemporary marriage is a wretched institution. It spells the end of voluntary affection, of love freely given and joyously received. Beautiful romances are transmuted into dull marriages, and eventually the relationship becomes constricting, corrosive, grinding, and destructive. The beautiful love affair becomes a bitter contract.

The basic reason for this sad state of affairs is that marriage was not designed to bear the burdens now being asked of it by the urban American middle class. It is an institution that evolved over centuries to meet some very specific functional needs of a nonindustrial society. Romantic love was viewed as tragic, or merely irrelevant. Today it is the titillating prelude to domestic tragedy, or, perhaps more frequently, to domestic grotesqueries that are only pathetic.

Marriage was not designed as a mechanism for providing friendship, erotic experience, romantic love, personal fulfillment, continuous lay psychotherapy, or recreation. The Western European family was not designed to carry a lifelong load of highly emotional romantic freight. Given its present structure, it simply has to fail when asked to do so. The very idea of an irrevocable contract obligating the parties concerned to a lifetime of romantic effort is utterly absurd.

Other pressures of the present era have tended to overburden marriage with expectations it cannot fulfill. Industrialized, urbanized America is a society which has lost the sense of community. Our ties to our society, to the bustling multitudes that make up this dazzling kaleidoscope of contemporary America, are as formal and superficial as they are numerous. We all search for community, and yet we know that the search is futile. Cut off from the support and satisfactions that flow from community, the confused and searching young American can do little but place all his bets on creating a community in microcosm, his own marriage.

And so the ideal we struggle to reach in our love relationship is that of complete candor, total honesty. Out there all is phony, but within the romantic family there are to be no dishonest games, no hypocrisy, no misunderstanding. Here we have a painful paradox, for I submit that total exposure is probably always mutually destructive in the long run. What starts out as a tender coming together to share one's whole person with the beloved is transmuted by too much togetherness into attack and counterattack, doubt, disillusionment, and ambivalence. The moment the once-upon-a-time lover catches a glimpse of his own hatred, something precious and fragile is shattered. And soon another brave marriage will end.

The purposes of marriage have changed radically, yet we cling desperately to the outmoded structures of the past. Adult Americans behave as though the more obvious the contradiction between the old and the new, the more sentimental and irrational should be their advice to young people who are going steady or are engaged. Our schools, both high schools and colleges, teach sentimental rubbish in their marriage and family courses.

The texts make much of a posture of hard-nosed objectivity that is neither objective nor hard-nosed. The basic structure of Western marriage is never questioned, alternatives are not proposed or discussed. Instead, the prospective young bride and bridegroom are offered housekeeping advice and told to work hard at making their marriage succeed. The chapter on sex, complete with ugly diagrams of the male and female genitals, is probably wedged in between a chapter on budgets and life insurance. The message is that if your marriage fails, you have been weighed in the domestic balance and found wanting. Perhaps you did not master the fifth position for sexual intercourse, or maybe you bought cheap term life rather than a preferred policy with income protection and retirement benefits. If taught honestly, these courses would alert the teenager and young adult to the realities of matrimonial life in the United States and try to advise them on how to survive marriage if they insist on that hazardous venture.

But teen-agers and young adults do insist upon it in greater and greater numbers with each passing year. And one of the reasons they do get married with such astonishing certainty is because they find themselves immersed in a culture that is preoccupied with and schizophrenic about sex. Advertising, entertainment, and fashion are all designed to produce and then to exploit sexual tension. Sexually aroused at an early age and asked to postpone marriage until they become adults, they have no recourse but to fill the intervening years with courtship rituals and games that are supposed to be sexy but sexless. Dating is expected to culminate in going steady, and that is the beginning of the end. The dating game hinges on an important exchange. The male wants sexual intimacy, and the female wants social commitment. The game involves bartering sex for security amid the sweet and heady agitations of a romantic entanglement. Once the game reaches the going-steady stage, marriage is virtually inevitable. The teen-ager finds himself driven into a corner, and the one way to legitimize his sex play and assuage the guilt is to plan marriage.

Another reason for the upsurge in young marriages is the real cultural break between teen-agers and adults in our society. This is a recent phenomenon. In my generation there was no teen culture. Adolescents wanted to become adults as soon as possible. The teen-age years were a time of impatient waiting, as teen-age boys tried to dress and act like little men. Adolescents sang the adults' songs ("South of the Border," "The Music Goes Round and Round," "Mairzy Doats"—notice I didn't say anything about the quality of the music), saw their movies, listened to their radios, and waited confidently to be allowed in. We had no money, and so there was no teen-age market. There was nothing to do then but get it over with. The boundary line was sharp, and you crossed it when you took your first serious job, when you passed the employment test.

Now there is a very definite adolescent culture, which is in many ways hostile to the dreary culture of the adult world. In its most extreme form it borrows from the beats and turns the middle-class value system inside out. The hip teen-ager on Macdougal Street or Telegraph Avenue can buy a

costume and go to a freak show. It's fun to be an Indian, a prankster, a
beat, or a swinging troubadour. He can get stoned. That particular trip
leads to instant mysticism.

Even in less extreme forms, teen culture is weighted against the adult
world of responsibility. I recently asked a roomful of eighteen-year-olds to
tell me what an adult is. Their deliberate answer, after hours of discussion,
was that an adult is someone who no longer plays, who is no longer playful.
Is Bob Dylan an adult? No, never! Of course they did not want to remain
children, or teens, or adolescents; but they did want to remain youthful,
playful, free of squares, and free of responsibility. The teen-ager wants
to be old enough to drive, drink, screw, and travel. He does not want to
get pushed into square maturity. He wants to drag the main, be a surf bum,
a ski bum, or dream of being a bum. He doesn't want to go to Vietnam,
or to IBM, or to buy a split-level house in Knotty Pines Estates.

This swing away from responsibility quite predictably produces frictions
between the adolescent and his parents. The clash of cultures is likely to
drive the adolescent from the home, to persuade him to leave the dead
world of his parents and strike out on his own. And here we find the central
paradox of young marriages. For the only way the young person can escape
from his parents is to assume many of the responsibilities that he so reviles
in the life-style of his parents. He needs a job and an apartment. And he
needs some kind of emotional substitute, some means of filling the emotional
vacuum that leaving home has caused. And so he goes steady, and sooner
rather than later, gets married to a girl with similar inclinations.

When he does this, he crosses the dividing line between the cultures.
Though he seldom realizes it at the time, he has taken the first step to
adulthood. Our society does not have a conventional "rite of passage." In
Africa the Masai adolescent takes a lion test. He becomes an adult the
first time he kills a lion with a spear. Our adolescents take the domesticity
test. When they get married they have to come to terms with the system
in one way or another. Some brave individuals continue to fight it. But
most simply capitulate.

The cool adolescent finishing high school or starting college has a skeptical view of virtually every institutional sector of his society. He knows that
government is corrupt, the military dehumanizing, the corporations rapa-
cious, the churches organized hypocrisy, and the schools dishonest. But the
one area that seems to be exempt from his cynicism is romantic love and
marriage. When I talk to teen-agers about marriage, that cool skepticism
turns to sentimental dreams right out of *Ladies' Home Journal* or the hard-
hitting pages of *Reader's Digest*. They all mouth the same vapid platitudes
about finding happiness through sharing and personal fulfillment through
giving (each is to give 51 percent). They have all heard about divorce, and
most of them have been touched by it in some way or another. Yet they
insist that their marriage will be different.

So, clutching their illusions, young girls with ecstatic screams of joy lead
their awkward brooding boys through the portals of the church into the

land of the Mustang, Apartment 24, Macy's, Sears, and the ubiquitous drive-in. They have become members in good standing of the adult world.

The end of most of these sentimental marriages is quite predictable. They progress, in most cases, to varying stages of marital ennui, depending on the ability of the couple to adjust to reality; most common are (1) a lackluster standoff, (2) a bitter business carried on for the children, church, or neighbors, or (3) separation and divorce, followed by another search to find the right person.

Divorce rates have been rising in all Western countries. In many countries the rates are rising even faster than in the United States. In 1910 the divorce rate for the United States was 87 per 1000 marriages. In 1965 the rate had risen to an estimated figure of well over 300 per 1000 in many parts of the country. At the present time some 40 percent of all brides are between the ages of fifteen and eighteen; half of these marriages break up within five years. As our population becomes younger and the age of marriage continues to drop, the divorce rate will rise to significantly higher levels.

What do we do, what can we do, about this wretched and disappointing institution? In terms of the immediate generation, the answer probably is, not much. Even when subjected to the enormous strains I have described, the habits, customs, traditions, and taboos that make up our courtship and marriage cycle are uncommonly resistant to change. Here and there creative and courageous individuals can and do work out their own unique solutions to the problem of marriage. Most of us simply suffer without understanding and thrash around blindly in an attempt to reduce the acute pain of a romance gone sour. In time, all of these individual actions will show up as a trend away from the old and toward the new, and the bulk of sluggish moderates in the population will slowly come to accept this trend as part of social evolution. Clearly, in middle-class America, the trend is ever toward more romantic courtship and marriage, earlier premarital sexual intercourse, earlier first marriages, more extramarital affairs, earlier first divorces, more frequent divorces and remarriages. The trend is away from stable lifelong monogamous relationships toward some form of polygamous male-female relationship. Perhaps we should identify it as serial or consecutive polygamy, simply because Americans in significant numbers are going to have more than one husband or more than one wife. Attitudes and laws that make multiple marriages (in sequence, of course) difficult for the romantic and sentimental among us are archaic obstacles that one learns to circumvent with the aid of weary judges and clever attorneys.

Now, the absurdity of much of this lies in the fact that we pretend that marriages of short duration must be contracted for life. Why not permit a flexible contract perhaps for one to two or more years, with periodic options to renew? If a couple grew disenchanted with their life together, they would not feel trapped for life. They would not have to anticipate and then go through the destructive agonies of divorce. They would not have to carry about the stigma of marital failure, like the mark of Cain on their foreheads. Instead of a declaration of war, they could simply let their contract lapse, and while still friendly, be free to continue their romantic quest. Sexualized romanticism is now so fundamental to American life—and is bound to become even more so—that marriage will simply have to accommodate itself to it in one way or another. For a great proportion of us it already has.

What of the children in a society that is moving inexorably toward consecutive plural marriages? Under present arrangements in which marriages are ostensibly lifetime contracts and then are dissolved through hypocritical collusions or messy battles in court, the children do suffer. Marriage and divorce turn lovers into enemies, and the child is left to thread his way through the emotional wreckage of his parents' lives. Financial support of the children, mere subsistence, is not really a problem in a society as affluent as ours. Enduring emotional support of children by loving, healthy, and friendly adults is a serious problem in America, and it is a desperately urgent problem in many families where divorce is unthinkable. If the bitter and poisonous denouement of divorce could be avoided by a frank acceptance of short-term marriages, both husbands and wives and ex-husbands and ex-wives treat each other decently, generously, and respectfully, their children will benefit.

The braver and more critical among our teenagers and youthful adults will still ask, But if the institution is so bad, why get married at all? This is a tough one to deal with. The social pressures pushing any couple who live together into marriage are difficult to ignore even by the most resolute rebel. It can be done, and many should be encouraged to carry out their own creative experiments in living together in a relationship that is wholly voluntary. If the demands of society to conform seem overwhelming, the couple should know that simply to be defined by others as married will elicit married-like behavior in themselves, and that is precisely what they want to avoid.

How do you marry and yet live like gentle lovers, or at least like friendly roommates? Quite frankly, I do not know the answer to that question.

MARRIAGE VERSUS THE COUNTER CULTURE

Gail Putney Fullerton

One of the most significant . . . [factors in] the communal counter culture is the preference . . . for consensual union rather than legal marriage. Some

From *Survival in Marriage: Introduction to Family Interaction, Conflicts, and Alternatives* by Gail Putney Fullerton. Copyright © 1972 by Holt, Rinehart and Winston, Inc. Reprinted by permission of Holt, Rinehart and Winston, Inc.

of the young people living in communes are married (some are even married to each other). But many are divorced or single, and in either case show little inclination to marry. Within the communal "family," consensual union permits flexibility. . . . Relationships are not expected to be permanent, the males may not be able to undertake the financial responsibility of a wife and children, the women may not want to tie themselves to men who are immature and often demanding.

Again, the counter culture has made virtue of necessity. The pair bond which marriage tends to create is seen as a divisive force within the communal "family." While it is possible for married couples to live in a communal setting, this is seldom the pattern. This is probably why, to the outside world, the commune looks like an experiment in group marriage or some kind of orgiastic cult. There are, however, surprisingly stable couple relationships in many communes, and the special relationship is recognized by a status: the Old Man or the Old Lady.

Within such a relationship, male is expected to be dominant. As Downing (1970) has remarked, the communal life style tends to restore the sharp differentiation between the sexes that the urban and suburban middle classes have abandoned. This is often the case in city communes.

> In the tribal families, while both sexes work, women are generally in a service role, such as waitress, masseuse, and secretary. Male dominance is held desirable by both sexes. The recognized dress is in a semi-rural or western style which emphasizes sexual differences. The women tend to wear long dresses and long hair, while the men tend toward the western or frontier clothing of boots, rough-woven cloths, and outdoor jackets. (Downing 1970:123)

The differentiation of sex roles is even more marked among the rural communal "families," for basic work roles require more division between "man's work" and "woman's work." The rural communes are in fact quite traditional: their life style has gone so far out that it has circled back; perhaps in value systems as in the universe itself, infinity is finite.

One of the ways in which the communal "families" have deliberately turned back toward the past is in the attempt to integrate work and life. The craft communes, and especially the rural communes, have tried to combine life-support and recreational activities in a single sphere, and to integrate the aspects of life that are usually fragmented in the larger society.

Hyman Rodman, writing of the misconceptions that the middle-class has of lower-class families, comments on the middle-class proclivity for ". . . viewing certain patterns as *problems* when, in reality, they can as easily be viewed as *solutions*" (1964:66). The comment can be applied equally to the middle-class way of viewing the communes. The voluntary poverty, the present-time orientation, the preference for consensual union, and other aspects of the communal life-style which are perceived as problems by many middle-class and middle-aged Americans are perceived by the young people who have chosen to live communally as solutions to problems they have encountered in the larger society.

THE LIFE-STYLE OF A RURAL COMMUNE

The particular rural commune that will be examined here has some features which are typical of most such groups and others which are unique. Typically, there has been an imbalance in the sex ratio throughout most of the commune's existence. The price of integrating work and family life is often relative poverty, which more young men than girls seem to be able to find romantic. An atypical feature of this commune is their attempt to integrate the work roles of men and women.

This commune has come close to achieving the ideal of "equality of all members in a freely giving, freely receiving cooperative" (Downing 1970: 20). Many communes that have achieved stability and duration have done so by accepting the leadership of an older man or woman who becomes the dominant family elder. This "family" has carefully avoided the evolution of a single leader, in part by specifically ruling out the participation in the group of any highly skilled or older individual.

The commune is located in the coastal mountains of southern Oregon on a 160-acre tract of second-growth timber. The "family" is buying the land on a ten-year mortgage. Most of their land is contained within a box canyon, and is steep and heavily timbered. But there are about five acres of meadowland suitable for a garden. A stream runs through the meadow, and there are several springs on the property. The men of the "family" built their large, octagonal lodge from logs they felled on their own land and hauled down to the site. (Their building technique seems to have been derived from their childhood experience with "Lincoln Logs," but the building is basically sound and quite spacious, centering on a large, open-hearth fireplace with a metal hood.)

The "family" has about a dozen members, some relative newcomers, all city-bred but one or two with a background of summer homes in the wilds. Members range in age from nineteen to twenty-nine, with most in their mid-twenties.

The two young people interviewed live as a couple, and are probably the two who would be considered the founders of the commune if they were willing to be singled out in that manner. The young man, whom I shall call Thad, is nineteen years old and the youngest member of the group. He graduated from high school at the age of sixteen, then spent about two years as a nonstudent at Berkeley, living in a succession of urban communes, some of which were little more than "crash pads" and some of which had more structure. His "Old Lady" is twenty-three years old. She dropped out of a large midwestern university in the last quarter of her senior year; she has been married, but left the more conventional relationship for reasons which she makes clear. I shall call her Jill.

Why They Chose the Commune

JILL: I met some people from Oregon and decided that I wanted to visit them and see what it was that they were doing, because being isolated and relatively free from the standards of our society, I thought that our chances for creating an alternative would be best. I didn't really know any of them, I came up to Oregon to visit, to see what it was like.

I felt that the life-style that was open to me in American society was not what I wanted. The only thing that I wanted to be was an artist and being a female and being an artist in that society, the chances are that I would have gone into teaching. Just for security, for one thing. And I didn't really want to teach, I wanted to make things. I tried working and it was totally unsatisfactory. I worked in various office jobs, on the campus, in the photography department, in the library—I have had probably ten or fifteen jobs.

I didn't want to live in the city, primarily because the atmosphere there was too negative for me. It could be called just the vibrations of day in, day out routine, and the fact that there is hardly anything living there. There are no trees, and most of the plants that live there are hybrids and appear artificial to me. I really can't identify with the city structure—the social games, the importance placed on money, for one thing, which is a totally abstract concept which really has very little relevance to human values.

I met Thad through a house I lived in—he was a friend of another fellow who lived there, and Thad had been in Mexico when we had been moving in with this fellow—or rather, he had moved and we moved and got a house together. And Thad was a friend of Steve's and came over to see Steve, and I had just come back from Oregon the first time I saw him. I was married at the time, and that is no longer existing. My ex-husband didn't want to live in the country, but when I saw this life-style, I knew that I wouldn't be happy living any other way. It was fundamental to my existence. And to my happiness. And so I met Thad, and Thad had been wanting to do this for quite a while—I guess for about a year he had been thinking about going to the country—and I met him and I said, "Let's go to Oregon."

At that time I was really enthusiastic and talking to everybody I met about it, and how it would be a chance to attempt to start something new, a positive alternative. And I met Thad and he came up and met the people at the Family of the Mystic Arts. They liked him a lot, but told us that we couldn't stay there. They were already full, they didn't need his skills, they didn't need his knowledge, and they didn't really want just another number. And they told us to go do it on our own. I was with him. They told us to go and do it on our own and we realized that that was probably best. Had we stayed there, we realized about four months later, there would have been a high probability that we would have left and probably not done this trip, because of the change of personnel there and what was happening.

So we went back to Berkeley. This was the end of June, the third week in June—and spent the summer, until the end of August, talking to people, people that we had known, people that were friends of ours, but not particularly close. We had none of us ever lived together. Some of us had lived with each other briefly, maybe. And Dick and Patricia and Steve had known each other when they lived in Connecticut for years, but nobody knew everybody. We all came at the time when we did because we didn't feel that there was anything else that we could do. For various reasons this was where we had to be, we couldn't be anywhere else, we had to make it here. There was no alternative, we couldn't go anywhere else. We were here with this piece of land and we had to make our life on it.

Thad and Dick and John came to Oregon and started going up and down the street to real estate offices and found a place where a man said he had land for about seventy-five dollars an acre, and maybe two or three hundred acres. They didn't even look at land, they came back down to the City and we got the money up for the down payment in a couple of weeks and came back up—I came with them—came out and looked at this piece of land first, and decided that this was it, even though we hadn't seen others. We went to see others as a token gesture, and decided on this land. There wasn't anything here, then.

Surviving in the Wilderness

JILL: There were only two girls at first, Patricia and I. And there were approximately—the number varied from four to six males. Steve was here sometimes, sometimes he wasn't. He didn't really move up here until the lodge was built. Dick was here, and Thad was here, and Walt and John and Tom, most of the time. So it varied from four to six. And they spent the first two and a half months we were here building the lodge, that was all they did. They hauled the logs down and built the lodge. They all centered their attention on that.

Patricia and I cooked—all day. There were only two of us and we were getting used to cooking on a wood stove. We had to haul water up from the stream and mainly cooked and did dishes.

We would get water from the stream. We had a big water bag that we would fill up, and it took eight trips of two buckets per person to fill it up. And we would use that up about every other day. I think we used about twenty-five gallons of water a day, for dishes and for cooking purposes and all that. We would get up and we would fix either cereal or pancakes. Primarily cereal and pancakes. Our diet when we got here until we went on food stamps was very high starch—entirely too high. We were living on surplus foods. We got here at the end of August so we didn't have a chance to put a garden in. We didn't have any vegetables, very few vegetables, things that were given to us by other communes. We couldn't afford to buy them. All the winter we only spent twenty dollars a month on food for ourselves, perhaps thirty in a good month. We didn't have any money to spend. We were feeding about eight or ten people on twenty dollars a month. We bought very little, we ate really quite badly. We would supplement with things like soy beans and have a grain cereal with raisins and nuts—it is fairly high in protein, theoretically you can live on it.

We chopped our own wood, Patricia and I chopped wood from the beginning. We didn't realize until months later when people visited from other communes that this was not done by the females—females don't chop wood in a lot of communes, the men do. Here the men would quarter it and we'd chop it from there. We'd chop wood in batches, generally getting up in the morning and chopping wood is a little too much, so we'd chop the wood the day before, or we'd chop up a stack for a couple of days, pile it by the stove which was under black plastic, which was our temporary kitchen.

Making breakfast started with making the fire and heating the water for coffee and cereal or for tea. And the actual meal wasn't very elaborate, so the time it would take—it would take about an hour and a half. It takes a while for the wood stove to heat up—we didn't know enough about wood stoves then, we didn't know as much as we do now. We can heat it up in half the time we could then. But it would take about an hour and a half to cook breakfast, sometimes two hours.

When we first got here we cooked over a campfire, for about the first three weeks, and did the dishes squatting on the ground. It took us about a month of squatting on the ground before we realized we could put them on the table—we had a temporary table there—and a few shelves in between trees. We had some nails on the trees and hung the cups there, and hung some pans on the trees. But it took us about a month before we realized that we didn't have to squat to do the dishes.

That taught us very clearly about pollution, though. The only thing that we had consciously done to pollute the ground here was to pour the dishwater out. And it would just go off down some little ravine there. It took about a month before it started to get really bad, polluted, and we realized we couldn't do that. We didn't know that until then. So it was good that we were dealing that directly with it. Now we have a sink and a drainage field, so it filters through the drainage field and we are working on a new drainage field which will have a grease pit, and that will take care of all of it.

I think the thing that brought us together originally as a group is our working together, our physically working together and creating the material aspect of our lives—building our shelter. That is the one part that I doubt a female could do—lifting the logs, notching them, cutting them out with a chain saw and putting them up is really heavy labor. It took four of them to lift a log, sometimes five. It really was too heavy work for us to do, and we had to cook. We were most beneficial cooking. They didn't need us to do the lodge, and they didn't have the time to cook.

We were here every day. We gave them a coffee break in the morning, we would bring up some sort of a snack and coffee and just sit around and look at what they had done, and they would talk about it, and also there were only two females and there were only two of us that weren't doing what they were doing, and it wasn't particularly complicated in the interaction, in talking to them. Had there been an equal number of males and females there could very easily have been a division of some sort, but with only two of us there wasn't. And also, we were working physically very hard, we were active physically and it was a thing that all of us were experiencing for the first time. None of us were in particularly good physical shape at all. We weren't aware that our muscles were actually used for anything, most of us. And so we did work, the same sort of plain, physical labor. The hardest thing about it was not being able to do anything else. It was just brute force, really, in the beginning, and we drove ourselves. We would get up and work for twelve hours a day, sunup until sundown.

We are working against time, and in fact we got the lodge up only about three days before it would have been too cold to do dishes outside. The timing has been good. We have a spring uphill from the lodge that we didn't know was there when we built the lodge. We discovered it and it is gravity-fed water that feeds right down in here so that we can have the sink inside. Had it been any closer it would not have flowed properly and had it been any farther away it would not have been possible, and it is the only spring in this area. So we were lucky. We have been lucky in a lot of ways.

Woman's Work and Man's Work: Changing Role Expectations

JILL: Our work schedule has changed a great deal since the beginning because Patricia and I did all of the cooking for months—I think about six months. Then we changed, and now everybody cooks. It was an inspiration. It was Thad's inspiration. I was blown out and had been really bitchy for a couple of weeks, not really being conscious of why I was so bitchy. And Thad said, "My God, if I had been in there—" and I said, "I don't want to go in that kitchen. I don't want to cook any more." And he said, "Well, you have been cooking every day since we have been here, there is no reason why males can't do it, that is discrimination, that's sex discrimination. You can learn how to do the jobs that we do, and we will learn how to cook." So since then we have been in the kitchen about once every eight days, or however many people there are here—and rotate. It's much better, and we do other things. And there is much more communication between the males and the females than there was before. Before we didn't have any common work patterns.

The only schedule we have is the kitchen duty because it's so complicated that it is hard to remember. But I think it is working out fairly well without a schedule, we don't really need it for other work. The goats get milked, the chickens get fed.

Later, I interviewed Thad and asked him about the origin of the sharing of kitchen chores.

THAD: At the beginning there were two chicks here and there were a whole bunch of cats, and we worked very hard building the log house and it was really not the sort of labor the chicks could do. Now, this situation went on. There were still very few females here and more males and after about six months I realized one day that if I had been here for six months—and this was a point where for some reason it was particularly dreary, the kitchen counters hadn't been finished and the kitchen was really intolerable at the time, and there was very little food, all we had was starches, it was the middle of the winter and we were eating commodities [that is, surplus commodities provided by the federal government to welfare agencies for distribution to the very poor] and we had no vegetables, no meat, all starches, and it was the same old thing every day. It was completely noncreative cooking. Nobody wanted to eat and nobody wanted to cook food. And I came to the realization that if I had been in the kitchen for six months, I would come out and I would say, "I'm not going to do this any more. I am not going to do this. I will work outside but I am not going to work in the kitchen any more."

Jill had been getting a little bitchy behind it, but she hadn't really considered saying this. And yet she was feeling it, she was feeling very trapped. But she couldn't really get it to the point of saying, "I am not going to do this," because there is the trip put on females in this society of, "You are supposed to work in the kitchen." It was also ingrained in her head, the feeling of "Even though I hate what I am doing, this is what I should be doing, this is my work." Whereas for me, as a male, I was a bit more objective and could say, "I would never do that, I'd walk out."

This was in the evening and that evening when I went to bed and talked to Jill, I said, "Jill, if I had been doing what you have been doing for the last six months, I would stand up and say, 'I'm not going to do this any more.'" And then she said, "There's nothing we can do about it until more chicks come." And I said, that's ridiculous, that there was no reason why cats couldn't work in the kitchen, there was no reason why chicks couldn't work outside, that it had happened in Israel.

Well, the next day this was brought up [in a "family" meeting] and nobody could say anything to it, there was simply no denying that that was the only correct way in which we could function. It was indeed a matter of a little bit of—chagrin, perhaps—that for six months we had been thinking all along on how well we were doing, and how unbigoted we were and all this time we had been maintaining this outrageous state of second-class citizen. And the chicks got with it, you know, getting out of the kitchen was an outrageous trip and the cats couldn't argue with it. It wasn't that they were necessarily pleased with it, but all of us agreed that it had to happen.

However, since some of us were not at a point where we would likely spontaneously go work in the kitchen, it was decided that that wouldn't really work, that we needed a list where we knew when it might be expected that we work in the kitchen to distribute the load evenly. The first while we worked two in the kitchen at a time. One person would get up and one person would help in the kitchen, so that while we had a schedule, nonetheless one chick would work every day, so the chicks were working more but this was looked upon as a learning process. And we learned how to bake bread, how to cook things. Baking eight, ten loaves of bread and cooking for ten people all day took a bit of coordination, but we got it. And that is the state of things now.

For some of us it is still a chore. Dick would never shirk his duty, Dick works in the kitchen, but nonetheless, Dick always, if possible, asks somebody to help him and if that person agrees, then that is not Dick's fault. But to him it is really very boring. He's got a number of other things that he is into and he hasn't really learned to be creative in cooking yet.

Then there is Steve, who never uses a recipe. Steve *never* uses a recipe. The bread we ate tonight was Steve's bread, baked completely without a recipe. He bakes cakes without recipes, pastries without recipes, cooks all kinds of things without recipes and sometimes he comes up with *strange* concoctions. They're not bad, they are just strange. You never tasted anything like it before, you don't know whether you like it, you don't know whether you might not want to eat it too often, but nonetheless you are eating it and it is an experience. And you know you haven't eaten one before and *not* liked it, because there is no chance that could have happened. [Note: One of the other boys had made a comment that afternoon which I had overhead about "that fried compost we ate for lunch," so perhaps Thad's enthusiasm for Steven's spontaneous creations is not uniformly shared.]

Our birthday cakes are a thing to experience. Completely from scratch, they are outrageous. They are the essence of birthday cake. They definitely don't cut with a feather, when you eat one you know that it was a cake, it was incredibly good, and you are *full*.

Now it is no longer, "What's for dinner, chicks? What's for dinner? Oh, its the same old thing." Now we all know what's going on, and we are all involved. And likewise, the chicks with things going on outside, like Patricia and Steve are fixing the bridge tomorrow. Now everyone understands every facet of the existence here, and it draws us much closer, because everyone has the totality of the experience in common.

Leadership and Group Process

THAD: We aren't completely balanced in skills, in fact there are great discrepancies in our skills. It is starting to level out but Dick and I are probably the two people who know most what is going on with the entirety of the place. We keep lists in our heads, and we are just now getting to the point where other people have the same list in their head, where you know that a new drainage field has to be dug, you know that the reason the old drainage field clogged up was because we didn't put a grease pit in, we know that a new shitter has to be dug, because we looked down the shitter.

But for a long time, to a very large degree, it was the two of us who bore the burden. It was a carefully controlled situation where it was never allowed to become a situation where people looked to us for the answer and we turned to them and gave it to them. It was always made clear, "All right, I may have thought this thing out, but it's up to all of us, and all of us have to understand it."

It all happens very much in the now, it is something that we are very concerned with right now and not the past and not the future, although these are not ignored. Avoiding leadership is very difficult, in that somebody will know more about a subject, but nonetheless if you can avoid it, if you can make an attempt not to put people in the category of leader and follower but leave it open, then the other person is open to catch up. It is very hard to look to your leader and say, "I am now ready to become co-leader." It simply is emotionally very hard, because you have gotten into the habit of looking up to this person, of looking to this person for the answer. And to look upon yourself as equal without having interrupted your relationship is very difficult. It can be done, but it is very difficult. But if it is left open, if it is never defined as such, then when that person is capable, that person simply starts assuming the responsibility. There is no formal change, it is simply that the other person starts doing it, too. And then we can both do it. And then I don't have to do it all the time and you don't have to do it all the time. That way we have time to do other things, and we aren't hung up doing an odious task or doing a really groovy task when someone else is stuck with an odious one.

The idea is that *everybody* can say, "Let's do it this way," except that it needs to be decided which way you are going to do it. And by everybody bringing it up, you don't get one person's idea, you get the best of everybody's idea. It takes the best thought of any one and adds the others, so that even if the others amount to nothing, it is still the best possible, and in this way there is no leader, everyone is leader. Everyone has one vote, issues are almost always resolved unanimously, although this isn't a rule, this almost always happens.

And our economic system is totally a communistic one. What is happening here is basically true to the original definition—not to the contemporary definition but true to the original definition of communistic democracy. Property is communal. There are exceptions, but the exceptions are not taken very seriously.

This is out of our heads. We wouldn't mind doing some reading, but this is out of our heads. I find that I am constantly rediscovering all kinds of stuff. We have learned a great deal from the recent history of the hip communes on this coast. To perceive the actual reality of people similar to me living together was perhaps the most realistic way to learn about it.

Adding to the "Family": Who May Join

We learned to be very careful about our numbers from observing the actual working process of other communes. Not too many new people at once because it completely destroys the group image. And not too many over all because it gets to the point where communication simply is not possible. You do not have time in the day to interrelate with everybody and soon there is a faction, soon you are divided. It may not be a malignant faction, it may simply be that you are into trip A and I'm into trip B, and that we do not interfere with each other, they are simply different. And no longer are we a unified group, we are now split and these people interrelate and have a very tight bond, we have two subcultures within the whole. And then no longer is the group who are into trip A completely aware of where group B's trip is at. At this point it falls apart.

In practice I think fifteen is a great number, when you first begin ten is much better. We built the lodge with between four and eight males and two chicks. And the maximum number is probably somewhere in the proximity of twenty. We grew very slowly, we are in no hurry to have people, we have quite sufficient people now. Ultimately, after the trip is very solid and you really understand each other, very slowly over a period of at least a year or two, perhaps twenty. And I would say any more is starting to push it.

Too many newcomers at once creates a newcomer faction. Too many newcomers at once and the newcomers don't understand what is going on, and there are enough of them that they really start interrelating and producing significant splinter groups. And this really creates a division. As far as a number of newcomers, probably two, at most three people. One is really preferable but then you have couples.

Within the first few minutes you know whether or not you want that person to stay for a day or two days, maybe, or whether you want them to leave immediately. You know, is this a person I want to talk to for five minutes and then I want them to exit, or is this someone I could really dig sitting down and having more leisurely interaction with this person. Assuming the person stays on, after a day or so we call a family meeting in which we explain ourselves to that individual, that we exist as a family, and here is the way in which we relate with each other, here is how we are likely to relate with you, here is what is going to put us uptight—likely—and where are you at? Why are you here? What are you looking for? How do you look upon yourself? And get it all up front and all out in the open immediately. Because we haven't always done this in the past, and we have blown it.

If a person stays here for about a month or a month and a half, we will make the decision as to whether or not they should become a member of the family or split, because after the end of a month we are pretty sure of what our opinion is. We simply do not have time to wait much longer than that to find out.

If a person is a member of the family and he interferes with the family and it is not an issue which can be resolved, nonetheless this is not looked upon as you have a *share*, you bought your share and "I'm going to carry it to my grave with me," what is looked upon as the most important thing is the trip, that comes first, not you. And if you interfere with the trip and there is no way of resolving it, then it is your place to split.

JILL: We are not really interested in people who just come here and blend in. Everybody has to be distinctly himself. A person that just comes and is innocuous isn't really a person that we want to live here. If you don't notice that they are there, why have them there? They are just extra baggage. Of course, if they are negative, that is noticed, too. But every person that is here is distinctly different, ways of looking at things, talents, and interests.

Everybody having their own peculiar way of looking at something, their own perspective, being exposed clearly and intimately is more important to us than to know a hundred people superficially. The element that holds our group together is the closeness of what I call—I call it age. We are close together in age, although in physical age there is ten years difference between the oldest and the youngest. But it is a mental and—it is really psychological—psychologically, we are about the same age. We can't have any inequality here, it is essential to our concept that everyone considers themselves equal.

LIVING AS A COUPLE IN THE COMMUNE

In a study of the "tribal family," Downing observes that the transitory "beginner family groups" in the urban setting usually have a high frequency of sexual expression, ". . . in the form of heterosexual intercourse on a casual basis. Among older groups, however, there is a marked preponderance of men over women, creating, in effect, a system of polyandry for several of the women, although others may have essentially monogamous relationships" (1970:127). The members of this "family" have all passed through the earlier stages and most have settled into monogamous relationships which seem to be semipermanent. That is, these relationships are consensual unions and could break and reform at any time, but in the nearly two years that this commune has been in existence, the pair relationships that existed at the beginning (basically, two couples) have remained intact. Some of the unattached males have gone away, some have acquired "Old Ladies."

Pair Relations and Group Relations

Each couple have their own house, and these houses are scattered through the wooded mountainside. These are basically sleeping quarters with a small living area. The large communal lodge is a cooking and dining commons, with a sleeping loft for guests. The central raised hearth is the setting for family meetings and much group interaction.

JILL: The couple aspect is minimized, in that when we are with the group we are not really aware that we are a couple. I don't really feel that much different toward Thad at this point than I do toward the other males here. It is compounded by the fact that we have had fewer females than males here. But the couple aspect is apparent, it is apparent because there are couples who have been here all along.

It has been necessary at times for the group to have a difference with one individual in a couple, while maybe the other half of that couple didn't agree. This has been rare and the people that this happened with left. But differences between the couple are at this time solved within the couple. Other than that, everyone is considered an individual. We work very hard on that, in fact we overemphasize the individual a bit and underplay the couple relationship because it has been so heavily opposite in the past that we are still reacting.

If there is any conflict, everybody here is aware of it and they don't like it. They live here now because they don't have to live with conflict. We have learned that we can control negative emotions. Fundamentally, we believe in getting it out in the open. We have a disagreement, we get it out in the open. We have family meetings and they are honest, if something is making people uptight they'll bring it out, and we will try to solve it. We have solved a lot of differences that way. The main thing is not repressing anything.

The houses are to be alone, but that is curious, the point that you brought up, you aren't alone if you are part of a couple, and so in a way that is an inconsistency—it is mainly a place to get off and sleep that is separate. Because the alternative would be everybody sleeping in one building, or several communal sleeping areas, which are all right, but we didn't prefer it that way.

The houses are thought of individually—I hear people say "Patricia's house" and I tend to think of it as "Dick and Patricia's." I think that most of us prefer living with a member of the opposite sex. Perhaps because we haven't broken down the concept of couples, maybe it is also nature. But the couple relationships are secondary. The thought of being part of a couple here is really not something that occupies my mind. There are not activities that couples take part in that others don't take part in, there is nothing that really distinguishes living as a couple except sharing the same house, which is mainly a sleeping activity, and of course talking to and knowing one individual better than you know other members of the group, but if we live together for a period of years we will eventually know everyone in the group equally.

I think it broadens our relationships in that through talking with, interacting with other people all of the time, when we talk to each other the perspective that we have gained from talking to other people is a lot greater. We enjoy talking to each other, we don't run out of things to think about or say. It is a rare couple that doesn't get bored with each other in the city.

In fact, our summer in the city showed both of us that there was a very high probability that we would not live together in the city. Our temperaments are such that—his definition of manhood is such that he can't express it in the city, he doesn't feel fulfilled. And my orientation is much more toward money, toward having possessions. I am more ingrained in that than he is. When we are in the city, I would feel a certain drive for him to succeed in the standard American way, even though I know that I basically don't agree with that. There is simply no other form of expression in the city. So we wouldn't live together there, I don't think. We would probably break up.

In practice, the couples do seem to have much more interaction with each other and much more joint activity than the group cares to admit. In many ways, their subgroup interaction is very similar to that of the conventional married couple. But the value perceptions are different. In the larger society, for example, the married couple is expected to settle its differences privately, and would resent the interference of neighbors and relatives. Here, the couple is likely to try to resolve differences in private, but the expectation is that they will bring their problems to the larger group, and such group resolution is not considered interference: the entire group has a stake in harmony in the subunits, because any dissension affects the group as a whole.

"What Is Addressed to Her Is Addressed to Me"

> THAD: We live together as couples, we live in houses together, but we are treated as individuals. As far as the group's relation to the couples, it is strictly as individuals. The only facet in which we are couples is that we happen to live together, we live in the same house, and share it. We are all individuals and we all relate to each other as individuals. The ties between couples are looked upon as "those two people live together," and that is all. There is no "Thad-and-Jill," although, "Thad and Jill went to the city together." When you concern yourself with one you concern yourself solely with one and not the other, although they very often appear in the same place at the same time. And, because we talk a lot to each other, often we have a very similar view. We have a tendency to talk to each other [as a couple] and we often settle matters in private, but this is only because it is more likely that we shall be somewhere else [that is, apart from the group] and also the object is to establish communication and it is not always the best possible environment to do this with the group. [I tried to suggest that he was apologizing for preferring the company of his old lady, but he seemed to feel the need to rationalize this behavior.]
>
> One of our main policies, one of the most important things, is a policy of constant up-frontness. You never sublimate things, you never push something down, if you have anything that is on your mind you bring it out, because to hold it in and push it down only twists things and makes it worse, because it all has to come out sooner or later. Almost invariably we bring it out in the form of a family meeting. We all sit down and discuss it. And if it is not brought out, it festers.
>
> Anybody can call a family meeting at any time about anything. It is the way in which we deal with things. If two people have a difference, the family meeting would most likely take the form of the two people starting to rap and the rest of us sitting and watching it and commenting and saying to someone, "That is a bullshit trip," you know, "That's a defense mechanism." Or, "I can perceive that, I can understand it," or, "The two of you are saying the same thing."
>
> We act as mediator, but as a mediator whom both parties respect. And actually not quite as a mediator, but as an integral part, because you become directly affected. Everybody has a stake, everybody is involved. They may not be emotionally involved with either side, however they are emotionally involved with the issue, because the issue is the peace of what's going on. The issue is that there is a disturbance here, and it must be worked out.

One of the young men who had been part of the group from the beginning had acquired a woman that the group felt it could not get along with, and when she was asked to leave, he left with her. In that instance the couple ties were apparently stronger than the group tie. I asked Thad to explain.

> THAD: None of us could accept his placing the couple tie above the group tie. This was very alien to us, and while we understood his doing it, it was something which separated him from us, because that was not like us. And as a result of doing that, he demonstrated to us that he did not belong here, that he was not ready for this, and that he had something else to do. Because he clung to the relationship in a way that none of us cling to anything, certainly not to a given individual.
>
> We addressed her and we explained ourselves one by one to her that we could not live with her, that it was a matter basically of incompatibility, that we had our trip and that we felt she had her trip and that we'd be better off and she'd be better off if we didn't live together, and that this was our place to stay and her place to go. And we turned to him and we said, "This is addressed to her and to her alone, to you it is our decision that if you wish to stay, we love you. If you wish to go, then go. But we by no means mean this to be addressed to you." And he said, "What is addressed to her is addressed to me," and split.
>
> Their relationship, incidentally, lasted at most a week after they left here. I doubt that he will ever come back, not so much on our behalf as on his behalf. I don't think he'd like to come back. As one might understand, in a relationship which is not all that secure, one clings all the more tightly. When a relationship really isn't very secure, a common reaction under pressure is to do the reverse. It is just that the trip in your head is the exact reverse of what is actually happening.
>
> This is an environment where there is no need to cling. Although we live as couples we are all as close as most couples in the society that surrounds us, all of us all together. And as couples we are certainly much closer than hardly any relationship I've seen outside. We view each other as individuals and looking upon ourselves as individuals, completely avoid the identity of, "I am his Old Lady" or "I am her Old Man."
>
> There is no longer a holding together, it is simply a resting together. There is no longer hanging onto each other, but simply standing side-by-side. Do you understand what I am trying to explain?

On Sex, Money, and Children

> JILL: Thad and I believe, or hope to believe, that the concept of the singular couple will be broadened here, that we aren't a bunch of individuals living together and that the family concept will eventually— it is still in theory, the actual practice hasn't come about—the family concept will be broadened to the point hopefully where I will love everyone here as much as I love Thad.
>
> We thought about plural marriage, it is the sort of thing that is so

emotionally charged, though, and at this time we have a lot of repressions and a lot of early training to unlearn before we feel that we will be capable of emotionally dealing with a sexual relationship as a group. We are feeling more and more able to deal with it without jealous hostility, bitterness, or rivalry. Without any of these basically meaningless emotions if everyone loves everyone concerned, it would merely be an expression of love. Thus far, this is pretty theoretical. It is something that we are working into very slowly.

We didn't even know each other when we got here. We are learning to know each other on more superficial levels first. We treat the physical aspect pretty seriously, because it has broken up a lot of communes. It has broken up a lot of couples and caused emotions that people aren't capable of dealing with. We want to be sure, or at least as sure as we can be theoretically, that we are capable emotionally of handling that situation before we get into it.

An individual sexual relationship is looked on as secondary to the group. If it threatens the group, then we'll postpone it or forget about it. But physical feelings have really been underplayed here, in a way. Free love and all that is very underplayed, and there aren't any big, flash emotional scenes between individuals that disperse and cause havoc in a couple.

Sex is a facet of our existence, but it is not the only one. That is why we designed a communal kitchen and eating area, and a communal crafts lodge. But mainly the eating and cooking area, so that there will be times when we are all together, very strong, and not just working with each other but sitting around and talking to each other, a communal, neutral place in which to meet that is everyone's.

I asked Thad about the problem of sexual jealousy as the group began to experiment with freer sexual expression.

THAD: There is no jealousy between us, and if there is, it is very quickly being eradicated and recognized as a meaningless emotion. If a chick moved in with someone else, I don't think it would be disruptive. It would be heavy, but then things are often heavy around here. When everything comes out and nothing is hidden, things are often heavy, but nonetheless it would not be allowed to be disruptive. And I would suspect that all the people involved would stay here. However, if it would be disruptive it wouldn't happen. If it is destructive to the group unity, it should not happen. At this point it is finally becoming acceptable without damage to the group, and is looked upon as a good thing if it brings us all closer. But as long as there was any possibility of it causing harm it has been avoided, because it was not worthwhile.

The poverty of this group is real, and it is not just a matter of lack of amenities; there has been a long period of malnutrition. I asked Jill to comment.

JILL: Money to us is not important in and of itself. The actual concept of money is something that has been perverted in this society and we really find that we don't need that money. We live on about two hundred dollars a month at this time. We have lived on less than that. All of us have come from middle-class America and we have had all of the possessions that we could ever want. We aren't interested in amassing possessions for possessions' sake, perhaps because we have already had it and we are able to give it up.

On a material level, money buys either security or it buys material possessions, sometimes it will buy travel, but that can be gained otherwise—hitching—you can hitch anywhere. It is harder, but to us being wealthy is having people around that I really love and communicate with. It is being able to care for ourselves.

There aren't very many goods that we need to buy. There are many things that we make or will make. The amount of clothing that a person actually wears out in a year's time isn't that much, but—in American society you spend a lot of money on clothes, on appearance. We all dress functionally. Occasionally we will dress up, but it is very rare, and they are often things that people have made. There is a value placed on how a person looks—it might be on the degree of difficulty in making a dress, for instance. In a way it is a flashback to earlier societies before the machine. It has only been very recently that people had more than three or four dresses.

We don't care. We have had it all and it didn't satisfy us. It didn't make us happy.

This is the same girl who had observed earlier that she felt differently in the city, that there she was more oriented toward material possessions. The rural setting is, she recognizes, a different mode of life, and she feels less torn about material things here.

Patricia had just learned that she was pregnant. There were no other infants or children and I raised the question of what a child might do to the group structure. Jill structured the question as an inquiry about the group's relations with the outside world.

JILL: That is a really great problem. We have until a child is eight years old in this area before we have to send them to school. We will not, unless it is totally impossible, we will not send a child to public school. We don't know how long we will live here, we don't know. Hopefully, ideally, we will be able to raise our children pretty much on our own, we don't know. It is possible that by that time we will have someone here with a teaching credential, then we will probably teach the children here—or use a correspondence school.

The child, the children, shouldn't have too much problem understanding the outside society in that they will be relating to a lot of individuals and we will try to be as clear as possible on why we are here. We don't know, we haven't tried it yet, and we will have eight years before we come into any direct confrontation with America. We don't want to raise our children and have them go back into the culture that we left—unless, of course, they want to. And perhaps being raised in this environment they could go back in and really create a lot of good if they wanted to.

It isn't even decided if children will live with parents past a certain age, maybe children will have their own place. The concepts of mother and father are really going to be underplayed. If you are a mother you won't have to spend twenty-four hours a day with your child, and when they are little it gets tiring, patience runs out, and negative effects are put on the child's head simply because it is taking up too much of your time. With a lot of people around, they will maybe spend three or four hours a day with the child. In the first few years the mother will spend more time with him, not after that. Everybody will be in charge of raising it, which will disperse the burden of child rearing.

I think it is a great burden to a female to have to raise a child on her own, she can't do anything else and for awhile it is really hard to do anything else at all, so hopefully that will be cut down. And the child should be happier. The mother won't dump on its head.

When asked about the potential effects of Patricia's pregnancy on the group, and what a child will mean, Thad had the following view.

THAD: This is looked upon by everybody as a pretty good trip. We feel that by the time she has it, we will be ready for it. It will be everybody's baby. And it will be raised in this way. Patricia will care for it most likely, more than other people for the first couple years of its life, but it nonetheless will be our baby. And is a concern of ours.

This is a place where you could express yourself more fully than you could any place else, be more an individual than you could any place else. And as total individuals, we are closer to each other than we could possibly be—it is the expansion of what I was talking about earlier in the couple relationship. We don't hold to each other, we stand side-by-side. And it is incredibly close. Because there is no clinging, there is no consequent pushing away.

Epilogue (one year after the above interviews were taped): Patricia's baby is a healthy boy with an Old Testament name who has been taken by his proud and still unmarried parents to visit his wealthy grandparents in the East. The goats and chickens have multiplied and the garden prospers. Group marriage is still a thing of the future, but sexual relationships are less monogamous.

"Thad" finished his house—a tower hung on poles sunk into the steep mountainside; it has a heavy beamed ceiling and a long view down the canyon toward the setting sun. And one afternoon in early winter, "Jill" hung herself from a ceiling beam. "Things are often heavy around here."

REFERENCES

Downing, Joseph, 1970. "The Tribal Family and the Society of Awakening." In *The Family in Search of a Future*, edited by Herbert A. Otto, pp. 119–135. New York: Appleton-Century-Crofts.

Rodman, Hyman. 1964. "Middle-Class Misconceptions about Lower-Class Families." In *Blue-Collar World: Studies of the American Worker*, edited by A. B. Shostak and William Gomberg, pp. 59–69. © 1964. Reprinted by permission of Prentice-Hall, Inc., Englewood Cliffs, N.J.

WHAT IS NORMAL SEX BEHAVIOR?

Albert Ellis

One of the many hornet's nests stirred up by Dr. Alfred C. Kinsey and his associates in publishing their first Report, "Sexual Behavior in the Human Male," is the problem of what is sexual "normality." Many of our statutes, in stating that various kinds of sex acts are "abnormal," or "perverse," or "crimes against nature," purportedly know exactly of what sexual "normality" consists. Many of our clergymen and philosophers, from their dogmatic assertions in this connection, also seem to know what, precisely, is "normal" sex behavior. The thesis of the present article, to the contrary, is that actually we have no absolute criterion of what is sexual "normality"; and, in fact, "normal" sex behavior is anything and everything which we—or which the societies in which we happen to live—declare and make it to be.

Before we can intelligently discuss what is "normal" sex activity, we must know what we mean by the term *normal*. For there are many different, and equally valid, definitions of this word. Thus, "normal" behavior may mean statistically prevalent behavior; or it may mean psychophysically healthy, well-adjusted, or mature behavior; or it may mean biologically appropriate behavior; or it may mean ethical, proper, or moral behavior. It is my thesis, however, that whichever of these definitions of "normality" we employ, whether it be any or all of them, "normal" sex behavior still boils down to socially accepted and culturally learned behavior; and that if our sex laws, customs, and writings are to be intelligently understood, we must clearly recognize this fact.

purpose

Let us examine, in turn, the statistical, adjustment, biological, and moral definitions of "normal" sex activity to see what are their basic derivations and implications.

STATISTICALLY "NORMAL" SEX BEHAVIOR

Let us assume that by "normal" we mean average or statistically prevalent sex behavior. If "normal" behavior is what the majority of any populace does, then sexual "normality" must differ radically in different parts of our existing world (not to mention different parts of our historical world). For in the United States, for example, we find masturbation almost ubiquitous among our young folk; while in many other parts of the world (where premarital sex relations are encouraged) it is uncommon. In our country, divorce is statistically rampant . . .; in Spain, it is rare. In America, petting without orgasm is exceptionally prevalent; in . . . [many] other parts of

Reprinted from *Complex*, Spring, 1952, 8, 41–51. By permission of the author, Dr. Albert Ellis, Executive Director, Institute for Advanced Study in Rational Psychotherapy.

the world, it is unusual. In our nation, officially acknowledged polygyny is non-existent; in Mohammedan countries, it is the rule. And so on . . .

The question may well be asked: *Why* are sex acts statistically "normal" in one part of the world and just as statistically "abnormal" in another part? The answer is fairly obvious: indirectly or directly the sex mores and laws of one people encourage certain sex acts, while the mores and laws of another group discourage these same acts. Thus, our romantic concept of marrying and remaining married only on the basis of mutual love is distinctly responsible for our high divorce rates; our banning of premarital sex relations is unquestionably one of the main causes for our high incidence of masturbation and petting; our ideas and laws on marriage are good reasons for the lack of polygynous marriage in this country.

In other words: what is statistically "normal" sex behavior is to a large extent *made* "normal" by the pro- and anti-sexual attitudes prevalent in a given culture in which such behavior is widely practised. Aside from coitus itself, few if any sex acts are performed by the majority of all, or even most, peoples of the world; and even coitus is culturally stylized in most regions, so that various positions and techniques which are utilized by large proportions of one group are virtually never used by members of another group. Consequently, what is statistically "normal" in one region is just as statistically "abnormal" in another region. . . .

HEALTHFULLY "NORMAL" SEX BEHAVIOR

Let us assume that by "normal" we mean healthy, well-adjusted, or mature sex behavior. If "normal" behavior is healthy sex activity, then any sex behavior which leads an individual to become unduly guilty, confused, anxious, tense, unhappy, upset, physically ill, or otherwise disturbed is obviously "abnormal." Whether the individual in question is consciously aware of his sexually-caused disturbance is beside the point: if he becomes in any way, consciously or unconsciously, upset by a certain sex act or a lack of this act, and if there is some possible alternative mode of sex activity he might perform which would alleviate his being thus upset, he is participating in psychophysically unhealthy and therefore "abnormal" sex conduct.

The fact remains, however, that sex behavior which is unhealthy for one person is hardly necessarily unhealthy for another; and that sex activity which is maladjusted or immature in one part of the globe is by no means necessarily so in another. Thus, the socio-economically lower level boy in our culture tends to worry seriously about masturbation, commonly becomes quite disturbed about resorting to it, and consequently it becomes an unhealthy act for him. At the same time, the college educated boy in our present-day culture may practise the same act of masturbation, very often, without being adversely affected by it. Again, the same lower level boy may worry very little about his fornicative relations, while the same college-level boy may worry very much about them, and actually become mentally ill because of his worry over them. Similarly: it is . . . [considered] unhealthy for an American male to be homosexual; but apparently it was . . . [considered] healthy for an Ancient Greek male to be an invert. A Scandinavian girl, again, may maturely and healthfully beget an "illegitimate" child; an American, Italian, or Spanish girl may be driven to a severe neurotic state if she begets one. And so on . . .

Again the question may be raised: *Why* are sex acts adjustedly "normal" for one person and not for another? *why* are they mature in one community and not in another? And again the answer seems to be that human cultures and sub-cultures actually *make* these acts healthy or unhealthy, mature or immature, adjusted or maladjusted. If our lower-level boy had been raised as was our college-level boy, he would have been *made* to feel disturbed over fornication, but not over masturbation. If the ancient Greek male had lived in our day, he would have been *made* to be upset over his homosexuality. Essentially, what is sexually healthy, or undisturbing, is what is (overtly or covertly) *accepted* by the group in which one is raised and continues to live; what is sexually unhealthy and disturbing, is what is *condemned* by this same group.

What, it may be asked, about the individual who practices the sex behavior extant in his group and who still becomes disturbed? Take, for example, the man who remains celibate, as his group demands, and then is bothered by headaches, insomnia, and nervousness. Isn't he unhealthy because of the inhibition of his biological "instincts" or drives rather than because of group mores and codes?

No, he is not. In the first place, it is questionable how many individuals would become seriously psychophysically disturbed if the groups in which they were raised and continued to reside *consistently* upheld a given set of sex mores. Naturally, in cultures like our own, where premarital sex relations, adulterous affairs, and many other sex acts are actually considered to be (as was pointed out in detail in my book, "The Folklore of Sex") both nasty *and* tasty, both frightful *and* delightful, the individual who sticks to the letter of our sex laws—and say, remains celibate—will often suffer intensely because many other individuals are obviously not sticking to the same letter of the same laws, and are having a good sexual time not so doing. He will be torn between the inconsistently held views of his own culture—and, more importantly, of himself—will regret both giving in and not giving in to sex bans, and will quite probably become more or less neurotic. It is doubtful, however, if this individual would become equally upset if he lived in a culture where *consistent* sex prohibitions were set up and held to by the great majority of the people, and where he himself learned to have such *consistent* sex views.

Even granting, however, that in any society where certain biological sex action-tendencies or drives are forbidden fruition, and where people consistently follow the bans that are set up against these drives, there will be some amount of psychophysical . . . [discomfort] on the part of sexually bottled-up individuals, it must still be remembered that the trouble will invariably stem not from the nature of the sex drives themselves, but from the *social* bans on them—in other words, from social *attitudes*. Thus, societies which forbid the acting out of biological sex impulses (e.g., societies which insist on celibacy for young people) or which make mandatory the extreme acting-out of these impulses (e.g., societies which insist that men of all ages shall have coital relations at least once a day for most of their lives) will . . . [encourage] some of their members to be distinctly disturbed. But the disturbances that are thus caused will not flow from the nature of man's sex drives in themselves, but from social attitudes which disrupt or interfere with many of the possible biologically appropriate expressions of these drives [and from the individuals *agreement* with these attitudes].

Here again, therefore, what becomes unhealthy or disturbing or immature for a member of such societies is that which, in the last analysis, the codes of these societies *make* unhealthy or disturbing or immature. The adjustment criterion of sex "normality" thus again boils down to a matter of the social acceptability of various kinds of sex acts.

BIOLOGICALLY APPROPRIATE "NORMAL" SEX BEHAVIOR

Let us assume that by "normal" we mean biologically appropriate sex behavior. By this, presumably, we mean that a man's sex act is "normal" when it most easily conforms to his basic physiological drives or "instincts." Thus, if an individual has very high sex drives, because he is blessed with potent hormones, it is presumably "normal" for him not to inhibit these drives; while if he has relatively low sex drives, it is "normal" for him to forego premarital sex relations, adultery, and other types of sex relations. Assuming that it were possible to carry such a biological standard of sex "normality" into consistent practice (and, within some reasonable limits, it might be) the fact remains that such a standard would, in the last analysis, depend largely on learned social norms rather than on innate biological tendencies.

The reason for this is that it would presently appear that . . . [much] of man's behavior is more dependent on social learning than on biological "instincts" or drives. Even man's hunger drives, which are certainly most important to his survival, are quite modifiable by ordinary human learning: so that we find that eating habits in various parts of the world, or even in various families living in the same community, are enormously different. Sex drives, it would appear, are more modifiable in this respect than are hunger drives: so that much of what is considered to be sexually pleasant in one culture is considered to be unpleasurable in another culture; and many of the outstanding sexual goals of one people are greatly different from the outstanding goals of another people.

Thus, the Trobriand Islanders favor a squatting position for sexual intercourse; some African natives greatly enjoy heterosexual anal intercourse; still other African tribesmen avidly seek sex relations with various animals; American women often obtain more pleasure from kissing than from active copulation; English homosexuals seem to favor anal relations, while American homosexuals prefer oral relations and French inverts prefer mutual masturbation. And so on . . .

It would seem, therefore, that although, in theory, man's sex "instincts" run wild, and move him to desire certain modes of sex relations rather than other modes, in practice this is rarely actually true, and his basic sex impulses are enormously influenced by his cultural upbringing. Not only, mind you, does man forbear many kinds of sex acts which are, theoretically, quite satisfying; more importantly, he even forbears *wanting* to try such acts.

The sex drives of humans, to the extent that they truly exist on a biological basis, appear to be drives toward *some* sex outlet rather than drives to a *particular kind* of sex outlet. Moreover, these drives are of such a nature as to be almost totally deflectable in many instances. Thus, many priests and other males in our culture are apparently able successfully to control virtually all their sex drives (although many other would-be celibates, of course, are not able successfully to exert such control); and in a less sexually inciting society than our own, many more males would possibly be able to conquer all or most of their sex desires. Again, in our present culture it would appear that literally millions of females are able to squelch their sex desires to such an extent as to be virtually sexless for many or most years of their lives. And this in spite of the great to-do we make about sex in our novels, films, radio and television shows, and other mass media.

Obviously, then, while the power of man's biological sex drives is not to be minimized, it is to a large extent controllable; and the direction of these drives—whether autosexual, homosexual, or heterosexual—seems to be . . . [largely] a matter of learning rather than innate "instinct." Consequently, even if men are to live primarily in accordance with their innate sex action-tendencies, and if this type of living is to be called "normal" sex activity, such "normal" behavior may be expected to vary widely from society to society and from family to family in a given society. It is true that, in this event, certain extreme modes of sex conduct—such as the espousal of complete abstinence for all legally unmarried individuals—would lead to some severe human psychophysical . . . [discomforts], but many differing less extreme sex codes—including codes which banned *or* permitted acts like homosexuality, heterosexual mouth-genital contacts, public sex acts, etc.—would be quite compatible with such a biologically "natural" code.

Some publicists have long contended that the only biologically appropriate sex code is one which bans all sex acts which are nonprocreative and which encourages those acts which do lead to procreation. The upholders of this code have rarely, if ever, carried it out to its logical conclusion: for it would obviously mean, if this were done, that such acts as homosexuality, masturbation, mouth-genital contacts, and exhibitionism would be taboo; but such acts as premarital sex relations and adultery, when carried on without benefit of contraception, would be quite permissible. Moreover, *all* forms of contraception—including even the rhythm method—would then presumably be taboo and "abnormal." So, too, would be coitus with an already pregnant wife.

More to the point in the present discussion, however, is the fact that such a procreative basis for sexual "normality" might, in theory, be consistently upheld—but it would then depend almost completely on social rather than biological rules of order. For the human race, quite patently, can survive, as it has for thousands of years, with both procreative and *non*-procreative forms of sex behavior. The only logical reason for calling procreative sex behavior "normal" and non-procreative behavior "abnormal" would therefore be for ideological, philosophic, religious, or other *social* purposes, and biology, per se, would have relatively little connection with these socially determined reasons. Here again, then, procreative behavior would become "normal" because men decided to *make* it "normal," and not because it had some intrinsic, inwardly necessary "normality" in its own sweet right.

It may be contended that the mode of sexual behavior is "normal" which makes for human survival and that mode "abnormal" which hinders survival. But here again it must be pointed out that man can easily survive—and so far has managed to do so—while performing every kind of sex behavior imaginable—including even, highly sadistic and masochistic modes of sex conduct. Moreover, since man, presumably, does not live *just* for survival, but for "happy" or "healthy" or "well-adjusted" survival, this biological norm of sex behavior actually boils down to the same criterion of psychophysical health or good adjustment which we have previously examined and found to depend largely on social concepts of living.

It may also be contended that sex "normality" should consist of that type of sex behavior which leads to maximum physical or somatic (rather than psychological or psychophysical) health and well-being. By this criterion, again, virtually all forms of sex activities except a few extreme acts (e.g., rape or sex murder) would presumably be termed "normal." But, as in the case of the human survival criterion of "normality," it must again be pointed out that man does not live for *physical* well-being alone, but for psychological and emotional satisfactions as well. All human acts, in fact, appear to be psychophysical ones, involving the *total* individual or organism. Basing sexual "normality" on the criterion of "physical" health alone, therefore, is totally unrealistic. If human health or adjustment is to be logically employed as a standard of sex "normality," the psychophysical health or adjustment of the entire organism must be the standard employed; and, by that criterion, as we have seen, sex "normality" becomes virtually equivalent to social acceptance of various "normal" sex acts.

In other words: biologically appropriate sex behavior, no matter how we conceive of it, seems to include virtually *all* kinds of sex activity, from mild kissing and petting to violent rape and sex murder. The only biologically consistent code of sex conduct would be one that permitted virtually *all* types of sex acts. Since, at least in some respects, such a consistent biological sex code would prove to be impractical and undesirable for all human beings to follow, it is clear that man cannot live by sex biology alone, and that quite apart from biological appropriateness he . . . [will] end up by designating some sex acts as "normal" and some as "abnormal." But such designations are invariably done on social, or biosocial, grounds.

All told, therefore, even the biological concept of sex "normality," which seems to be one of the most promising ones for which absolute, universally consistent standards of conduct might be developed, turns out to be a concept that, in effect, is dependent on social, and quite relative, values. Just as he *makes*, in different times and climes, what is statistically and healthfully "normal" sex behavior, so man also for the most part makes what is biologically "normal" sex activity.

MORALLY "NORMAL" SEX BEHAVIOR

Let us assume, finally, that by "normal" we mean "good," "proper," or "moral" sex behavior. In this event, it should be obvious to all thinking persons of this day and age that, since no absolute moral law has ever been shown to exist, and since morality varies most widely from culture to culture, sex acts which are "normal" in that they are moral are invariably *made* both "normal" and moral by the socially approved codes of the society in which they occur.

It is true, of course, that many individuals and sects throughout world history have claimed to know some absolute code of morality by which sex (and all other human) acts could be judged to be "normal." Unfortunately for such individuals and sects, they have never been able to agree among themselves as to the exact composition of this moral code; so that its existence remains, to the present day, undeniably unproved. Until it is just as undeniably proved, we shall have to continue to assume that it does not exist, and that all sex codes based on moral laws are, in the last analysis, based upon what groups of human beings *deem* moral, and hence "normal." In other words, sex "normality" used as a synonym for sex morality means "normality" by human fiat—by social learning.

IN CONCLUSION

To sum up: "normal" sex behavior, from whatever point one views it, amounts in the last analysis to *socially approved* sex behavior. Statistically "normal" sex activities are activities which society has *made* statistically prevalent. Healthfully "normal" sex acts are acts which society has *caused* to be healthy. Biologically "normal" sex behavior is behavior which various social groups have extracted from the whole range of possible sex behavior and have come to *view* as biologically appropriate. Morally "normal" sex conduct is conduct which society has *declared* or *legislated* to be moral.

For any group to state, therefore, that certain sex acts are "abnormal," or "immature," or "against nature," or "immoral," or "biologically unsound," is for this group to *make* this act what it has declared it to be for most of the individuals living within the group who (consciously or unconsciously) are influenced by its statements. Or, in other words, those who *learn* that a given sex act is "normal" come to think of it as "normal" and to perform it in a "normal" (statistically prevalent, healthful, biologically appropriate, and moral) manner; those who learn that it is "abnormal," or who inconsistently learn that it is both "normal" and "abnormal," get into various degrees of difficulty with themselves and their fellows when they perform this same sex act. Sex "normality" is a relative, culturally conditioned phenomenon, and *no* mode of sex behavior is absolutely, finally, and for all times and places "normal" or "abnormal." Groups which *think* various types of sex behavior "abnormal" automatically tend to *make* them so. Or, as the French say *Honi soit qui mal y pense!*

Part Four Psychological Aspects of Poverty

In the consideration of poverty as a social and human tragedy, rather than merely as an economic problem, two issues repeatedly arise. The first has to do with the relationship between race and poverty; many people, both blacks and whites, regard being poor as synonymous with being black. It is true, of course, that blacks are disproportionately represented among the poor, but it is not true that all of the poor are black—roughly 80 percent of the poor are white and, in addition to blacks, the remaining 20 percent includes Mexican-Americans, Indians, Asian-Americans, and other non-white people. Similarly, it remains to be seen whether merely being non-white will continue to be a barrier to economic advancement. The Equal Rights Movement has resulted in broadened economic opportunities for non-whites and there is every reason to believe that this trend will continue. Dr. James O'Kane, in his article, *Ethnic Mobility and the Lower-Income Negro*, discusses these and related topics from a rather controversial perspective that you may not have encountered before.

The second of the two issues that arise in the consideration of poverty involves the role of education as a route out of poverty. It is generally assumed that education is the key to jobs and that it is therefore the key to the whole problem. Even if things were that simple, which they are not, the fact is that poor children often do not do well in school and that the drop-out rate is distressingly high. In her article, *Some Impediments to the Education of Disadvantaged Children*, Dr. Norma Radin examines the complex reasons why education fails to be the cure-all that we, perhaps over-optimistically, have expected it to be.

ETHNIC MOBILITY AND THE LOWER-INCOME NEGRO: A SOCIO-HISTORICAL PERSPECTIVE

James M. O'Kane

In recent years it has become academically fashionable to analyze and interpret the plight of the lower-income Negro in urban ghettoes as though this were an entirely novel situation in American life. Reference has been made to the "problem of the Negro," as one which is intrinsically unique and fundamentally different from the predicament of all previously lower-income minority groups. This mode of analysis implies that the difficulties which the Negro urbanite faces as a result of his inferior position on the lowest rungs of the social ladder are infinitely more complex, more paradoxical, and less amenable to solution than anything encountered by the Irish, the Pole, the Jew, and the Italian. The problem's specific interpretation in these terms has consequently resulted in social scientists abandoning, or at least side-stepping, the socio-historical relationships relevant to the routes of upward mobility for minority groups in American life.

The resultant myopic interpretation has subsequently led social observers to view the problem of the lower-income Negro as essentially a *racial* problem. Hence the Negro has been differentiated from previous lower-class minority groups on the basis of so-called racial differences and distinctions. The argument runs as follows: the Negro cannot be likened to the immigrant groups of the nineteenth century simply because of his ascribed *racial* qualities. The former slave status and legal disenfranchisement from American social life have necessitated the realization that the Negro is in a category distinct from all previous societal rejects. His situation and problems are unique; they are literally larger and more incomprehensible than anything of a similar vein witnessed in our history, and the old answers will be irrelevant to the amelioration of the Negro's situation.[1]

Such a position betrays not only a pessimistic, but also a tempo-centric view of the lower-income Negro and his supposed uniqueness at the bottom of urban society. Yet, *how* different is this urban Negro from his Italian

From *Social Problems*, 1969, *16*, 302–311. By permission of The Society for the Study of Social Problems and the author, Dr. James M. O'Kane, Associate Professor and Chairman, Department of Sociology, Drew University, Madison, New Jersey.

[1] *The Report of the National Advisory Commission* has subscribed to this approach, stating: "Racial discrimination is undoubtedly the second major reason why the Negro has been unable to escape from poverty. The structure of discrimination has persistently narrowed his opportunities and restricted his prospects. Well before the high tide of immigration from overseas, Negroes were already relegated to the poorly paid, low status occupation. . . . European immigrants, too, suffered from discrimination, but never was it so pervasive as the prejudice against color in America which has formed a bar to advancement, unlike any other." *Report of the National Advisory Comission on Civil Disorders*, New York: Bantam Books, 1968, pp. 278–79.

counterpart of sixty years ago? *How* distinct is the so-called female centered household of the lower-income Negro from that of the Irish a century ago? *How* different is the inequality and discrimination which the Negro ghettoite presently faces from that of his Jewish predecessors? Basically the differences are secondary. To become absorbed in analyzing only the differences between these groups implies a certain degree of ignorance of the structural supports of ethnic and class mobility which have been similar for all the minority groups in American urban life.

Presently it might indeed be more fruitful to view the plight of the lower-income urban Negro in terms of *class* and *ethnic* factors rather than *racial* factors. The social unrest and turmoil evident in the urban ghettoes are consequences of lower-class membership and, to that degree, are not specifically related to racial factors. John and Lois Scott (1968) in a recent article have paraphrased this relationship:

> Most racial antipathy in America is not pure racism but derives from the disdain of higher classes for those below them. The tragedy of race in this country . . . is that visible genetic differences, superficial in themselves, have become generally reliable clues to a person's class position —his education, his income, his manners. . . . Events of the last 20 years have done much to modify the legal and political aspects of this subordination, but the more general effects of the past remain: black Americans are disadvantaged and poor, and their culture—so much a "culture of poverty"—is offensive to more affluent classes.

The lower-income Negro thus represents the most recent ethnic group in urban America and, like his forerunners from other ethnic minorities, has migrated from agricultural poverty to industrial poverty. Essentially he has moved from the lowest position in an agricultural caste society to the lowest position in an urban class system; in the former environment caste characteristics exerted primary importance while in the latter they are secondary and of limited consequence in either defining or labeling the plight of the Negro.

The Negro, like all the lower ethnic minorities in America's past, comes from an agricultural background. He has been forced from the land and consequently drawn to the cities primarily because of agricultural technology and impoverishment which have destroyed his economic usefulness in an agricultural society. In this respect he differs little from the Irish, the Pole, and the Southern Italian. To observe that each came from a different historical, social, and cultural heritage does not alter the fact that their primary reasons for migration were similar.

So also with the lower-income Negro. It is of little concern to the unemployed Harlemite that his greatgrandfather was a slave. His concerns are with survival in a modern urban metropolis. To dwell solely on the past glories and past humiliations of the Negro, of his African heritage, of his slave status and freedom from bondage, is an irrelevant point. All the immigrant minorities had similar exposures to cultural pride and historical trauma, yet this heritage had little to do with their realistic position in poverty. Each of these minorities also fought and pushed its way into a dominant American society which had made it quite evident that the group concerned was not socially acceptable. The Irish, the Jews, and the Italians —all faced the reality of exclusion from the dominant middle-class society yet each in turn maneuvered its way into the economic, political, and social mainstream. There is no reason to suggest that the Negro will not do similarly, for if the lessons of history are correct, he will be successful.

Yet how is the Negro slum dweller to move away from his socially inferior lower-class position? Through what methods will he be able to partake of the status and affluence of the middle-class dominant groups? What routes of upward social mobility lie open to him? The historical and social realities of America's past suggest answers to these questions, for strangely enough, the lessons of our own history provide us with the clues necessary for the understanding of the present situation.

One factor remains constant: no minority group ever achieved acceptance through dependence upon the benevolence and good will of the dominant American society. Each of the immigrant groups started at the bottom of American society and eventually forged its way into economic, political, and—ultimately—social equality with the dominant society. They had not been invited, and it has been adequately documented that their presence was ridiculed and resented in America. Naturally there were those few voices in the established society which bemoaned the cruel and harsh treatment of the immigrant minorities, yet these dissenters from middle-class propriety were too few and too powerless to effect any real change. Hence, the Irish and the Jews, the Italians and the Slavs—all faced the same basic dilemma of removing themselves from the poverty of the lower class and simultaneously gaining a foothold in the door of the socially accepted classes.

However, the socially approved routes of upward mobility bear little semblance to the daily reality of life in the slums. Being economically and socially ostracized, the newcomers were forced into seeking routes of upward mobility which were not totally explainable in terms of the Horatio Alger form of success. Prejudice and discrimination prevented these minority groups from succeeding in the acceptable manner and consequently other forms or modes of mobility evolved. But what were these routes of mobility? What form did they take?

Each of the minority groups utilized three core modes of movement from the lower classes to the dominant society, each of which is interrelated and interdependent. These can be identified as labor, crime, and politics. Each of these offered a route of upward mobility to the newcomers and their children. This is not to imply that no other modes were present. Hence, for specific ethnic groups such as the Irish, the clergy became an "occupational" source of prestige and power. For other groups, particularly the Negro and Puerto Rican, professional sports and entertainment became alternative methods of success.[2] Yet these alternative forms served as corollary forms of mobility while the primary forms remained labor, crime, and politics. In discussing the progress of the immigrants and their relationship to the Anglo-Saxon Establishment, Baltzell writes, "as the traditional ways to wealth and respectability in business or the professions were more or less monopolized by Protestant Americans of older stock, many of the more talented and ambitious members of minority groups found careers in urban politics, in organized crime, or for those of the Catholic faith, in the hierarchy of the church (Baltzell, 1966). Thus the analysis of ethnic upward mobility somehow encompasses the relationships between these three factors of labor, crime, and politics.

LABOR

The economic expansion of the nineteenth century provided the most obvious channel of upward mobility for the recent immigrants, for it was this industrial expansion which required the abundant supply of cheap and unskilled labor. Each of the ethnic minorities had been forced through societal exclusion to work at the most menial and underpaid types of employment— digging canals, working in the garment sweatshops, building subways and railroads, working in unskilled construction, and literally thousands of other tasks which had been deemed economically and socially unfit for the dominant classes. Yet these jobs provided the newcomer with a relative degree of economic security, a ray of hope perhaps not for himself but possibly for his children. Certainly he was mistreated and underpaid, yet his meager, but growing, savings enabled him to initiate the ever-so-slow process of mobility from the ethnic slum and the conditions of pauperization. In time, each of the minorities accepted this pattern and subsequently realized that the American norms of thrift, hard work, advancement, and progress were integral parts of the American ethos. They were the keys to status and respectability in the new nation and the immigrant's desire for upward mobility necessarily required the internalization of these ideals (Handlin, 1962). Hence, labor in the unskilled and semi-skilled professions provided the immigrant with a beginning from which he could at least maintain himself and his immediate family. Physical labor was in economic demand and it furnished the newcomer with the "tool" necessary for an entry into the labor market.

---

[2] Oscar Handlin (1962) writes, "In the theatre, art, music and athletic worlds, talent was more or less absolute; and discrimination was much less effective than in other realms. This accounted for the high incidence among Negroes and Puerto Ricans to seek these pursuits as a way up; and it accounted also for the popularity and high status among them of prize fighters, musicians and the like, a popularity of which the incidence of reference in magazines and newspapers is a striking index." Oscar Handlin, *The Newcomers*, Garden City: Doubleday, 1962, p. 72.

ETHNIC CRIME AND ETHNIC POLITICS

It would be fruitless and unrealistic to speak of the ethnic political movements of the nineteenth and early twentieth centuries without realizing
the close connection between these movements and the criminal organizations of that era. Ethnic crime and ethnic political structures formed a
symbiotic relationship which is perhaps best epitomized by the success of
Tammany Hall in New York City. In his book, *The Gangs of New York*, the
noted social observer Herbert Asbury (1929) comments on this relationship:

> The political geniuses of Tammany Hall were quick to see the practical
> value of the gangsters, and to realize the advisability of providing them
> with meeting and hiding places, that their favor might be curried and
> their peculiar talents employed on election days to assure government of,
> by and for Tammany. . . . [p. 37].

Commenting on this symbiotic relationship between political parties and
gangsters, Cloward and Ohlin (1960) write,

> The gangsters and racketeers contributed greatly to the coffers of political
> parties and were rewarded with immunity from prosecution for their
> various illegal activities. As the political power of the ethnic or nationality
> group increased, access to legitimate opportunities became enlarged and
> assimilation facilitated. . . . Blocked from legitimate access to wealth,
> the immigrant feels mounting pressures for the use of illegal alternatives
> (p. 196).

Accordingly, a working relationship emerged in each of the ethnic groups
between crime and politics. Illegality provided an attractive means of upward mobility and social advancement, and its success was insured through
an established, though sometimes tenuous and uneasy relation to the local
neighborhood political structure (Handlin, 1962, p. 26; Herberg, 1960, p. 17).
The vast majority of the specific ethnic groups worked their way out of the
lower classes by saving their "pennies and dimes" and eventually, in two or
three generations, their descendants achieved middle-class status and respectability.

Productive labor was but one factor. Concurrent with it there existed the
profound impact of ethnic crime and politics which supplied the finances
and the political acumen necessary for the mobility of the entire group.
Ethnic consciousness and ethnic solidarity were thus created, the cultural
heroes of each of these groups being both the political bosses and the
gangsters. These "models" demonstrated to the masses of the lower class
that an individual could achieve success and power and that the ethnic
group itself, as a collective entity, constituted a force with which the
dominant elites would have to reckon.

IMPLICATIONS

What about the Negro? How do the channels of employment, crime, and politics affect his opportunities for upward mobility? What relationship, if any, exists between the lessons of historical mobility and the conditions of Negro lower-income life?

The answers to these questions are both interrelated and complex; it would be an oversimplification and, indeed, a gross misrepresentation of reality to say that the Negro should pursue these routes of mobility. The fact remains that he *is* pursuing these routes. It takes no profound insight to see that in crime and politics the Negro has been working his way into the higher positions of power. Yet, like the Jew and the Italian before him, he has been forced to contend with the established criminal and political elites, for mobility in the political and the criminal realm is demonstrably as difficult, if not more so, than mobility in the occupational realm. . . .

Political considerations are also operative. The recent black political successes in Gary, Indiana and Cleveland, Ohio underscore the contention that the traditional path of ethnic political power is being utilized. Among both black militants and moderates, there is a growing awareness that the key to success lies not in violence and disorder but rather in political mobility. In a recent interview, Timothy Still the late president of the United Community Corporation of Newark stated:

> Newark is a city that is 60 percent colored, and we are going to inherit this city. And so we cannot let fools destroy the city we are going to inherit. The guys who were trying to start all this trouble were those who were lost, hopeless, those who had no chance. I can understand their feelings, but you can't destroy the whole city. It is *our* city, and we are not going to let you do that (Cook, 1968, p. 31).

Still's comments point to the increasing recognition on the part of the black community of the need for political awareness and political power. Black power and black consciousness thus can be considered as necessary intermediary means to the politicalization of the Negro population (Leventman, 1968). If present demographic projections hold true, the major urban centers of America will be predominantly black and consequently the population base for Negro political leverage will be present. Ethnic solidarity thus becomes the key to the subsequent political power and political mobility of the entire group. Again, the lessons of America's past are in evidence, for the Negro is presently actualizing what other minorities historically have accomplished.

A closer examination of the employment route, however, reveals the presence of one all important factor which has blocked the potential for upward mobility for the Negro. Unlike all his predecessors, the lower-income Negro faces one enduring fact of contemporary economic structure—the relative disappearance of unskilled occupations. The lower-income Negro increasingly can be classified as economically useless (Willhelm and Powell, 1964). Economic and technological development since World War II have eliminated precisely those positions which the Negro might have utilized as leverage for subsequent mobility. Without these jobs he cannot even hope to climb the class ladder. Without them he has little chance of removing himself from the lower class, for employment in these occupations constitutes the barest minimum necessary for ethnic mobility. . . .

However, class factors are evident in the employment situation confronting the Negro. The unavailability of unskilled jobs does not affect the middle-class Negro and, to that degree, its members participate in the economic and social prosperity so characteristic of contemporary American society. The Negro has been victimized not primarily by his color, not by his former slave status, but by his lower-class position. In this he remains no different from his Puerto Rican, Mexican-American, or Appalachian white counterpart. All are substantially represented in the lower class, and upward mobility is increasingly very difficult due to the economic structural forces beyond their control. Thus, the degree that unemployment in the unskilled jobs diminishes, to that same degree will the lower-income Negro be cut off from the possibilities of upward mobility. The recent urban disorders in scores of cities have underscored this problem of class. In many of the cities, the rioters demonstrated the same hostility towards middle-class Negroes as they did towards white policemen, firemen, and business proprietors. It should also be emphasized that lower-income Negroes were not the only group to participate in urban disorders. New York City, in the summer of 1967, and Paterson, New Jersey, in the summer of 1968, witnessed small scale community outbreaks. The rigidity of lower-class positioning and the increasing uncertainty of upward mobility thus create tensions in those individuals cut off from the prospects of improving their societal lot. Given the proper environment, these tensions erupt in violence and destruction. As the Riot Commission has pointed out, the typical rioter was *better* educated, *better* informed, and geographically *more stable* than the non-rioter of the same neighborhood. He perhaps had more reason to hope for subsequent upward mobility yet the inevitable workings of an economic structure which cannot, or will not, use his labor has confronted him with the realities of the American class structure. His behavior bears the marks of vengeance, of lashing back at a society which has promised him much yet has removed the routes to the rewards. It may be surmised that the non-rioter comprises an American variation of the Marxian "lumpenproletariat" —that group which has been so suppresssed that appeals to revolution and retaliation become meaningless and hollow.

The problems and the styles of life encountered in the lower-income Negro are not basically distinguishable from those of other ethnic groups, past or present. Certainly his family structure, his beliefs, and his values are different from those of the middle class. Yet, how distinct are these same traits from other lower-income ethnic groups such as the Puerto Rican? The similarities found in our current lower-class ethnic minorities greatly out-weigh the differences and to magnify the differential styles and values of these respective groups is to place undue emphasis for poverty and de-privation on the wrong factors. . . .

Racial considerations add little to the analysis of these issues; all too often they act as smoke screens which mask the real problems. If race and racial considerations exerted primary importance, it would be increasingly difficult to interpret the values and styles of life of the Negro *middle-class* popula-tion. These values are vastly different from the Negro lower class, yet they are essentially similar to the values and life styles of the white middle-class population. The gap exists between the classes, not the races; it is between the white and black middle class on one hand, and the white and black lower class on the other. Skin color and the history of servitude do little to explain the present polarization of the classes.

Social class thus assumes a primary position in defining and explaining the relationship between upward mobility and the behavior of specific ethnic groups, while racial stigmatization can be considered as relatively secondary in importance. Class differentials, not racial differentials, explain the pres-ence and persistence of poverty in the ranks of the urban Negro. It becomes superfluous to speak of the problem in moral terms, in the rhetoric of brotherly love and social equality. However noble these answers may be, they ignore the reality of ethnic mobility, for no group has ever achieved parity unless it followed the well-traversed route of labor, crime, and poli-tics. Only *after* each of the groups achieved relative success and power in these ventures were they "accepted." Social acceptance and social integra-tion were the last steps, and perhaps the easiest steps, in the long journey from the bottom. In contemporary America, many well-meaning individuals and groups have placed the cart before the horse. They have argued for social acceptance first, from which ultimately should come economic equal-ity and political power, rather than the converse. To argue in this manner merely aggravates the situation, for it deflects the forces of change from the economic and structural considerations and wastes them in moral reform and spiritual catharsis.

The Head Starts, the community action programs, and the educational pilot projects function, but they remain unrelated to the roots of the prob-lem of poverty in the Negro ghettoes. The facts speak for themselves: none of the existing programs attack the problem at its structural foundation, employment. What difference does it make if all these programs do not create employment for the presently unskilled? What contribution is made by a Job Corps that trains youth for non-existing jobs? What difference does it really make for a lower-income Negro to get a high school diploma when the available statistics suggest that his unemployment rate remains dispro-portionately higher than whites with or without the diploma? These are the crucial questions which must be answered if the Negro is to move in American society. His odyssey is essentially no different from that of previous ethnic minorities; it only remains for American society to provide the employment necessary to make the journey productive and rewarding.

REFERENCES

Asbury, Herbert. *The Gangs of New York: An Informal History of the Underworld.* New York: Knopf, 1929, 37.

Baltzell, E. Digby. *The Protestant Establishment.* New York: 1966, 49.

Cloward, Richard & Ohlin, Lloyd. *Delinquency and Opportunity.* Glencoe: Free Press, 1960, 196.

Cook, Fred. It's our city, don't destroy it. *New York Times Magazine,* June 30, 1968, 31.

Handlin, Oscar. *The Newcomers.* Garden City: Doubleday, 1962, 49.

Herberg, Will. *Protestant, Catholic, Jew.* Garden City: Doubleday Anchor, 1960, 17.

Leventman, Seymour. Black power and the Negro community in mass society. Paper presented at the annual meeting of the American Sociological Association, Boston, August, 1968.

Willhelm, Sidney M. & Powell, Edwin. Who needs the Negro? *Transaction, 1,* Sept.-Oct., 1964, 3–6.

Scott, John F. & Scott, Lois H. They are not so much anti-Negro as pro-middle class. *New York Times Magazine,* March 24, 1968, 46.

SOME IMPEDIMENTS TO THE EDUCATION OF DISADVANTAGED CHILDREN

Norma Radin

In our industrial society, the educational institution is virtually the only legitimate channel to upward mobility for young people from families of very low socioeconomic status. Literacy and an understanding of the basic mathematical functions are the minimum requirements for any but the most dead-end jobs. Self-restraint, reliability, and punctuality are also expected and the most conclusive proof of their existence to employers is a high school diploma. Thus, if children of the extremely poor are to share in an affluent society's material and symbolical rewards as adults, plans for their future must include a high school education.

The foundation for academic success at high school age is laid by the time the child is 8 or 9 years of age. If the foundation is weak, the edifice constructed upon it will be extremely shaky. The tragedy is that the public school system is often far from effective in laying this foundation in children from families of very low socioeconomic status. I refer here and throughout this article not to families of blue-collar workers such as the man on the

From *Children,* 1968, *15,* 170–176.

automobile assembly line, but to families characterized by chronic unemployment, underemployment, and disorganization—the problem-ridden families who live in dilapidated, overcrowded housing and suffer from poor health, powerlessness, and despair. Even then I do not mean to imply that all such families are alike, and that none of their children can surmount the educational difficulties presented. I recognize, too, that in the past few years State and Federal funds available to the schools for compensatory education—especially those appropriated under Title I of the Elementary and Secondary Education Act—are producing some changes, but it is still too early to determine how effective or pervasive these changes are. However, the statements that follow probably still apply to most of the schools in this country that are in neighborhoods where large numbers of seriously disadvantaged children live.

Many discerning educators and research workers are focusing their efforts on strategies for making school programs more effective generally with the children of such families. These efforts, however, have been directed in many different directions sometimes producing contradictory results. Rosenthal and Jacobson (1967) have found that the teacher's initial expectations about a child's achievement correlate with the child's subsequent achievement. Coleman and associates (1966) found that mixing children from middle-income families with children from very low socioeconomic backgrounds in school classrooms seems to increase the school performance of the latter. Clark (1965) believes that if teachers raise their standards for children of very low socioeconomic status their performance will improve. Cloward (1967) found that using children from low socioeconomic backgrounds to tutor young students of similar backgrounds improves the achievement of both groups. Suppes (1966) sees a need for computerized instruction. Berciter (Carnes, 1968) noted 20-point gains in the IQ's of children who were included in a highly structured preschool program focused on language development.

Schafer (1965) has found that the structure of the school system pushes children out of the classroom. The Flint (Mich.) school system is trying out community schools as a solution to the problem. Litwak and Meyer (1966) suggest that linkages between the school and the child's family are needed. Others attest to the importance of a small pupil-teacher ratio, remedial reading programs, better teacher training, better pay for teachers, and community control of the school.

Where is the pattern in all of these findings and suggestions? Can *an* answer be found to the problem presented by children who are educationally handicapped by the time they enter school? My contention is that there is no *one* answer to the problem. The basis for the school's ineffectiveness in educating children of very low socioeconomic status is not to be found in any one area or segment of our educational institutions but in a whole complex of factors.

This paper will attempt to delineate some of these factors. They arise from many aspects of our society and from the intrapersonal and interpersonal realms of the child's life, and they can be grouped under four general heads: cultural factors; social organizational factors; primary group or family; and the individual child.

CULTURAL FACTORS

Five points about our society in general affect our educational system and its relevance to young people growing up in our inner-city slums.

1. Of prime importance is the nature of our technology. As machines become increasingly complex and pervasive, little room remains for the unskilled laborer. Even floor polishers and lawn mowers today necessitate some ability to handle delicate and potentially dangerous machinery. In addition, there is every indication that the trend to mechanization and automation will increase as the use of computers grows and invades more sectors of our economy. Thus, there is little gainful employment available today for the unskilled, the unreliable, or the semiliterate in contrast to the past. Even entry jobs often require high school diplomas as evidence of diligence and a fair degree of competence.

2. Value is placed primarily on instrumental, goal-oriented activities. Although a poet, an artist, or a philosopher is occasionally honored, this happens rarely. Thus children who are artistically gifted but who find academic work dull are likely to run into trouble in the classroom.

3. The "Protestant ethic" of hard work and self-sacrifice, as delineated by Weber (McClelland, 1967), is highly respected while indulgence in sensual pleasures without concern for the future is generally denigrated.

However, in describing a subculture found among people of very low socioeconomic status, Walter Miller (1958) has emphasized two aspects that conflict with the value system dominant in our society: (1) the attribution of great value to toughness (endurance, physical prowess, bravery) rather than to cognitive abilities; (2) the belief that luck or fate—not hard work— is responsible for success. While these views have survival value for disadvantaged people, they can prevent a child from adapting to the classroom.

4. The mass media, particularly TV, are ubiquitous, even in the homes of families of very low income. Through such media children of the poor are constantly and vividly reminded of the comforts and luxuries enjoyed by children of more affluent families. As a result they often develop a sense of bitterness, frustration, and self-denigration. The relation between self-rejection and poor academic performance appears to be a close one (1957).

5. The generally racist nature of our society has an additional detrimental effect on Negro children. Clark and Clark (1952) have shown that such children absorb at an early age society's view that a black skin is demeaning. The militant civil rights movement may be altering the picture of self-hatred among Negroes, but the effects of the movement on personality development have yet to be researched.

No discussion of the cultural effects on educational achievement is complete without an exposition of the relevant aspects of knowledge and technology that are missing. We do not really know how young children learn. We know very little about the appropriate techniques for fostering the development of the cognitive structure. We know very little about the best way to present new material so that it will be comprehended and integrated into knowledge already absorbed. We do not really know how to help children organize the information they have already accumulated.

We *do* know that some children will learn regardless of how the material is presented; other children, of normal intelligence, will have severe difficulties no matter what we do. Because teachers "teach" is no guarantee that students learn. We also do not know what specific child-rearing practices are related to specific types of behavior. Much research is now being carried on in all these areas, but much remains to be done.

ORGANIZATIONAL FACTORS

The school system, the major organization with which the child has contact, affects him as soon as he enrolls in kindergarten. The demands on the child as a student in the typical public school are rather subtle and never clearly spelled out. Usually if the student is to perform adequately, he must display initiative and curiosity in relation to subject matter but be complying and passive in relation to school authorities. He is expected to interact with the other students in a positive fashion, exerting leadership when he can; yet he must never overstep the bounds of approved verbal behavior or become physically aggressive. If he wishes to fight, he must wait until he gets off the school grounds.

In school the child is encouraged to stand up for himself, but verbally not physically. He must follow rules, yet understand how to use his own judgment as to when the rules do not apply. He must accept his teacher as his superior, yet feel free to think for himself and express his own thoughts. He must use language that his teacher considers appropriate for school in sentences she can comprehend. However, at home he is free to talk in any way acceptable to his parents. Thus the child meets with many expectations and restrictions requiring different and seemingly conflicting responses.

In middle-class families, the mother is familiar with the demands made on the child in his role as a student, having herself internalized them—that is, made them part of her own expectations of herself—and performed the role adequately herself. Thus she has little difficulty in explaining the complexities of the role to her children. In contrast, in a family of very low socioeconomic status, the mother may never have internalized the demands of the role and may not understand them completely.

One aspect of the student's role is to communicate in a complex language structure, which Bernstein (1965) has likened to an elaborate code. The child of very low socioeconomic background may never have learned this means of communication and may use what Bernstein calls a restricted code exclusively. An elaborate code must be attended to carefully, for it transmits a number of particular messages adding up to detailed information. A restricted code fosters in-group cohesion, but it transmits only stereotyped messages that are very familiar to all the members of the group.

According to Bernstein, children from middle-class families can "switch codes," using the restricted code with their friends or members of their family on some occasions and the elaborate code when they want to transmit specific information. The disadvantaged child can use the restricted code only. Thus, when the child from the low-status family enters school, he is unaccustomed to the linguistic code his teacher is using and is unable to comprehend what she is saying—for example, when she is giving a complex set of directions. Even more serious is his inability to communicate his own bewilderment to her.

The role of the teacher also creates an obstacle to effective teaching of disadvantaged children. Throughout their training, teachers are taught that the goals of education are not measurable, that teachers are educating the "whole child," and that the degree of their success therefore is not researchable. They are told that the teacher "knows" when she is doing a good job, but no one else can really tell. This orientation has created two difficulties. It prevents the teacher from attempting to delineate her specific goals in operational terms that are measurable on a daily, weekly, or monthly basis rather than in general terms. It also has impeded research in the field of education. Only recently, with the introduction of programmed instruction, have educators begun to analyze the tiny steps that are necessary for children to develop skill in arithmetic, spelling, or reading, or to comprehend the complex concepts presented in geography and science.

The role of the school administrator has similarly impeded effective education of the disadvantaged child. It involves errors of omission as well as commission. A serious omission is that neither the principal, assistant superintendent, nor superintendent is required to form linkages with the community or with the student's parents. The parent-teacher association is the only formal avenue for involving people other than educators in the schools' efforts and generally its structure has become so rigid that its original function of serving as a two-way communication channel between the school and the parents seems unlikely ever to be restored. The errors of commission involve the use of school administrators as building managers, book rental-fee collectors, milk machine repairmen, and the like, thus cutting into the time and energy they have for serving as curriculum experts and supervisors of the instructional staff. In too many schools, the principal does little to deal with the fact that many children are having severe learning difficulties or that the curriculum is inappropriate for some students.

The usual structure of the school itself interferes with learning in children of low socioeconomic background. Students are taught in large groups of 25 to 35 children, making it impossible for the teacher to attend to their individual needs so that each child can progress at his own pace. They are promoted or retained a full grade except in a few schools that have experimental ungraded programs. Even in these programs, the teachers do not have the training or the material to be able to teach each child at his own level.

Nearly all teachers have tenure rights after a probationary period of a year or two. Removing a teacher once he has tenure is almost impossible. So teachers may remain in the school system who are not sympathetic to children from the slums or who are sympathetic but do not understand either their emotional or cognitive needs.

Interpersonal relations between teacher and student are critical in determining whether progress will occur. Rosenthal (1967) has shown that the expectations teachers have of their students affect student performance. Other studies have shown that the student who feels his teacher likes him does better. Other less definitive findings suggest that children of very low socioeconomic background generally need a more firmly controlled classroom than other children because they have not developed the kind of self-discipline required for learning.

Most school systems provide little or no inservice training for teachers to help them understand the behavior and needs of the disadvantaged child. Teachers tend to resist supervision, but even if this were not so there is no time during their working day for participation in a continuing education program, for in the hours they are not teaching, they must plan their work and grade papers. Many teachers also resist working overtime to increase their skill or knowledge. Hence, if inservice training is to be offered, time for it must be made available either by closing school, which is not in the student's interest, or by paying teachers to attend the program after hours, on weekends, or during the summer. Few school districts can afford to do this. Other methods of inducing teachers to continue their education, such as offering them higher pay for taking additional university courses, do not motivate all teachers and do not direct the teachers to the kinds of courses they need most.

Few, if any, school systems have training programs built into their structure specifically focused on how to deal with disadvantaged children and required of all teachers who have such children in their classrooms. Moreover, few teacher training institutions offer such courses and even fewer offer student teacher assignments in schools in the city slums, where many of their graduates will teach.

The teacher's role, like the principal's, is deficient in failing to demand that a linkage be formed with the students' parents. Most teachers welcome parents to the school when they come for conferences at times designated by the teacher. But they tend to regard parents who do not show up for such conferences as uncooperative no matter what may be preventing them. Teachers today rarely, if ever, visit parents at their homes; they have no time during their regular working hours for making such visits even if they wished to do so. The absence of a two-way channel of communication between teachers and the parents of low socioeconomic status creates two problems: the teacher is unaware of the kind of environment the student lives in and the parents are unaware of what they can do to reinforce and support the child's efforts to learn in class.

THE PRIMARY GROUP

Of all the influences on the child's educational achievement, the primary group in the child's life—his family—is perhaps the most critical. It is in the family that the beliefs of a culture are transmitted. It is also in the family that the attitudes, skills, and motivation essential for academic achievement are or are not fostered.

Too often, families of low socioeconomic status lack role models of successful students for the child to emulate. But there are more specific differences between most middle-income and very low-income families that tend to effect differences in their children's school performance. My own research (Radin & Kamii, 1965) has indicated that mothers in families of low socioeconomic status often do not foster the development of internal controls in their preschool-age children. They try to protect their children from the dangers they see in the external world and to suppress the dangers they feel are arising from within the child, such as aggressiveness and sexuality; but they do not prepare their children to cope with problems. For example, they set down specific rules for behavior, but do not explain the reasons for the rules. The child is taught to follow the orders of recognized authority, not to make judgments for himself.

One consequence of this pattern of child rearing may be seen in the classroom among children who are passive in the presence of the teacher and obstreperous when there is no teacher in the room or when they have a substitute teacher whose authority they do not recognize. Even more important are the consequences for cognitive development. The child does not learn to inquire, to doubt, to think for himself.

The importance of cognitive stimulation for future intellectual development is well known. Hunt (1961) highlighted this factor in his famous book, "Intelligence and Experience." Children of low socioeconomic backgrounds generally have few intellectually stimulating experiences before entering school and they generally do not have the advantage of the kind of "hidden curriculum" commonly present in middle-class homes. Parents in middle-class families are constantly teaching their children, in the normal course of their family life. Shapes, colors, numbers, names of objects, words on signs are all part of a continuous input of information to the child. Books are read, stories are told, intellectual curiosity is rewarded, and efforts to learn are praised. Thus the mother in the middle-class family incorporates components of the teacher's role in her own functioning as a parent; but the mother of low socioeconomic status tends to confine herself to meeting the child's physical and emotional needs.

Hess and Shipman's (1965) work has emphasized another generally differing aspect of parent-child relations in the two socioeconomic groups. The mothers' teaching styles are not the same. Mothers in middle-class families usually try to help a child solve a new problem by first explaining the entire problem and the goals to be achieved. They then respond to the child's specific moves, correcting errors and explaining why they are errors. Mothers of low socioeconomic status tend merely to give the child specific directions without any explanation. Again they rely on specific rules rather than principles.

The physical conditions in most homes in low-income families also impede the children's education. A recent study in which I was involved indicated that the homes of such families are not only far more crowded than those of the middle-income families but they also are usually very poorly lighted. Often the TV din is continuous and there is no surface on which to write, making it practically impossible for a child to read or do homework.

THE INDIVIDUAL CHILD

Hunt (1961) and others have found that the developing intellectual ability of the child is not solely the result of constitutional factors but is derived from the interaction of hereditary characteristics with the environment. Piaget (1964) postulates that the more learning the child has already assimilated, the more new material he is able to assimilate. Rosenzweig and associates (1964) have shown that distinct anatomical differences exist in the cortex of rats raised in a stimulating environment and those raised without access to stimulating "toys." Hence there is reason to believe that raising a child in an unstimulating environment produces a youngster with more limited intellectual ability than he might otherwise have had. According to Bloom (1964), a large fraction of the intelligence of the child is already fixed by the age of 5. He doubts that environmental change beyond that point can raise a child's intellectual ability appreciably.

One characteristic frequently found in preschool children of low socioeconomic status is an inability to engage in social-dramatic play, to pretend that an object is present that is not, or to take on another's role in a reciprocal relationship. This inability to pretend has been found by Smilansky (1965) among children in Israel as well as by teachers in compensatory preschool programs in this country. It may be related to the lack of games of pretending between mother and child at home. The ability to imagine situations which do not exist is critical for understanding in reading, geography, history, and many other subjects. Piaget (1954) finds it essential for concept formation.

The school problems of children from low-income families, however, are not derived solely from their lack of skills other children develop at home. They also are derived from special skills such children possess that interfere with academic achievement. One is an ability to tune out undesirable words and sounds—a very useful ability in a crowded home but a distinct impediment to learning in the classroom. Another is an ability to express one's emotions in movement rather than words—a source of much of the discipline problem in schools, which are not geared to this mode of expression.

There is some disagreement among researchers as to whether or not motivation to achieve exists at all among many children from the lowest socioeconomic groups. The suggestion has frequently been made that such children *do* want to achieve but in the realm of toughness, physical power, and athletic skill rather than in academic work. But Cohen and associates (1967) found that when delinquent boys of low status were offered concrete rewards for academic achievement, their will to learn eventually became internalized. This suggests that a rechanneling of the motivation to achieve can be induced much later than most psychologists once believed possible.

To summarize, many factors are impeding the effectiveness of schools in educating children from the lowest socioeconomic groups. Some of these factors are societal in nature; some, organizational; some, familial; and some, individual. No one remedy will be sufficient to resolve the problem, nor will an attack on any one aspect of it. What is clearly needed is a massive attack on all the factors involved, along with the opening of new legitimate channels of upward mobility for the few children who even then would be unable to advance educationally. The costs of such a program would be enormous but not so great as the cost of doing without it.

REFERENCES

Bernstein, B. A socio-linguistic approach to social learning. In J. Gould (Ed.) *Penguin survey of the social sciences.* Baltimore: Penguin Books, 1965.

Bloom, B. *Stability and change in human characteristics.* New York: John Wiley & Sons, 1964.

Clark, K. *Dark ghetto.* New York: Harper & Row, 1965.

Clark, K. & Clark, M. Racial identification and preference in Negro children. In G. Swanson et al. (Eds.) *Readings in social psychology.* New York: Holt, Rinehart & Winston, 1952.

Cloward, R. Studies in tutoring. *Journal of Experimental Education.* Fall, 1967.

Cohen, H., et al. *Case I: an initial study of contingencies applicable to special education.* New York: Educational Facility Press, 1967.

Coleman, J. S., et al. *Equality of educational opportunity.* Washington, D. C.: U. S. Department of Health, Education, and Welfare. Office of Education, 1966.

Group for the Advancement of Psychiatry. *Psychiatric aspects of school desegregation.* New York, 1957.

Hess, R. & Shipman, V. Early blocks to children's learning. *Children.* Sept.-Oct., 1965.

Hunt, J. McV. *Intelligence and experience.* New York: Ronald Press Co., 1961.

Karnes, M. A research program to determine the effects of various preschool intervention programs on the development of disadvantaged children and the strategic age for such intervention. Paper presented at the 1968 convention of the American Educational Research Association, Chicago, Illinois. (Unpublished).

Litwak, E. & Meyer, H. J. A balance theory of coordination between bureaucratic organizations and community primary groups. *Administrative Science Quarterly.* June, 1966.

McClelland, D. C. *Achieving society.* New York: The Free Press, 1967.

Miller, W. Lower class culture as a generating milieu of gang delinquency. *Journal of Social Issues.* 1958, *14(3)*.

Piaget, J. *The construction of reality in the child.* New York: Basic Books, 1954.

Piaget, J. *Six études de psycholgie.* Geneva: Editions Gonthier, 1964.

Radin, N. & Kamii, C. The child-rearing attitudes of disadvantaged Negro mothers and some educational implications. *Journal of Negro Education.* Spring, 1965.

Radin, N. & Weikart, D. A home teaching program for disadvantaged children. *Journal of Special Education.* Winter, 1967.

Rosenthal, R. & Jacobson, L. Self-fulfilling prophecies in the classroom. Paper presented at the 1967 meeting of the American Psychological Association, Washington, D. C., (Unpublished).

Rosenzweig, M., et al. Cerebral effects of environmental complexity and training effects among adult rats. *Journal of Comparative and Physiological Psychology.* June, 1964.

Schafer, W. Student careers in two public high schools: a comparative cohort analysis. Unpublished doctoral dissertation. The University of Michigan. Ann Arbor, 1965.

Smilansky, S. Promotion of preschool "culturally deprived" children through "dramatic play". Paper presented at the 1965 meeting of the American Orthopsychiatric Association, New York (Unpublished).

Suppes, P. Logical and mathematic concept formation in children. Paper presented at the 1966 meeting of the American Psychological Association, New York (Unpublished).

Part Five   Drugs and the Drug Experience

It is very difficult to select a sane set of readings about drugs. At the one extreme, there is an abundance of true and fanciful stories about tragic involvements with drugs; stories that ought to serve as warnings about the dangers of drug use. At the other extreme, there are a few true and fanciful descriptions of drug experiences; descriptions that ought to make it clear why so many people use drugs. Somewhere in between these two extremes there is a growing number of scientific reports that generally are not biased one way or the other. The first three of the four readings that follow are selected from this latter category— the unbiased scientific reports. The fourth is very biased in favor of marijuana, but its credentials are sufficient to justify its being included here.

The first article, Dr. Leon Greenberg's *Intoxication and Alcoholism: Physiological Factors*, despite its rather formidable title, is a simple description of alcohol's influence on the human body. On the assumption that at one time or another you are likely to use the Western world's favorite drug, it will stand you in good stead to know how much is too much, how alcohol calories will influence your stoutness-reduction program, and a thing or two about alcoholism.

The second article, Dr. John Kramer's *Introduction to Amphetamine Abuse*, examines the real and mythical effects of "speed."

The third article describes the obstacles to and the results of one of the first objective attempts to investigate the physiological and psychological effects of marijuana on humans. A great deal of research has been done since this study was first reported but, for the most part, the results have been pretty much the same as those reported by Drs. Norman

Zinberg and Andrew Weil in *The Effects of Marijuana on Human Beings.*

The final reading, *The Marihuana Experiences of Mr. X*, is an unabashed endorsement of marijuana. It is taken from Dr. Lester Greenspoon's excellent and authoritative *Marihuana Reconsidered.* The reading is included because it contains the thoughtful reflections of a mature, responsible man as he recalls his experiences with marijuana. While many people find it easy to ignore the favorable descriptions of marijuana experiences that are written by "heads" brushing them aside as mere propagandistic mutterings of pot smoking degenerates, it is less easy to ignore the measured, reasonable opinions of a man of Mr. X's stature.

INTOXICATION AND ALCOHOLISM: PHYSIOLOGICAL FACTORS

Leon A. Greenberg

It is not surprising that even in the earliest efforts to deal with the use—and especially the misuse—of alcoholic beverages, attention has been directed to the properties of alcohol for, obviously, if alcohol did not have these properties—if it had those of orange juice or milk—there would be no problem. In the atmosphere of anxiety and emotionalism surrounding these problems there has grown an abundance of misconceptions and fallacies, particularly since many have lent themselves well to the technique of the psychology of fear often used in efforts to solve the problems. But more recent research has provided a body of scientific information about the actions of alcohol. The present article will deal with this. . . .

METABOLISM OF ALCOHOL

The metabolism of alcohol refers to its fate in the body. On imbibing alcohol its effect is exercised only after it is absorbed. Absorption refers to its passage through the walls of the alimentary tract into the tissues and fluids of the body. Unlike most foods, alcohol requires no digestion before it can be absorbed. However, since the function of the stomach is mainly that of digestion, alcohol like most other ingested substances must pass into the small intestines in order to be rapidly and completely absorbed. It is only the alcohol which is absorbed and carried by the circulating blood to the brain that exercises an intoxicating effect. That which remains unabsorbed in the alimentary tract—no matter how great the amount—is without effect.

From *The Annals of The American Academy of Political and Social Science*, 1958, *315*, 22–30. Copyright 1958 by the American Academy of Political and Social Science, and reproduced by permission of the Academy and the author.

The speed with which the alcohol leaves the stomach, and therefore the rate of absorption, depends on the amount of food in the stomach, on the kind of beverage drunk, and on individual constitutional factors.

Food in the stomach retards the passage of alcohol into the intestines, delaying its absorption. It is not an uncommon observation that a single cocktail taken on an empty stomach—before eating—has a substantial "kick"; two or three after dinner are without effect. The cocktail hour traditionally precedes the dinner for a good reason. The kind of food in the stomach is also important. The intoxication-minimizing effect of ingesting fatty substances such as olive oil before drinking is surpassed by some proteins; a few glasses of milk is a good bulwark against the results of an overenthusiastic session of "social drinking."

Some beverages, such as beer, contain food substances which themselves slow absorption. Thus the same amount of alcohol consumed as beer has less effect than that consumed as whisky. Some carbonated alcoholic beverages, such as champagne, are known for the speed with which they "go to one's head." Carbon dioxide expedites absorption. . . .

After absorption, alcohol is distributed by the circulating blood to all of the tissues of the body. Actually the alcohol becomes dissolved uniformly in the water of the body. The body consists of about 70 per cent water; some tissues, such as blood, contain a large proportion of water, other tissues such as muscle a moderate proportion, and still others such as bone a small amount. The concentration of alcohol in each of these will be correspondingly large or small. But human bodies all contain essentially the same proportions of the various tissues and water, and it is therefore possible to predict quite accurately from the concentration of alcohol found in the blood the total amount present in the whole body. Thus in a person of average size weighing about 150 pounds, an ounce of whisky or a 12-ounce bottle of ordinary beer will yield a concentration in his blood of 0.02 per cent; and conversely a finding of 0.02 per cent of alcohol in the blood would indicate that he has consumed at least this much alcohol. When a blood test reveals a concentration of 0.15 per cent, indicating that the body contains ½ pint of whisky or 8 bottles of beer, the overworked "two-beer" alibi of the drunken driver in court becomes incredible.

Once absorbed, alcohol starts to undergo destruction and elimination. Only about a tenth of the ingested alcohol is eliminated unchanged from the body, mainly through the kidneys and lungs. The concentration of alcohol in both the urine and breath bears a fixed relationship to that in the blood. Chemical analysis of either urine or breath is thus useful for the indirect but accurate estimation of the alcohol content of the blood. The major part of the alcohol is destroyed in the body.

Oxidation

Alcohol is destroyed in the body by oxidation. Oxidation is the process by which all foods liberate their chemical energy in the body in the form of heat and work. The rate at which the ordinary foods—fats, proteins, carbohydrates—are oxidized is determined by the body's need for energy; the more work that is done the faster the oxidation to provide the energy. But the rate of oxidation of alcohol is independent of the body's energy expenditure and is essentially constant and similar for all people. In the average person this amounts to the equivalent of approximately ¾ of an ounce of whisky each hour. Thus one could sip whisky at this rate for 24 hours, a total consumption of over a pint of whisky, without accumulating alcohol in the body and without intoxication. Consuming this same amount in 1 or 2 hours would have quite a different result; it is not recommended.

As a drug, alcohol is thus unique in that, like the ordinary foodstuff, it can provide a rich source of energy in the body. In its oxidation an ounce of whisky provides about 75 calories of energy. A highball or cocktail containing 1½ ounces of whisky liberates the same number of calories as 6 teaspoons of sugar, 2 pats of butter or 1½ slices of bread. This is all a matter of straightforward bodily energy dynamics. To speculate that use of the calories liberated from alcohol is rejected by the body tissues, one must invoke a new philosophy of cellular morality. The energy liberated from alcohol can, indeed, replace that from the oxidation of ordinary foods. And to the extent of such replacement the oxidation of the ordinary foods is curtailed and the unoxidized food is stored in the body as fat. Thus the moderate consumption of alcohol without a corresponding curtailment in the regular meals may be fattening. The afternoon or evening cocktail is as threatening to the lady's figure as the nibbling of bonbons.

With the heavy drinker the story is a different one. The daily consumption of large quantities of alcohol results in a marked decrease in the amount of ordinary food eaten, just as the appetite is "spoiled" by eating too much sugar candy. A pint of whisky liberates about 1,200 calories. The average man expends about 3,000 calories daily. The excessive drinker who satisfies a large part of his caloric requirements with alcohol will correspondingly curtail his daily intake of ordinary foods; his appetite declines; he is "drinking his meals." Ordinary foods provide the minerals, proteins, and vitamins essential to bodily health; alcohol does not. Although the individual may be in caloric balance, he is not satisfying his other nutritional needs. Such dietary deficiencies result in nerve degeneration and other deficiency diseases such as pellagra and beriberi. Many of these diseases in alcoholics were formerly thought to be due to a direct damaging action of alcohol on bodily tissues.

Some way of hastening the disappearance of alcohol from the body and thus diminishing intoxication has been sought for widely; the efforts have been unrewarded. Many drugs which greatly increase bodily metabolism and oxidation of other foods have no effect on the rate of alcohol oxidation; nor is the inhalation of oxygen effective. The common belief that alcohol can be disposed of and intoxication "worked off" by exercise has no basis except to the extent that exercise takes time. And sobering up is a matter of time that might just as well be spent in relaxation. Stimulant drugs may counteract some of the depressant actions of alcohol, altering behavior. Such changes are not uncommonly interpreted as sobering. Thus the inebriate, frequently prone to fall asleep, is stimulated by the caffeine in the "black coffee"; he is now merely a wide-awake drunk instead of a sleepy one.

PHYSIOLOGICAL EFFECTS OF ALCOHOL

The actions of alcohol with which we are concerned here are those relevant to intoxication and alcoholism. Little more than fifty years ago this matter was settled with superb simplicity. You took a tumbler of alcohol and the white of an egg. You broke the egg into the alcohol. The albumen turned white, coagulated and shriveled. By analogy the man who imbibed became the tumbler and its contents. His brain and his liver were the white of the egg. What happened to the egg happened to him. His gray matter clotted and shriveled, his nerves dried up; he stumbled over his toes when he walked and slurred his words when he spoke. His liver dried up until it resembled the sole of an old boot with the hobnails showing—the "hobnail" liver. Nothing remained to be added to the physiology of alcohol; it was all very simple, very graphic, very satisfying.

Since then, orderly research has provided more reliable facts. These are worthy of examination. Pure alcohol is intensely irritating and damaging to all living tissues. A 40 or 50 per cent solution of alcohol, as in whisky, is also irritating. A drop placed in the eye would provide convincing evidence of this. Below 15 or 20 per cent, alcohol is only slightly irritating; below 5 or 6 per cent, there is no irritation. Attention is called to these facts because, as shall be seen soon, the concentration of alcohol prevailing in the body tissues, even in extreme intoxication, is a small fraction of that tolerated by the tissues without irritation. The highest concentration of alcohol ever attained in the living body is far lower than that which can cause organic damage or destroy, corrode, dissolve, or dry out the body cells. This includes the cells of reproduction; alcoholism is not genetically transmissible.

The prime action of alcohol in the body is its depressant action on the function of the central nervous system, the brain. This is an anesthetic action no different from that of ether or chloroform. The part of the brain affected and the degree of impairment depend on the concentration of alcohol in the blood and therefore acting on the brain. Although this action is entirely on the brain, disturbance in behavior is manifested in the organs controlled by the particular brain areas affected. Speech is thick, hands clumsy, knees sag, the person appears drunk—not because of the presence of alcohol in his tongue, hands or knees, but because it has depressed those parts of his brain controlling these organs.

In a person of average size, 2 or 3 ounces of whisky present in the body will produce 0.05 per cent of alcohol in the blood. With this amount the uppermost levels of brain functioning are depressed, diminishing inhibition, restraint, and judgment. The drinker feels that he is "sitting on top of the world"; many of his normal inhibitions have vanished; he takes many personal and social liberties as the impulse prompts; he is long-winded and has an obvious blunting of self-criticism. At a concentration of 0.10 per cent of alcohol in the blood, resulting from 5 or 6 ounces of whisky in the body, function of the lower motor area of the brain is dulled. The person sways perceptibly; he has difficulty putting on his coat; he fumbles with the key at the door; words stumble over a clumsy tongue.

Illusion of Stimulation

The states so far described are popularly designated as mild intoxication or "feeling high." The significant feature of these states is depression and dulling of sensory and motor function and, contrary to popular belief, not stimulation. The illusion of stimulation is given by the increased tempo and altered quality of behavior occurring when the normally prevailing inhibitions and restraints are removed by alcohol. The effect may be compared to releasing the brakes rather than stepping on the accelerator. Notwithstanding this illusion there is actually measurable reduction in sensitivity, impaired discrimination, and diminished speed of motor response. The drinker, however, often denies that this occurs; often asserts, on the contrary, that after a few drinks his reactions, perception, and discrimination are better. This is an important effect of alcohol; his judgment about himself and his own activities is blunted, allowing for an inflated feeling of competence and self-confidence.

With increasing concentrations of alcohol in the blood there is a corresponding progression of impairment of functions. At 0.20 per cent, resulting from about 10 ounces of whisky, the entire motor area of the brain is profoundly affected. The individual tends to assume a horizontal position; he needs help to walk or undress. At 0.30 per cent, from the presence of a pint of whisky in the body, sensory perception is so dulled that the drinker has little comprehension of what he sees, hears, or feels; he is stuporous. At 0.40 per cent, perception is obliterated; the person is in coma, he is anesthetized. At 0.60 or 0.70 per cent, the lowest, most primitive levels of the brain controlling breathing and heartbeat cease to function and death ensues. Throughout this entire progression the concentrations of alcohol in the body are far too low to cause any direct organic damage to the tissues. The disturbance is entirely one of nerve function and is reversible; short of death, when the alcohol disappears the effect goes with it.

With these facts about the metabolism of alcohol and the effects of various concentrations in the blood, the relationship of these to the various beverages can be expressed in Table 1.

Supplementary Physiologial Effects

So far only the depressant, intoxicating action of alcohol on the nervous system has been considered. Intoxication is but one of a series of events

Table 1

The Effect of Alcohol Beverages

Amount of Beverage Consumed	Concentration of Alcohol Attained in Blood	Effect	Time Required for All Alcohol to Leave the Body
1 highball (1½ oz. whisky) or 1 cocktail (1½ oz. whisky) or 3½ oz. fortified wine or 5½ oz. ordinary wine or 2 bottles beer (24 oz.)	0.03%	No noticeable effects on behavior	2 hrs.
2 highballs or 2 cocktails or 7 oz. fortified wine or 11 oz. ordinary wine or 4 bottles beer	0.06%	Feeling of warmth—mental relaxation—slight decrease of fine skills—less concern with minor irritations and restraints	4 hrs.

Beverage	Blood alcohol		Effect	Time
3 highballs or 3 cocktails or 10½ oz. fortified wine or 16½ oz. (1 pt.) ordinary wine or 6 bottles beer	0.09%	Increasing effects with variation among individuals and in the same individuals at different times	Buoyancy—exaggerated emotion and behavior—talkative, noisy or morose	6 hrs.
4 highballs or 4 cocktails or 14 oz. fortified wine or 22 oz. ordinary wine or 8 bottles (3 qts.) beer	0.12%		Impairment of fine coordination—clumsiness—slight to moderate unsteadiness in standing or walking	8 hrs.
5 highballs or 5 cocktails or (½ pt. whisky)	0.15%		Intoxication—unmistakable abnormality of gross bodily functions and mental faculties	10 hrs.

For those weighing considerably more or less than 150 lbs. the amounts of beverage indicated above will be correspondingly greater or less. The effects indicated at each stage will diminish as the concentration of alcohol in the blood diminishes.

that reinforce and perpetuate each other in a vicious circle in the phenomenon called alcoholism. Intoxication alone is not alcoholism. There are other physiological effects of alcohol seen in the disturbed functions of other organs. These often persist after intoxication. While they are not due to the direct action of alcohol upon the organs involved, but rather indirectly to disturbance of their nervous control, they are nevertheless important features in alcoholism.

Alcohol affects the pituitary gland whose hormonal secretions in turn affect the activity of other glands and functions. The pituitary influences growth; it influences sexual development, and sexual cycles; it acts on kidney functions; it influences the adrenal glands. The adrenal glands control the balance of mineral salts and water in the body. Alcohol affects important functions of the liver. During and after intoxication the liver is often seen to be swollen and yellow, an event caused by a disturbance of chemical and hormonal states in the body essential to the normal handling of fat by this organ. Frequent repetition of this may underlie the genesis of liver cirrhosis in alcoholism.

Intoxication affects the so-called water balance of the body. It was believed—and still is by many—that alcohol dries out the body, giving rise to the intense thirst of the hangover. Actually, the water of the body is not depleted but merely shifted from within the cells to the spaces about the cells, giving rise to a sensation of thirst and the "wet brain." With this dislocation of body water, there is a corresponding alteration in the distribution of salts within the various compartments of the body structure, a change which itself causes a host of other malfunctions.

Clearly, intoxication represents not only a disorientation of the whole individual in relation to the realities of his external environment, but also a disorganization of the complexly poised interrelationship of organic functions and biochemical states constituting his internal physiological environment—a disturbance of the normal homeostasis. This internal organic disruption and the attendant malfunctions often persist after intoxication; they are the physical components of hangover. In the prolonged and repeated inebriety of the alcoholic, just as his deviant performances increasingly injure his normal relationships with his external environment, his disrupted internal environment injures tissues and organs of his body. Repeated injury to tissues results in persisting damage—the cirrhotic liver, degenerated nerves, delirium tremens.

CURE OF ALCOHOLISM: HOPES AND REALITY

Needless to say, the alcoholic is sick—sick physiologically as well as emotionally and socially. It is pointed out here that research in the metabolism and acute physiological effects of alcohol itself, and in the indirect effects of excessive use and repeated inebriety, has given to therapy a better knowledge of these disabilities and a more rational and effective basis for their medical treatment.

The immediate purpose of medical treatment is to alleviate threatening and painful symptoms. But the ultimate goal of medical progress is to discover and remove the cause of these symptoms. Although the concept of alcoholism as an illness is relatively new, or perhaps because it is new, hypotheses as to its physiological etiology have already been proposed. One of these attributes the cause of excessive and addictive drinking to vitamin deficiency—a vitamin inadequacy based not on any normal standards of vitamin needs, but on a postulated genetically inherited extraordinary need for vitamins. This hypothesis was undoubtedly inspired by the observation that alcoholics are frequently in a state of vitamin deficiency, a condition, as we now know, resulting from inadequate nutrition common in excessive drinkers.

The other hypothesized physiological etiology attributes alcoholism to improper function of the adrenal glands. This theory, too, originated in the observation that among the organic disturbances in alcoholics some were indicative of adrenal malfunction.

Both of these hypotheses are examples of the classic error in reasoning—"post hoc, ergo propter hoc"—alcoholics suffer vitamin deficiency and adrenal malfunction, therefore the latter are the cause of alcoholism. The proponents of both theories have competed in promises of the quick eradication of alcoholism. In clinical application, unfortunately, these promises have not been realized. What these hypotheses lack in reality they seem to make up in simplicity.

Alcoholism is indeed a complex phenomenon involving both in its origin and manifestations subtle and devious interplay of physiological, psychological, and social factors. Definition of the etiology of alcoholism in the exclusive terms of any one of these disciplines is, under present knowledge, as inadequate as a similar explanation of the entire manifestation would be. In fact, present knowledge of physiology offers no certain answer as to the cause. But to deny entirely a physiological etiology would be to deny psychosomatic concepts. When we have learned the physiology of thought, emotion, motivation, and social behavior, then will we, perhaps, know the physiological etiology of alcoholism.

INTRODUCTION TO AMPHETAMINE ABUSE

John C. Kramer, M. D.

Though regular, oral use of amphetamines may cause difficulties, including paranoid psychosis and a disabling dependence, it is less likely to lead to these effects than is intravenous use. Colonies of intravenous stimulant users have gathered in such areas as San Francisco, New York, Los Angeles, and perhaps elsewhere. At present the developmental history of the intravenous amphetamine user is typical enough to warrant a general description.

He has tried amphetamines orally; he may have liked them or not. He has used other drugs perhaps moderately, perhaps extensively, and he has been moving either in marijuana-psychedelic drug-using circles or in heroin-addict circles. His first intravenous use of amphetamine is an ecstatic experience and his first thought is "where has this been all my life." The experience somehow differs from the effects of oral amphetamines not only quantitatively but also qualitatively. Early his use of the drug is intermittant; doses probably equivalent to twenty to forty milligrams per injection may be taken once or a very few times over a day or two. Days or weeks may intervene between sprees. Gradually the sprees become longer and the intervening periods shorter; doses become high and injections more frequent.

After a period of several months, the final pattern is reached in which the user (now called a "speed-freak") injects the drug many times a day, each dose in the hundreds of milligrams, and remains awake continuously for three to six days getting gradually more tense, tremulous and paranoid as the "run" progresses. The runs are interrupted by bouts of very profound sleep (called "crashing") which last a day or two. Shortly after waking after crashing, the drug is again injected and a new run starts. The periods of continuous wakefulness may be prolonged to weeks if the user attempts to sleep even as little as an hour a day.

Though amphetamine used intravenously is a powerful reinforcer, there are individuals who have tried it once or several times and have chosen not to continue. Nevertheless, like heroin and cocaine, it is a form of drug use which may overwhelm even a casual dabbler.

It is interesting to note that in experiments (Pickens, Meisch, and

Reprinted from the *Journal of Psychedelic Drugs*, 1969, 2, 1–16. By permission of the Haight-Ashbury Free Medical Clinic and the author.

The kind assistance of the following people is gratefully noted: Mr. Robert Cravey, Orange County Pathologist's Office; Mrs. Leah Jaffe, Smith, Kline and French Laboratories; Dr. Thomas Noguchi, Los Angeles County Coroner; Dr. David Smith, Haight-Ashbury Medical Clinic; and Dr. Henry Turkel, San Francisco County Coroner. Burroughs-Welcome donated Methedrine brand amphetamine.

This work was supported in part by Grant C-67-10 of the Committee on Problems of Drug Dependence of the National Research Council.

McGuire, 1967; Pickens and Harris, 1968) in which rats had the opportunity for self-injection of amphetamines intravenously, the drug proved to be strongly reinforcing and the self-administration was characterized by periods of intake and abstinence entirely analogous to that seen in human amphetamine users.

Effects The intravenous use of amphetamines produces a syndrome with a variety of behavioral and physical effects some of which, particularly the insomnia and the anorexia [loss of appetite], may themselves produce symptoms or alter the effects specifically attributable to the drug. The high dose user thus is not merely responding to a drug, but also to altered sleep patterns, to undernourishment, to malnourishment, and often to infection. And amphetamines are seldom, if ever, used exclusively: "downers"— opiates, . . . [tranquelizers] and sedatives—are regularly used, as is cannabis and occasionally psychedelics. A surprising miscellany of other substances may be used experimentally and the "speed" itself is seldom pure and probably contains by-products not extracted during illicit manufacture, as well as those added afterward to "cut" the product.

The Flash and the Euphoria A few seconds following the injection, the user experiences a sudden, intense generalized sensation which has both physiological and psychological characteristics. It is ineffable and ecstatic, yet may differ in intensity and in quality from time to time. Because different batches of the drug produce a different intensity and quality of flash and because the pure, commercially produced products do not give a good flash, it seems likely that the flash may to a great extent depend upon substances other than the methamphetamine.

The euphoria can be viewed as having both primary and secondary characteristics. Part of the sense of well-being seems purely internal and part stems from the feelings of ability and of invulnerability which are produced. Suddenly, magically, volubility and gregariousness appear and boredom departs.

These desired effects are extremely vulnerable to the impingement of tolerance. It takes ever more drug to recreate this chemical nirvana. It is the desire to re-experience the flash and the desire to remain euphoric, and to avoid the fatigue and the depression of the "coming down" which drives the users to persist and necessarily to increase their dose and frequency of injection. And it is this persistence of use and these large doses which bring on all the other effects of these drugs.

Anorexia One of the medical uses of amphetamines is to induce anorexia to aid in weight reduction. In doses ordinarily prescribed, five to thirty milligrams per day, the anorexia produced is moderate and some have questioned whether a placebo effect is responsible rather than a drug effect. With the large doses taken during abusive use, there is no question but that anorexia is produced. Users uniformly lose weight during periods of abuse. Appetite suppression may be so profound that users may find the very act of swallowing difficult. Some users diligently force themselves to take small amounts of highly nutritious foods or inject themselves with vitamins and other dietary supplements.

Upon arising from the profound sleep which follows a run, either immediately or perhaps a few hours later, the user becomes voraciously hungry. Though he has eaten little or nothing for several days, . . . [appetite] like this seems to be related to release from the drug effect in large measure, because in the instance of non-drug assisted starvation appetite is diminished after several days starvation.

Undernutrition and malnutrition result and undoubtedly complicate all the other effects of high dose amphetamine use. . . .

Insomnia Even early in this pattern of drug abuse the users remain awake for a day or two at a time. These periods gradually become longer so that the runs tend to last three to six days. Though longer runs have been reported, they are generally isolated events. Some users will force themselves to lie down, close their eyes and drift into a half-sleep for perhaps an hour or two. With this the user may be able to persist in a run for several weeks before crashing.

There is no question but that sleep deprivation (or perhaps dream deprivation) alone can produce deterioration in performance, misperceptions, hallucinations and other phenomena. All these occurred in one sleep deprivation experiment (Pasnau et al., 1968), but it was the impression of Pasnau et al. that withholding all stimulants from their subjects during the eight-and-one-half days of wakefulness, permitted the subjects to cope better with these effects.

It is likely that both the insomnia and the drug contribute to the syndrome, and as with other aspects of this phenomenon, are inextricably intertwined. The observation that many of the physical and psychological symptoms are largely dissipated after sleeping for a day or two suggests that the insomnia alone is a major contributor to the syndrome. The fact that some symptoms persist after weeks or months of abstinence indicates that sleep deprivation is not alone responsible.

Considering that the usual pattern seen during well established high dose abuse is of three to six days of wakefulness followed by one to two days of sleep, then users spend about one-fourth of their time in sleep, about the same proportion as non-users only distributed differently. Whether the REM time is different has not been investigated and may be of consequence even if the total sleeping time of users equals that of non-users.

Tolerance develops to many of the effects of amphetamine, including that of producing wakefulness. When drug use is well developed very large doses will be necessary to keep the user awake. At times when tremulousness develops after several days of wakefulness, users describe taking a moderate dose of their drug to calm them sufficiently so that they can relax and sleep. A "moderate" dose in this instance may be as much as several score milligrams.

Paranoia A paranoid psychosis can be precipitated by either a single large dose or by chronic moderate doses of amphetamines. Two surveys of patients entering psychiatric units have suggested that amphetamines may be causal or at least a precipitating event in the psychiatric hospitalization of patients not otherwise identified as users of amphetamines (Johnson and Milner, 1966; Rockwell and Ostwald, 1900). The presenting symptoms are those of paranoid psychosis.

High dose intravenous users of amphetamines generally accept that they will sooner or later experience paranoia. Aware of this, they are usually able to discount for it. Moderate persecutory ideas and visual illusions will seldom be acted on because of their intellectual awareness of their nature and origin. However, when drug use has become very intense or toward the end or a long run, even a well practiced intellectual awareness may fail and the user may respond to his delusional system.

Leake (1958) has suggested in the past, and Ellinwood (1967, 1968) more recently, that the effect of amphetamine is to release underlying psychotic trends. Griffith, Cavanaugh and Oates (unpublished) however, precipitated a paranoid psychosis in all four subjects given d-amphetamine (120-220 mg. per day for 24-120 hours) enciting psychosis. All had previously been diagnosed as having a moderate personality disorder.

Though there may be individual differences in sensitivity to the psychotogenic effects of amphetamines, it appears that anyone given a large enough dose for a long enough time will become psychotic. Though this hypothesis may be untestable, given the experiences of a large number of high dose amphetamine users, it seems likely, more so than the view that psychosis is precipitated only in those already so inclined.

As mentioned earlier, the paranoia does not usually start during the first few months of high dose intravenous use. When it does finally begin, it is mild, easily controlled and is largely dissipated upon waking after crashing and it usually does not start again until after two or three days on a new run. As time goes on, it may start earlier in a run and may persist to some extent even after crashing. In some instances, the first injection after a period of sleep will bring about a return of the paranoia. Once an individual has experienced amphetamine paranoia, it will rather readily return even after a prolonged period of abstinence.

Violence Public concern over use of psychoactive drugs often centers on the assumption that among the effects of a specific drug is its tendency to induce unwarranted violence. Clearly, opiates do not possess this characteristic pharmacologically. Though an opiate user could, for instance, commit an act of violence during a robbery, there is nothing in the drug effect which would so incline him. If anything, opiates are more likely to inhibit any tendency toward violent behavior.

From all evidence, amphetamines do tend to set up conditions in which violent behavior is more likely to occur than would be the case had an individual not used it. Suspiciousness and hyperactivity may combine to induce precipitous and unwarranted assaultive behavior. Under the influence of amphetamines liability of mood is common—the user abruptly shifting from warmly congenial to furiously hostile moods for the most trivial of reasons.

Most high dose amphetamine users describe involvement, either as aggressor or victim, in episodes in which murder or mayhem was avoided by the slimmest of margins. There are, of course, instances in which violence actually occurred. From descriptions of a number of these events, it is clear that they would not have taken place had it not been for the use of amphetamines. . . .

Compulsivity Perhaps the most curious effect of amphetamine is its capacity to induce behavior which is persisted in or repeated for prolonged periods. If the user is not too disorganized the activity may, on the surface at least, be useful. Dwellings may be cleaned, automobiles polished or items arranged to an inhuman degree of perfection. Or these activities may be partially completed when another compulsively pursued task intervenes. The behavior may be bizarre as in the elaborate but nonfunctional reconstruction of mechanical or electrical devices, or it may take on a destructive character as in skin picking which may produce extensive ulcerations. . . .

Over-amping The term "over-amping" was probably derived during the year when commercially produced ampoules of methamphetamine were widely used. Users prefer this word to the word "overdose" which carries the connotation of an overdose of heroin, a condition which produces an entirely different set of symptoms. A variety of events may occur when the dose of amphetamine taken far exceeds the tolerance of the user. Descriptions have been too few in number for a clear pattern to emerge. One or several symptoms may occur, including chest pain which lasts minutes or hours. Unconsciousness, again lasting minutes or hours, may occur, the user waking and occasionally finding himself aphasic or paralyzed for hours or days in a manner suggestive of the pattern seen following a cerebralvascular accident. More frequent is the situation in which the user remains conscious, his mind racing with a myriad of thoughts, often in an ecstatic mood but unable, or perhaps unwilling to move.

Under these circumstances the user's friends attempt to nurse him and may use opiates or sedatives in an attempt to counteract the effects of over-amping.

Death The motto "Speed Kills" is cute, short enough to fit on a button, and carries a message of concern. It is not altogether accurate. Very few deaths have been recorded in which overdose of amphetamines has been causal.

Though viral hepatitis and other infections are common and persistent among intravenous amphetamine users, again, only a few deaths related to infection have been recorded. Death by violence might add still a few more names. The San Francisco County Coroner revealed that only one or two deaths per year in each county could be attributed to overdose and a like number to other events which might be related to amphetamine use.

The rarity of death may be due to the tolerance produced by these drugs and the relatively high ratio of effective dose to fatal dose. Dr. David Smith of the Haight-Ashbury Clinic and Amphetamine Research Project indicates that the two deaths he has seen were both in individuals who were relative novices in amphetamine use. . . .

Recovery Though a Japanese report (Tatetau, 1963) suggests that some high dose amphetamine users may become chronically psychotic, what has been most striking in our experience has been the slow but rather complete recovery of users who, according to their own descriptions and that of others, had become rather thoroughly disorganized and paranoid prior to their detention. Though the most florid symptoms are dissipated within a few days or weeks, some confusion, some memory loss, and some delusional ideas may remain for perhaps six to twelve months. After that time, though there may be some residual symptoms, they are slight and not disabling and are noticed primarily by the (now abstinent) user himself. Most commonly, ex-users report slightly greater difficulty in remembering.

As a group they describe being more open and talkative than they had been prior to their use of amphetamines. They like the result and declare with certainty that it is due to their experience with amphetamines.

Anyone concerned with the welfare of amphetamine users and the users themselves should recognize that most, if not all, can recover from even the most profound intellectual disorganization and psychosis given six months or a year of abstinence.

Treatment The care of amphetamine users poses some special problems. In them are combined the problems of management of the hooked drug user and the paranoid personality. Though suffering with severe medical and psychiatric symptoms they are generally fearful of hospitalization.

Some crises may yield to phenothiazine tranquilizers of first aid, but abstinence is probably the most important therapeutic device, and that may be difficult to attain. Many users who attempt abstinence find it difficult because of the fatigue which results, extreme at first, gradually diminishing but persistent, perhaps for months.

Abstinence for many is forced by a stay in prison or jail or commitment to a psychiatric hospital or civil addict program. No data has yet been collected to indicate the long term value of such enforced abstinence. Certainly, many who have been incarcerated have returned to their drug use upon release. A concerned person is in a bind. Users do not readily volunteer for care, but commitment programs offer little besides enforced abstinence. Should the user be permitted to live in the limbo of his drug or forced into the limbo of an institution? Can voluntary programs be devised which are sufficiently useful and attractive that users will seek them out and persist in their program? Can commitment programs be devised which do not resemble slightly benign prisons? Or, do we just let the user seek heaven or hell on his own terms while the community offers help only on its own terms.

REFERENCES

Pickens, R.; Meisch, R.; and McGuire, L. E.: Methamphetamine Reinforcement in Rats, Psychon. Sci. 8:371–372, 1967.

Pickens, R.; and Harris, W. C.: Self-Administration of d-Amphetamine by Rats, Psychopharmacologia (Berl) 12:158–163, 1968.

Pasnau, R. O.; et al.: The Psychological Effects of 205 Hours of Sleep Deprivation, Arch. Gen. Psychiat. 18:496–505 (Apr) 1968.

Johnson, J.; Milner, G.; Psychiatric Complications of Amphetamine Substances, Psychiatrics Acta Scandinavica 42:252–263, 1966.

Rockwell, D. A.; Ostwald, P. F.: Amphetamine Use and Abuse in Psychiatric Patients, Arch. Gen. Psychiat. 18

Leake, C. D.: The Amphetamines—Their Actions and Uses, Springfield, Chas. C. Thomas, 1958.

Ellinwood, E. H. Jr.: Amphetamine Psychosis: I. Description of the Individuals and the Process, JMND 144:273–283, 1967.

Ellinwood, E. H. Jr.: Amphetamine Psychosis: II. Theoretical Implications, J. Neuropsychiat 4:45–54 (Jan-Feb) 1968.

Griffith, J. D.; Cavanaugh, J.; and Oates, J.: Schizophreniform Psychosis Induced by Large-Dose Administration of D-Amphetamine, Nashville, Vanderbilt University, No date, mimeo.

Tatetau, S.: Methamphetamine Psychosis, Folia Psychiat Neurol Jap Suppl. 7: 377–380, 1963. (Reported in Ref. 7).

THE EFFECTS OF MARIJUANA ON HUMAN BEINGS

Norman E. Zinberg and Andrew T. Weil

Unlike most Bostonians on April 19, 1968, we celebrated Patriots' Day by violating Section 200 of the Commonwealth of Massachusetts. The law reads: "A physician or a dentist, in good faith and in the course of his professional practice only, for the alleviation of pain and suffering or for the treatment or alleviation of disease may prescribe, administer, and dispense narcotic drugs. . . ." What we did on the evening of the 19th was to administer marijuana (a narcotic drug under Massachusetts law) to volunteer subjects, not for the alleviation of suffering or disease, but in order to find out what marijuana does to people who smoke it. The legislators of the Bay State had simply not provided a statute to authorize this research.

The event itself, which took place in a pleasant laboratory at the Boston University School of Medicine, was of greater scientific than legal consequence because it was the start of the first human experiments with mari-

New York Times Magazine, May 11, 1969, p. 28. © 1969 by The New York Times Company. Reprinted by permission.

juana ever designed according to modern principles of drug testing. We had received permission to investigate the drug only after a full year of the most frustrating negotiations with Federal agencies and the administrative bureaucracies of two universities (B.U. and Harvard). We were not about to give up when our mid-April deadline came around because of an oversight in state law, even though our lawyer warned us that we might be prosecuted. (Shortly after we began work, he succeeded in extracting a promise of immunity from prosecution from the Attorney General of the Commonwealth, who hinted wryly that the last such request he had received concerned the ill-fated "Titicut Follies"—a film documentary about the state prison for the criminally insane at Bridgewater, Mass.) Nine weeks and some 60 marijuana cigarettes later, we had obtained the first "hard" data on the acute effects of the drug on human beings, and we then began to analyze our results. These were published last December in a long article in the journal *Science* and have generated considerable discussion.

Our report in *Science* began: "In the spring of 1968 we conducted a series of pilot experiments on acute marijuana intoxication in human subjects. The study was not undertaken to prove or disprove popularly held convictions about marijuana as an intoxicant, to compare it with other drugs, or to introduce our own opinions. Our concern was simply to collect some long overdue pharmacological data." Nevertheless, the report has given rise to vigorous debate about the harmfulness of marijuana. In both scientific and nonscientific circles our results have been taken to indicate that the "seriousness" of the drug has been overrated. For example, in an editorial, titled "Boston Pot Party," *The New Republic* wrote: "While pot heads may legitimately ask, 'So what else is new?' the study may have a pacifying influence on parents and officials who fear the drug on the basis of unsubstantiated horror stories. According to the *Science* report, 'no adverse marijuana reactions occurred in any of our subjects.'" And our experimental findings have already been introduced as evidence in several court challenges to the current harsh laws on possession of marijuana.

Consequently, we feel an obligation to explain what we think is the significance of our study as well as to point out what is and is not known about the effects of marijuana.

It is worth reiterating that very little is reliably known about the effects of marijuana. In studying a drug of this sort there are two ways a researcher can go about getting information: he can ask users of the drug what effects they get from it or he can actually give marijuana to subjects in a laboratory and watch what happens. The trouble with the first kind of information is that it is grossly unreliable. As we have learned more about drugs that affect the mind, it has become all too clear that the pharmacological action of the drug (that is, what a pharmacology text says it should do) is but one of three factors that determine how a given person will react to that drug on a given occasion. The other factors are called "set" and "setting," and they are at least as important as the drug. Set is the psychologist's term for an individual's expectations of what a drug will do to him; it includes much of what we commonly call "personality." Setting is the total environment—physical and social—in which a drug is taken.

It is quite possible for the combined effects of set and setting to overshadow completely the pharmacological action of a drug. Thus, a barbiturate, which pharmacology texts tell us is a "sedative," can produce stimulation under certain conditions of set and setting. And amphetamine, a "stimulant," can cause sedation under other special circumstances. The vaguer and less predictable are the pharmacological effects of a drug, the greater is the importance of set and setting. Hence the danger of relying on information about marijuana from people who use it. What they say may apply to them, but whether it is pharmacologically accurate and can be applied to other persons is never clear.

Unfortunately, nearly all of the voluminous scientific literature on marijuana consists entirely of this kind of unreliable information. It is a collection of rumor, anecdote, and secondhand accounts. Much of it has been culled from other countries where set and setting are drastically different from set and setting in, say, an American college community. In India, for example, hemp drugs (usually more potent than U.S. marijuana) are in great disrepute and are used only by the lowest socioeconomic classes, often as an escape from the dreariness of everyday life. Observations on these users simply have no relevance to the situation in our country.

This is not to say that experimental laboratory information is always "right," and information from users is always "wrong." In fact, laboratory information has its own problems. The essence of the experimental method is manipulation of the environment so that an observed effect may be ascribed with some confidence to a known cause (in this case the administration of a drug). Consider a simple example. About 9 out of 10 marijuana users we have interviewed (we have now interviewed many hundreds) have told us they are certain marijuana dilates the pupils of their eyes when they are high.

An even higher percentage of law-enforcement agents have told us the same thing. But pupil size depends on other things besides what drug you may happen to have inside you. One obvious determinant is the surrounding illumination: The dimmer the light in a room, the larger are one's pupils. A less obvious factor is the distance at which one's eyes are focused; pupils constrict as part of the eye's accommodation for near vision. Therefore, if a researcher wishes to measure the effect of a drug on pupil size, he is obliged to hold the other factors constant—to control them. He must measure the pupils before and after administration of the drug under constant, standard illumination with the eyes focused at a constant, standard distance.

Observations made by users or law-enforcement agents at pot parties are not likely to be this scrupulous. When we finally did the appropriate experiment in Boston, we were not surprised to find that pupil size was not changed at all by marijuana. (Since the lighting at marijuana parties is often dimmer than usual, it is also not surprising that participants commonly have large pupils.)

The curious problem of the experimentalist, however, is that as he controls the laboratory environment more and more carefully, so as to maximize his confidence in ascribing observed effects to known causes, his laboratory becomes less and less like the real world, which is what he set out to study. Indeed, control can proceed to the point that the experimental results are scientifically impeccable, but their relevance to anything in the real world is lost. Then, if someone comes along and says, "So what?"— as happens all too infrequently in science—the experimentalist will be stuck for an answer.

What little laboratory research has been done on marijuana is defective in just this way. Recently a chemical called THC (for tetrahydrocannabinol) has been isolated from marijuana and synthesized. To date, it has not been established that this chemical is the sole active ingredient of hemp, but it has been so advertised in the scientific literature. In 1967 this drug was given to human beings in a well-designed experiment in the Addiction Research Center in Lexington, Ky. With high doses (probably many times higher than users commonly absorb from marijuana cigarettes) the drug caused psychotic reactions in subjects recruited from a prison population of former opiate addicts. This result was widely interpreted in both scientific and lay journals to mean that marijuana is not such a harmless drug after all—a wholly unjustified conclusion. The only legitimate conclusion is that unusually high doses of a compound that may or may not reproduce the effects of marijuana cause acute psychotic reactions in former opiate addicts. No one spoke up with the "So what?" that was called for.

In our experience, and that of all users we have talked to, true acute psychotic reactions to marijuana are rare to the point of being psychiatric curiosities—at least in persons who have not previously taken hallucinogenic drugs like LSD. This real world observation casts further doubt on the relevance of the findings with THC.

It would seem that the marijuana researcher must steer a middle course between his desire for scientific accuracy and his obligation to make his findings relevant to the world beyond his laboratory. We made a great effort to do this in our Boston University experiments.

One of our first decisions was to administer the drug to subjects in the form of cigarettes. Up to now, most researchers have given the drug in some form to be swallowed. Their argument is that doses are hard to standardize in smoking since different subjects inhale in different ways. In other words, the results are more "scientifically accurate" if the drug is swallowed.

We would agree if we felt the effects of the drug were the same regardless of route of administration. But, in fact, it appears that swallowed marijuana is qualitatively different from smoked marijuana. We have collected massive evidence from interviews suggesting that marijuana causes more powerful, longer-lasting effects when it is eaten, and this does not appear to be due simply to differences in dose. Possibly, components of the plant that are destroyed by the heat of smoking get into the body when the drug reaches the stomach. And since in the real world marijuana is usually smoked, we were willing to risk some inaccuracy in standardizing dose in order to preserve the relevance of our data. We also used doses of marijuana that made users very high in their own judgment; we did not use the very high doses of THC that some researchers have used in the past (as much as 1,000 times the .18 mgm. of THC we estimated subjects received in our experiment as a high dose of marijuana), resulting in florid psychotic or other toxic responses.

In order to minimize variation in the set of our subjects, we used, primarily, a group of nine young men who had never tried marijuana previously; their attitudes toward the drug were explored before the start of testing in an intensive psychiatric interview. (Interviews were repeated six months after the end of the experiment to see whether any of these subjects had "moved up" to other drugs; only two of the nine had tried marijuana subsequently and those on only one occasion each. None had tried any other psychoactive drugs.) The setting of the experiment was as "neutral" as possible. Subjects were made comfortable and secure in a suite of laboratories and offices but no attempt was made to provide them with an enjoyable experience. Interactions with the staff were few and formal, and no subject was permitted to discuss the experiment until he had finished it.

In properly designed research, the number of subjects needed is determined entirely by the kinds of data one wants to collect. For our purposes, nine marijuana-naive subjects were more than sufficient. Each was tested four times. First we held a practice session with tobacco to teach a standardized technique of inhaling and to allow subjects to become familiar with the tests. By instructing the subjects to hold each inhalation for 20 seconds as timed by a stop watch, we achieved fair standardization of intake. Five volunteers never got past the practice session. Although they had regarded themselves as heavy cigarette smokers, they experienced acute toxic nicotine reactions during this regime of rigorous inhalation. (Indeed, these nicotine reactions were the most impressive physiological responses of the entire experiment.)

Then came three "drug" sessions in which subjects smoked—in random order and at weekly intervals—either high or low doses of marijuana, or inert placebos, prepared from portions of male hemp stalks that contained no pharmacological activity. These sessions were "double-blind"—that is, neither we nor the subjects knew what was being smoked each evening— a precaution against possible contamination of the results by whatever preconceptions we, ourselves, held about marijuana. No previous research with the drug had employed this necessary safeguard.

We also studied a comparison group of eight heavy users of marijuana who were tested only once and only on high doses. (We could not use the double-blind method here because no one has yet found a placebo good enough to fool heavy users.) Interesting differences in the reactions of the two groups showed up; we will discuss them in a moment.

As a result of the care we took in planning these experiments, our results, we think, have more to say about marijuana than those of all earlier studies. Here is what we did, starting on Patriots' Day, 1968.

When we sat down to plan the experiments, we outlined three major areas of investigation. We wanted to clarify the effects of marijuana on the body during a high; we wanted to study psychological performance while under marijuana influence; and we wanted to assess the long-range effects—if any—of heavy marijuana use. Our first tactical decision was to postpone study of the third area simply because accurate measurement of the effects of chronic use of a drug requires far more elaborate procedures and far more time than we had available.

In planning experiments on acute physical effects, we were faced with the problem of not knowing what to look for. Unlike most drugs that affect consciousness, marijuana does not seem to do very much to the body, and we had few clues as to what tests would be likely to pay off. We looked at heart rate because previous studies had consistently found an increase. We studied pupil size because no one had ever done the simple measurement described above. We examined blood-sugar levels because low blood sugar has been invoked as an explanation of the increased appetite users commonly report when they are high. We looked at the whites of the eyes because marijuana allegedly reddens them. And we measured respiratory rate because it is an easily measured vital sign and depression has been reported.

We could have studied other physiological variables (such as level of adrenaline in the blood) but to do so would have been a random approach based on no hypotheses. We feel strongly that mindless experiments of that sort are inconsistent with the principles of good laboratory investigation and that results from such studies merely clutter the scientific literature with facts of obscure significance. Hence our amusement when a biochemist on one of the Harvard committees that got itself into endless muddles over our proposal criticized our experiments for lack of sophistication in that they did not include measuring of "other physiological and biochemical parameters." (Another member of the committee asked why we couldn't do the experiments on rats or pigeons to avoid controversy.)

Our results were clear-cut. Marijuana caused a moderate increase in heart rate, but not enough to make subjects conscious of a rapid pulse, and it reddened whites of eyes. It had no effect on pupil size, blood sugar, or respiratory rate. Possibly the drug has a few other effects on the body (we think it decreases flow of saliva and tears and are about to start new experiments to document these changes), but it is unlikely that other major effects will be found. The significance of this near-absence of physical effects is twofold. First it demonstrates once again the uniqueness of hemp among psychoactive drugs, most of which strongly affect the body as well as the mind. Thus the mental effects of LSD are accompanied by a panoply of neurological and physiological changes including widely dilated pupils, altered reflexes, abnormal reactions of involuntary muscles, and so forth.

Second, it makes it unlikely that marijuana has any seriously detrimental physical effects in either short-term or long-term usage. The influence of marijuana smoke on the lungs is unknown, but aside from the possibility of local irritation, marijuana has not been accused of having adverse medical effects, even in countries like India and Egypt where government agencies actively campaign against the drug. As recently as 1967, on the basis of no evidence whatever, the American Medical Association told physicians in a statement in its *Journal* on the hazards of marijuana that "hypoglycemia" (chronic low blood sugar) was a consequence of repeated use of the drug, but our research has undercut that claim. All in all, we think it is fair to say that in terms of medical dangers only, marijuana is a relatively harmless intoxicant.

In approaching the question of psychological effects of the drug, we again had a difficult time deciding what tests to use. The great mystery about marijuana seems to be the enormous discrepancy between its subjective and objective mental effects. Persons who smoke the drug experience great changes in their consciousness, but they seem to have nothing to show for it. Previous researchers have found that if tests are made complicated enough or if doses of the drug are made high enough, subjects will show across-the-board impairments in psychological performance, especially if they are not very familiar with the drug. But these impairments are nonspecific; they are the sort seen with any drug that influences alertness, for example. No one has shown any specific way in which a person, high on marijuana, is different from one who is not.

We used several standard psychological tests and one or two unorthodox ones. The Digit Symbol Substitution Test is a simple test of cognitive function often used on I.Q. tests. . . . [See the example of the Digit test on the next page.]

The Continuous Performance Test measures a subject's capacity for sustained attention. In our study, the subject was placed in a darkened room and directed to watch a small screen upon which six different letters of the alphabet were flashed rapidly and in random order. The subject was instructed to press a button whenever a specific critical letter appeared. Errors of commission and omission were counted over a five-minute period. The test was also done with a strobe light flickering at a distracting rate. Normal subjects make no or nearly no errors on this test either with or without strobe distraction, but sleep deprivation, organic brain disease and certain drugs (like chlorpromazine, an antipsychotic drug) adversely affect performance.

A third standard test we used was the Pursuit Rotor, in which the subject's task is to keep a stylus in contact with a small spot on a moving turn-

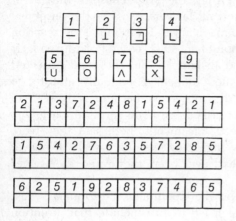

On a signal from the examiner the subject is required to fill as many of the empty spaces as possible with the appropriate symbols (top two lines). The code is always available during the 90-second test.

table. It measures muscular coordination and attention. Finally, we collected a "verbal sample" from each subject before and after he smoked the test cigarettes. The subject was left alone in a room with a tape recorder and instructions to describe "an interesting or dramatic experience" in his life until he was stopped. After exactly five minutes he was interrupted and asked how long he thought he had been in the recording room. In this way an estimate of the subject's ability to judge time was also obtained. (After intoxication, time sense was significantly slowed. Some subjects guessed the five-minute period to be as long as 10 or 12 minutes.)

The first three tests were chosen because they are standard tests for specific mental functions we thought might be altered during a marijuana high. The verbal sample was taken because we had a hunch—on the basis of careful interviews with and observations of chronic users—that speech undergoes changes when one is high, and we wanted to see if we were right.

In several ways the results of the psychological tests were surprising. Our first observation was that persons who had never tried marijuana previously had minimal subjective reaction to the drug in our neutral setting— even after smoking high doses that made their hearts beat faster and their eyes turn red. They simply did not get high. By contrast, all the users got high on the same dose, even though many of them thought our setting was extremely negative and were set not to have a pleasant time.

We were struck by the difficulty of recognizing when a subject is high, unless he tells you that he is. As a splendid example of the problem, we should mention that at the end of our study we arranged a demonstration session, in which two of our user subjects volunteered to go through the tests again for the benefit of a party of observers from the Federal Bureau of Narcotics and Dangerous Drugs, the Massachusetts Bureau of Drug Abuse and Drug Control, and several lawyers. Most of the observers had never seen anyone smoke marijuana before. Their universal reaction was extreme disappointment—disappointment that nothing happened. It was not clear what they had expected to happen, but they had expected something. When our subjects continued to behave normally and to go through the tests without difficulty, the observers became restive. "Are you sure they were inhaling right?" one asked. "Are you sure the marijuana is any good?" said another. The subjects, meanwhile, both said they were quite stoned. When asked to rate how high they were on a scale of one to ten, with ten being the highest they had ever been, they rated themselves at eight and nine.

Both groups did exactly the same on the Continuous Performance Test after smoking the drug as before, which led us to conclude that attention as measured by the C.P.T. is unaffected by marijuana. On the Digit Symbol Substitution Test an interesting difference appeared. The naive subjects did worse after smoking, and the degree of impairment was related to the dose smoked: A little made scores go down a little; a lot made scores go down a lot Here again is the nonspecific effect noted above. But the users improved slightly on the D.S.S.T. when they were high—even though they started out from good baseline scores. They showed a similar improvement in the Pursuit Rotor test. Especially interesting to us was the surprise users expressed on finding how well they could perform when stoned. Most of them were very apprehensive about taking the tests after smoking because they felt so high; some even asked to be excused from them. But when they tried, they were delighted to find they could perform well. This reaction is quite the opposite of the false sense of improvement subjects have under some psychoactive drugs (like alcohol) that actually impair performance.

What do these results mean? Apparently, getting high on marijuana is a much more subtle experience than getting high on alcohol: perhaps it is something that must be learned, so that most persons who take the drug for the first time cannot recognize the changes it causes in their consciousness. This hypothesis is consistent with the evidence that marijuana seems to affect little in the brain besides the highest centers of thought, memory and perception. It has no general stimulating or depressive action on the nervous system (hence the absence of neurological as opposed to psychological changes during a high), no influence on lower centers like those controlling the mechanical aspects of speech and coordination (hence no slurred words or staggering gait). As a result it seems possible to ignore the effects of marijuana on consciousness, to adapt to them, and to control them to a significant degree.

If you pour enough alcohol into a person who has never before had alcohol, he may not have a pleasant time, but at some time he will be unable to ignore the fact that he is intoxicated: he will *feel* that his nervous system is behaving in an abnormal fashion. Not so with marijuana: A first-time smoker can consume enormous amounts and have the physical reactions to the drug without any mental effects at all. As with most intoxicants, as one becomes familiar with alcohol, he can learn to compensate for the drug's adverse effects on performance—but only to a point; alcohol imposes absolute limits on the speed of nervous functioning by its direct pharmacological action. Again, not so with marijuana: Users appear to be able to compensate 100 per cent for the nonspecific adverse effects of ordinary doses of marijuana on ordinary psychological performance (including driving, according to the findings . . . [of a] . . . study conducted by the Department of Motor Vehicles of the state of Washington and the University of Washington). A person intoxicated on alcohol, on the other hand, has a hard time acting sober.

Again the question arises: How is a person high on marijuana psychologically different from one who is not? And there is still no answer. In fact, the only way to know someone is high on marijuana is still to have him tell you so.

Our hunch that speech might be an area in which to find a change seems to have paid off, but further experiments must be done before we can spell out the exact nature of the change. We were able to show in our user population that the nature of a verbal sample changed in several important ways after the subjects smoked marijuana. For example, before smoking, in response to the instructions, most subjects told a story about past events. After smoking, the same subjects abandoned narrative format and tended to talk about the present—things going on in their immediate environment. They also tended to become more intimate and to think in free associative patterns rather than according to everyday logic. The imagery they used became less concrete and more dreamlike.

To illustrate this point, here are two excerpts from one subject's verbal sample before and after he smoked marijuana:

Predrug: "Well, I guess the most interesting event recently that I can think of would have to do with turning my draft card in, which happened Jan. 29, 1968, and—uh—one of the most interesting things to me about handing in my draft card to the Resistance was that I hadn't planned to do so before I did it. . . ."

Postdrug: ". . . Oh—[clears throat]—you know, the tro- . . . the trouble is that—uh—the present is more interesting now than events in the past. I mean the idea of sitting here and talking about something that's already happened instead of—uh—you know—instead of happening now—instead of just being now—the present—is kind of ridiculous. . . ."

We are going to pursue these differences in an expanded investigation of language under marijuana influence and also want to search for other possible differences between being straight and being high—particularly in the areas of immediate memory and "secondary perception," that is, what the brain decides to do with incoming sensory information. In the meantime, what can we say about the dangers of marijuana from a psychological standpoint? From our own study and from other studies now in progress, it would seem—in short-term usage only—that usual doses of marijuana do not impair a user's ability to carry out successfully a wide range of tasks of ordinary complexity. But higher than usual doses, especially in novice smokers might be expected to cause performance decrements.

The real debate about the merits or evils of marijuana ought to focus on the long-range psychiatric effects of the drug, if any. This is the main area of controversy because there are still no data at all. We have no information on the subject from our own study, and we regret the continuing lack of any good research on it. What is needed is a decent prospective study of persons—say, medical students—who are setting out to become regular marijuana users matched against a similar group not using the drug. Each group should be followed and tested serially for 5, 10, or more years. If such a study is not organized soon, it may be too late. Marijuana use is becoming so extensive in some sections of the country that within certain age ranges, persons who do not use the drug are so unusual as to constitute what statisticians call a biased sample.

We hope that our own study has significantly weakened this trend. In view of the ease with which we carried out the tests once they were underway and the lack of harm to any of the participants, we hope that our project will be used as a precedent.

We also hope that state laws obstructing marijuana research will rapidly be amended. For society will never be able to develop an effective and sensible policy on the use and abuse of psychoactive drugs unless it permits the free collection of information on the actual effects—whether harmful or beneficial—these drugs have on the mind.

Anyone attempting research in an area as hotly immersed in controversy as marijuana use knows that he cannot expect his findings to be received with neutrality or scientific objectivity. Nevertheless, even with this in mind we have been surprised at the extent to which we are asked to jump from one experiment concerning a small area of information about marijuana into large political and philosophical questions. We are repeatedly asked, "Should marijuana be legalized?" or, "If it is 'harmless,' do you advocate people trying it?" We don't know the answers. The first question is out of our ken and neither question could be answered until our most important recommendation is implemented. What we proved is that research can be done with this substance. What we recommend is that individuals and institutions in conjunction with the legal authorities do it.

THE MARIHUANA EXPERIENCES OF MR. X.

Anonymous
(Reported by Dr. Lester Grinspoon)

The following biography is approximately accurate. Mr. X is a professor
at one of the top-ranking American universities, head of an organization
producing important new research results, and is widely acknowledged as
one of the leaders in his specialty. In his early forties, X has lectured at
virtually every major American university, and his scientific and popular
books have been best-sellers of their kind. His productivity has steadily
increased over the last decade. He has won many awards and prizes given
by government, university, and private groups, is happily married, has a
wife and children, and asks that his anonymity be respected. I am grateful
to another scientist for putting me in touch with Mr. X. . . .

"It all began about ten years ago. I had reached a considerably more
relaxed period in my life—a time when I had come to feel that there was
more to living than science, a time of awakening of my social consciousness
and amiability, a time when I was open to new experiences. I had become
friendly with a group of people who occasionally smoked cannabis, ir-
regularly, but with evident pleasure. Initially I was unwilling to partake,
but the apparent euphoria that cannabis produced and the fact that there
was no physiological addiction to the plant eventually persuaded me to
try. My initial experiences were entirely disappointing; there was no effect
at all, and I began to entertain a variety of hypotheses about cannabis
being a placebo which worked by expectation and hyperventilation rather
than by chemistry. After about five or six unsuccessful attempts, however,
it happened. I was lying on my back in a friend's living room idly examining the pattern of shadows on the ceiling cast by a potted plant (not cannabis!). I suddenly realized that I was examining an intricately detailed
miniature Volkswagen, distinctly outlined by the shadows. I was very
skeptical at this perception, and tried to find inconsistencies between
Volkswagens and what I viewed on the ceiling. But it was all there, down
to hubcaps, license plate, chrome, and even the small handle used for
opening the trunk. When I closed my eyes, I was stunned to find that
there was a movie going on on the inside of my eyelids. Flash . . . a simple
country scene with red farmhouse, blue sky, white clouds, yellow path
meandering over green hills to the horizon. Flash . . . same scene, orange
house, brown sky, red clouds, yellow path, violet fields . . . Flash . . . Flash
. . . Flash. The flashes came about once a heartbeat. Each flash brought
the same simple scene into view, but each time with a different set of colors
. . . exquisitely deep hues, and astonishingly harmonious in their juxtaposi-

tion. Since then I have smoked occasionally and enjoyed it thoroughly. It amplifies torpid sensibilities and produces what to me are even more interesting effects, as I will explain shortly.

"I can remember another early visual experience with cannabis, in which I viewed a candle flame and discovered in the heart of the flame, standing with magnificent indifference, the black-hatted and -cloaked Spanish gentleman who appears on the label of the Sandeman sherry bottle. Looking at fires when high, by the way, especially through one of those prism kaleidoscopes which image their surroundings, is an extraordinarily moving and beautiful experience.

"I want to explain that at no time did I think these things 'really' were out there. I knew there was no Volkswagen on the ceiling and there was no Sandeman salamander man in the flame. I don't feel any contradiction in these experiences. There's a part of me making, creating the perceptions which in everyday life would be bizarre; there's another part of me which is a kind of observer. About half of the pleasure comes from the observer-part appreciating the work of the creator-part. I smile, or sometimes even laugh out loud at the pictures on the insides of my eyelids. In this sense, I suppose cannabis is psychotomimetic, but I find none of the panic or terror that accompanies some psychoses. Possibly this is because I know it's my own trip, and that I can come down rapidly any time I want to.

"While my early perceptions were all visual, and curiously lacking in images of human beings, both of these items have changed over the intervening years. I find that today a single joint is enough to get me high. I test whether I'm high by closing my eyes and looking for the flashes. They come long before there are any alterations in my visual or other perceptions. I would guess this is a signal-to-noise problem, the visual noise level being very low with my eyes closed. Another interesting information-theoretical aspect is the prevalence—at least in my flashed images —of cartoons: just the outlines of figures, caricatures, not photographs. I think this is simply a matter of information compression; it would be impossible to grasp the total content of an image with the information content of an ordinary photograph, say 108 bits, in the fraction of a second which a flash occupies. And the flash experience is designed, if I may use that word, for instant appreciation. The artist and viewer are one. This is not to say that the images are not marvelously detailed and complex. I recently had an image in which two people were talking, and the words they were saying would form and disappear in yellow above their heads, at about a sentence per heartbeat. In this way it was possible to follow the conversation. At the same time an occasional word would appear in red letters among the yellows above their heads, perfectly in context with the conversation; but if one remembered these red words, they would enunciate a quite different set of statements, penetratingly critical of the conversation. The entire image set which I've outlined here, with I would say at least

100 yellow words and something like 10 red words, occurred in something under a minute.

"The cannabis experience has greatly improved my appreciation for art, a subject which I had never much appreciated before. The understanding of the intent of the artist which I can achieve when high sometimes carries over to when I'm down. This is one of many human frontiers which cannabis has helped me traverse. There also have been some art-related insights —I don't know whether they are true or false, but they were fun to formulate. For example, I have spent some time high looking at the work of the Belgian surrealist Yves Tanguey. Some years later, I emerged from a long swim in the Caribbean and sank exhausted onto a beach formed from the erosion of a nearby coral reef. In idly examining the arcuate pastel-colored coral fragments which made up the beach, I saw before me a vast Tanguey painting. Perhaps Tanguey visited such a beach in his childhood.

"A very similar improvement in my appreciation of music has occurred with cannabis. For the first time I have been able to hear the separate parts of a three-part harmony and the richness of the counterpoint. I have since discovered that professional musicians can quite easily keep many separate parts going simultaneously in their heads, but this was the first time for me. Again, the learning experience when high has at least to some extent carried over when I'm down. The enjoyment of food is amplified; tastes and aromas emerge that for some reason we ordinarily seem to be too busy to notice. I am able to give my full attention to the sensation. A potato will have a texture, body, and taste like that of other poatoes, but much more so. Cannabis also enhances the enjoyment of sex—on the one hand it gives an exquisite sensitivity, but on the other hand it postpones orgasm: in part by distracting me with the profusion of images passing before my eyes. The actual duration of orgasm seems to lengthen greatly, but this may be the usual experience of time expansion which comes with cannabis smoking.

"I do not consider myself a religious person in the usual sense, but there is a religious aspect to some highs. The heightened sensitivity in all areas gives me a feeling of communion with my surroundings, both animate and inanimate. Sometimes a kind of existential perception of the absurd comes over me and I see with awful certainty the hypocrisies and posturing of myself and my fellow men. And at other times, there is a different sense of the absurd, a playful and whimsical awareness. Both of these senses of the absurd can be communicated, and some of the most rewarding highs I've had have been in sharing talk and perceptions and humor. Cannabis brings us an awareness that we spend a lifetime being trained to overlook and forget and put out of our minds. A sense of what the world is really like can be maddening; cannabis has brought me some feeling for what it is like to be crazy, and how we use that word 'crazy' to avoid thinking about things that are too painful for us. In the Soviet Union political dissidents are routinely placed in insane asylums. The same kind of thing, a little more subtly perhaps, occurs here: 'Did you hear what Lenny Bruce said yester-day? He must be crazy.' When high on cannabis I discovered that there's *somebody inside* in those people we call mad.

"When I'm high I can penetrate into the past, recall childhood memories, friends, relatives, playthings, streets, smells, sounds, and tastes from a vanished era. I can reconstruct the actual occurrences in childhood events only half understood at the time. Many but not all my cannabis trips have somewhere in them a symbolism significant to me which I won't attempt to describe here, a kind of mandala embossed on the high. Free associating to this mandala, both visually and as plays on words, has produced a very rich array of insights.

"There is a myth about such highs: the user has a illusion of great in-sight, but it does not survive scrutiny in the morning. I am convinced that this is an error, and that the devastating insights achieved when high are real insights; the main problem is putting these insights in a form acceptable to the quite different self that we are when we're down the next day. Some of the hardest work I've ever done has been to put such insights down on tape or in writing. The problem is that ten even more interesting ideas or images have to be lost in the effort of recording one. It is easy to under-stand why someone might think it's a waste of effort going to all that trouble to set the thought down, a kind of instrusion of the Protestant Ethic. But since I live almost all my life down I've made the effort—successfully, I think. Incidentally, I find that reasonably good insights can be remem-bered the next day, but only if some effort has been made to set them down another way. If I write the insight down or tell it to someone, then I can remember it with no assistance the following morning; but if I merely say to myself that I must make an effort to remember, I never do.

"I find that most of the insights I achieve when high are into social issues, an area of creative scholarship very different from the one I am generally known for. I can remember one occasion, taking a shower with my wife while high, in which I had an idea on the origins and invalidities of racism in terms of gaussian distribution curves. It was a point obvious in a way, but rarely talked about. I drew the curves in soap on the shower wall, and went to write the idea down. One idea led to another, and at the end of about an hour of extremely hard work I found I had written eleven short essays on a wide range of social, political, philosophical, and human bio-logical topics. Because of problems of space, I can't go into the details of these essays, but from all external signs, such as public reactions and expert commentary, they seem to contain valid insights. I have used them in university commencement addresses, public lectures, and in my books.

"But let me try to at least give the flavor of such an insight and its ac-companiments. One night, high on camnabis, I was delving into my child-hood, a little self-analysis, and making what seemed to me to be very good progress. I then paused and thought how extraordinary it was that Sigmund

Freud, with no assistance from drugs, had been able to achieve his own remarkable self-analysis. But then it hit me like a thunderclap that this was wrong, that Freud had spent the decade before his self-analysis as an experimenter with and a proselytizer for cocaine; and it seemed to me very apparent that the genuine psychological insights that Freud brought to the world were at least in part derived from his drug experience. I have no idea whether this is in fact true, or whether the historians of Freud would agree with this interpretation, or even if such an idea has been published in the past, but it is an interesting hypothesis and one which passes first scrutiny in the world of the downs.

"I can remember the night that I suddenly realized what it was like to be crazy, or nights when my feelings and perceptions were of a religious nature. I had a very accurate sense that these feelings and perceptions, written down casually, would not stand the usual critical scrutiny that is my stock in trade as a scientist. If I find in the morning a message from myself the night before informing me that there is a world around us which we barely sense, or that we can become one with the universe, or even that certain politicians are desperately frightened men, I may tend to disbelieve; but when I'm high I know about this disbelief. And so I have a tape in which I exhort myself to take such remarks seriously. I say 'Listen closely, you sonofabitch of the morning! This stuff is real!' I try to show that my mind is working clearly; I recall the name of a high school acquaintance I have not thought of in thirty years; I describe the color, typography, and format of a book in another room. And these memories do pass critical scrutiny in the morning. I am convinced that there are genuine and valid levels of perception available with cannabis (and probably with other drugs) which are, through the defects of our society and our educational system, unavailable to us without such drugs. Such a remark applies not only to self-awareness and to intellectual pursuits, but also to perceptions of real people, a vastly enhanced sensitivity to facial expressions, intonations, and choice of words which sometimes yields a rapport so close it's as if two people are reading each other's minds.

"Cannabis enables nonmusicians to know a little about what it is like to be a musician, and nonartists to grasp the joys of art. But I am neither an artist nor a musician. What about my own scientific work? While I find a curious disinclination to think of my professional concerns when high—the attractive intellectual adventures always seem to be in every other area—I have made a conscious effort to think of a few particularly difficult current problems in my field when high. It works, at least to a degree. I find I can bring to bear, for example, a range of relevant experimental facts which appear to be mutually inconsistent. So far, so good. At least the recall works. Then in trying to conceive of a way of reconciling the disparate facts, I was able to come up with a very bizarre possibility, one that I'm sure I would never have thought of down. I've written a paper which mentions this idea in passing. I think it's very unlikely to be true, but it has conse-quences which are experimentally testable, which is the hallmark of an acceptable theory.

"I have mentioned that in the cannabis experience there is a part of your mind that remains a dispassionate observer, who is able to take you down in a hurry if need be. I have on a few occasions been forced to drive in heavy traffic when high. I've negotiated it with no difficulty at all, although I did have some thoughts about the marvelous cherry-red color of traffic lights. I find that after the drive I'm not high at all. There are no flashes on the insides of my eyelids. If you're high and your child is calling, you can respond about as capably as you usually do. I don't advocate driving when high on cannabis, but I can tell you from personal experience that it certainly can be done. My high is always reflective, peaceable, intellect-ually exciting, and sociable, unlike most alcohol highs, and there is never a hangover. Through the years I find that slightly smaller amounts of cannabis suffice to produce the same degree of high, and in one movie theater recently I found I could get high just by inhaling the cannabis smoke which permeated the theater.

"There is a very nice self-titering aspect to cannabis. Each puff is a very small dose; the time lag between inhaling a puff and sensing its effect is small; and there is no desire for more after the high is there. I think the ratio, R, of the time to sense the dose taken to the time required to take an excessive dose is an important quantity. R is very large for LSD (which I've never taken) and reasonably short for cannabis. Small values of R should be one measure of the safety of psychedelic drugs. When cannabis is legalized, I hope to see this ratio as one of the parameters printed on the pack. I hope that time isn't too distant; the illegality of cannabis is outrageous, an impediment to full utilization of a drug which helps produce the serenity and insight, sensitivity and fellowship so desperately needed in this increasingly mad and dangerous world."

Correlation Chart

Many of the readings in this text can be used to supplement other introductory psychology textbooks which are currently in use. On the following pages we have provided a correlation chart that suggests which chapters in our text supplement chapters in other texts. We have listed our authors' names on the left hand side of the page, and the supplementary chapters of the other texts in the columns below the respective author(s).

REFERENCES FOR CORRELATION CHART

HARRISON, ALBERT A. *Psychology as a Social Science*. Monterey, Calif.: Brooks/ Cole Publishing Company, 1972.

HILGARD, ERNEST R., ATKINSON, RICHARD C., and ATKINSON, RITA L. *Introduction to Psychology*. 5th ed. New York: Harcourt Brace Jovanovich, 1971.

KAGAN, JEROME, and HAVEMANN, ERNEST. *Psychology: An Introduction*. 2d ed. New York: Harcourt Brace Jovanovich, 1972.

LANDAUER, T. K. *Psychology: A Brief Overview*. New York: McGraw-Hill, 1972.

LANA, ROBERT E., and ROSNOW, RALPH L. *Introduction to Contemporary Psychology*. New York: Holt, Rinehart and Winston, 1972.

MCKEACHIE, WILBERT J., and DOYLE, CHARLOTTE L. *Psychology: The Short Course*. Reading, Mass.: Addison-Wesley Publishing Company, 1972.

MCNEIL, ELTON B. *Being Human: The Psychological Experience*. San Francisco: Canfield Press, 1973.

MORGAN, CLIFFORD T., and KING, RICHARD A. *Introduction to Psychology*. 4th ed. New York: McGraw-Hill, 1971.

MUNN, NORMAN L., FERNALD, L. DODGE, and FERNALD, PETER S. *Introduction to Psychology*. 3d ed. Boston: Houghton Mifflin Company, 1972.

Psychology Today. 2d ed. Del Mar, Calif.: CRM Books, 1972.

RUCH, FLOYD L., and ZIMBARDO, PHILIP G. *Psychology and Life*. 8th ed. Glenview, Ill.: Scott, Foresman and Company, 1971.

RUCH, FLOYD L., and ZIMBARDO, PHILIP G. *Psychology and Life*. Brief 8th ed. Glenview, Ill.: Scott, Foresman and Company, 1971.

Authors	McKeatchie & Doyle (Short Course) Chapters	Morgan & King Chapters	Harrison Chapters	Landauer Chapters	Psychology Today Chapters	Munn Chapters	Lana & Rosnow Chapters	Ruch & Zimbardo (Brief) Chapters	(Hardback) Chapters	McNeil Chapters	Hilgard Chapters	Kagan & Havemann Chapters
Skinner	1	1	1 & 14	1	1	1 & 22	1	1	1	15, 20	1	1
Miller	1	1	1 & 14	1	1	1 & 22	1	1	1	15, 20	1	1
Gibson	6	8	4	5	14	7	3	2, 3, 6	2, 3, 7	–	6	7 & 15
Lipscomb	6	8	4	5	13	6	3	2	2	–	5	6
Bower	9(1)	4	–	8	10	10	–	5	6	–	9	3
Skinner	5	3	4	7	3	8	4	4	5	–	8	2
Seligman	5	3	4	7	3	8	4	4	5	–	8	2
Hunt &												
Lunneborg	10	10	6	3	5, 6	16	7	3	4	–	15 & 16	14 & 15
Sommer	14	14	5	2 & 6	25	12	13	3	4	19, 8	22	16 & 2
Gilula &												
Daniels	14	14	5 & 12	2 & 6	–	12 & 13	13 & 2	3	13	9	13	10 & 2
Tiger	14	14	5	2 & 6	22, 33	12 & 13	13	3	13	11	22	2

Rogers	13	11	7	4	22, 23	18	9	9	10	–		19	11
Smith	13	13	10	4	30, 33	19	9	11	15	–		21	12
Meadow	9(2)	5	6	8	7	20	6	3 & 5	4 & 6	–		11	5
Vernon &													
Koh	9(2)	5	6	8	7	20	6	3 & 5	4 & 6	–		11	5
Baratz	9(2)	5	6	8	28	20	6	3 & 4	4 & 6	6		11	5
Rokeach	15	15	11	2 & 9	26, 28	21	10	8	12	18		22	16
Rockower	10	7	–	–	24	11	–	–	8	–		11	5
Cadwallader	Appendix 1 / 12	–	6	6	27	13	13	7	9	13		4	–
Fullerton	Appendix 1 / 12	–	6	6	27	13	13	7	9	13, 16		4	–
Ellis	Appendix 1 / 12	6	6 & 10	6	18, 27	12 & 13	13	7	9	12		4 & 12	–
Radin	2	–	8	2	28	21	11	–	13	4, 6, 7		23	16
O'Kane	2	15	8	2	28	21	11	–	13	4, 6, 7		23	16
Greenberg	Appendix (2)	19	–	6	34	7	2	Appendix	Appendix	Appendix D	5	7	1
Kramer	Appendix (2)	19	–	6	34	7	2	Appendix	Appendix	Appendix D	5	7	1
Zinberg &													
Weil	Appendix (2)	19	–	6	34	7	2	Appendix	Appendix	Appendix D	5	7	1
Grinspoon	Appendix (2)	19	–	6	34	7	2	Appendix	Appendix	Appendix D	5	7	1

Index

A

Adaptation, 86–90
  human, 86–87
  and theories of aggression, 87–90
Aggression, 87–93, 99, 107
  biological–instinctive theory of, 87–88
  and catharsis theory, 93
  frustration theory of, 88–89, 92
  social learning theory of, 89, 92–93
  and testosterone levels, 107
Alcohol, 235, 236, 237, 238, 239, 240, 241, 242
  absorption of, 236
  blood concentration of, 236, 237, 238, 239
  caloric value of, 237
  as a depressant, 238–239
  effects of "black coffee" on, 238
  and the hangover, 242
  and illusion of stimulation, 239
  metabolism of, 235–238
  oxidation of, 236–237
  physiological effects of, 238–242
  and psychological behavior, 238–239
  and tissue damage, 238, 242
  and "wet" brain, 242
Alcoholism, 242–243
Amphetamines, 244–249
  abuse, 249
    and recovery, 249
    and treatment, 249
Assassination, 90–91
Associability, 47–48, 49, 50, 57, 58–59
Association, 42–44, 45, 46, 47–48, 51
  in mnemonic methods, 42–44, 45, 46
Attitudes, 167, 172, 210
  change in, 167, 172
  about sex, 210
"Autoshaping," 54
Aversive conditioning, 50–51, 52, 58

B

Baratz, Joan, 144, 160
Behavior, control of, 6–11, 12–20
Binet, A., 65–67
Binet intelligence test, 65–67
Bonding, social, 109, 110, 112
Bower, G. H., 37, 38
Bright children, 69–70